THE ORIGIN OF LANGUAGE

The Origin of Language

Tracing the Evolution of the Mother Tongue

Merritt Ruhlen

JOHN WILEY & SONS, INC.

This text is printed on acid-free paper.

This publication is designed to provide accurate and authoritative
information in regard to the subject matter covered. It is sold
with the understanding that the publisher is not engaged in
rendering professional services. If legal, accounting, medical,
psychological, or any other expert assistance is required, the
services of a competent professional person should be sought.
ADAPTED FROM A DECLARATION OF PRINCIPLES OF A
JOINT COMMITTEE OF THE AMERICAN BAR ASSOCIATION AND
PUBLISHERS.

Library of Congress Cataloging-in-Publication Data:

Ruhlen, Merritt.
      The origin of language: tracing the evolution of the mother tongue /
   Merritt Ruhlen
         p.   cm.
      Includes bibliographical references and index.
      ISBN 0-471-15963-8 (paper: acid-free paper)
      1. Language and languages—Origin.   2. Language and languages—
   Classification.   3. Human evolution.   I. Title.
   P116.R85   1994
   401–dc20

                                                            93-39009

Printed in the United States of America

10 9 8

For my twins,

Marian, Ricky & Johnny

Preface

One day in the early 1980s, I was startled by a story in a popular magazine about a mathematical theorem that was so complex it had taken dozens of mathematicians decades to prove it. As a linguist, I was especially impressed by the fact that many different people had collaborated on a single aim, which took years to attain. In linguistics these days, each scholar is expected to have his own "theory of grammar" and such extensive collaborative efforts among linguists are rare. Or so I thought when I first read the article.

Several years later, I realized that linguists had, in fact, worked together, for at least two centuries, to prove something of even more fundamental importance than this famous mathematical theorem. What these linguists had done, was to show that all the languages now spoken on earth (roughly 5,000 by my count) are descendants of a single ancestral language.

Yet I also realized that most linguists (indeed, virtually *all* linguists) were unaware that this proof existed in the linguistic literature. In fact, almost all linguists who hold the Ph.D. degree believe that such a proof not only *does not exist*, but *cannot* exist for (alleged) reasons that will be examined in the course of this book. In my opinion, such beliefs are so fervent primarily because this is what almost all linguists have been taught in the course of their professional training. Very few of them have ever bothered to examine the evidence first-hand.

Furthermore, there is a great temptation to accept the views of experts in fields outside one's own as valid, a temptation to which virtually everyone succumbs. The notion that European languages are somehow special and unrelated to the rest of the world's languages has persisted—indeed flourished—throughout the twentieth century despite abundant evidence to the contrary. As you will see in the course of this book, the actual evidence has often taken a back seat to the well-entrenched expectations of experts. I hope that one salutary aspect of this book will be to show how foolish supposed experts can sometimes be. In this book you, the reader, will discover things that distinguished scholars consider beyond their capabilities. The classification of human languages—the subject of this book—is such a simple task that, in the words of the twentieth century's greatest taxonomist, "to really screw up classification you almost have to have a Ph.D. in historical linguistics. Ordinary folks, with no training, inevitably arrive at the correct solution."

Merritt Ruhlen
Palo Alto, California
March 1994

Contents

Prologue

What Do We Mean by the Origin of Language?

For centuries the question of the origin of language has fascinated laymen and scholars alike. Unfortunately, the topic is usually discussed in such imprecise terms that one cannot even be sure what exactly is at issue, and several entirely different questions are often confused. In one sense the origin of language is taken to mean the evolution of the *capacity* for speech in our biological ancestors (or perhaps cousins), such as Neanderthal Man, *Homo erectus*, *Homo habilis*, and the celebrated Lucy, who is thought to have lived around three million years ago. But because even the most recent of these creatures, Neanderthal Man, became extinct almost 35,000 years ago—some 30,000 years before the invention of writing by the Sumerians in the fourth millennium B.C.—we have no information on the languages or even the linguistic abilities of these earlier hominids. Nor are we ever likely to.

Despite these seemingly insurmountable obstacles—or perhaps because of them—there has been no shortage of speculation about how and when language developed. One popular theory has been that language began with gestures, to which

1

grunts and other sounds were later added, and this expressive stew in turn developed into human language. The fact that chimpanzees, monkeys, and other primates address each other with gestures and calls lends plausibility to this hypothesis, and gestures are part of everyone's face-to-face language today, but the gap between these rudimentary communication systems and human language is enormous, and how that gap was bridged, and when and where it was bridged, are questions that are not really resolved by the theory of gestural origins, even if it should be correct.

How, When, and Where

One aspect of the problem of the origin of language is the *pace* at which human language may have developed. Here one might contrast a cultural scenario with a biological scenario, though the two are not really mutually exclusive, and there may well have been feedback between the two over a long period of time. According to the cultural scenario, human language is simply a cultural artifact (like knives, clothes, and television sets) that may well have developed quite recently, say within the past 100,000 years. There is good archaeological evidence that human culture has become progressively more complex over this time span, especially within the last 50,000 years. Some scholars have sought to identify the origin of fully modern human language with this cultural expansion, sometimes called the "Sapiens explosion." According to this view, the possession of a fully developed language would have provided modern humans with a distinct advantage over the Neanderthals, whom they replaced. But there is currently considerable debate on the linguistic abilities of Neanderthals—some scholars maintain that they were not capable of the fully modern languages we possess, others that their languages may not have been substantially different from ours—so we cannot be certain that language played a crucial role in the disappearance of the Neanderthals in Europe (and of similar populations elsewhere). Furthermore, even if language did play a pivotal role in their extinction, it does not necessarily follow that fully modern language developed just before the extinction. Still, Neanderthals need not be the issue: the possession of language undoubtedly played a key role in the dramatic development and spread of human culture.

The biological scenario, by contrast, sees human language as the result of a very long period of evolutionary development, probably going back to our hominid ancestors hundreds of thousands, if not millions, of years ago. According to the biological scenario, human languages spoken 100,000 years ago would *already* have evolved to an advanced state, one not qualitatively different from that displayed by modern languages. Earlier human ancestors, such as *Homo habilis* and *Homo erectus*, would likely have possessed less developed forms of language, forms intermediate between the rudimentary communicative systems of, say, chimpanzees and modern human languages. Still, it is difficult to imagine what form these intermediate stages might have taken, and we have no way of associating any particular stage, no matter how speculative, with any particular ancestor. We know a good deal about what our ancestors looked like, and how they lived, but their minds and languages remain shrouded in the mists of the past. I personally believe that the biological scenario is probably closer to the truth than the cultural scenario, which I find implausible. Human language is simply too complex a phenomenon—and too intricately enmeshed with other human cognitive abilities—to have developed as quickly, or as late in human evolution, as the cultural scenario would have it.

Another perplexing question about the origin of language is that of *monogenesis*, the theory that all modern languages have evolved from a single earlier language, which itself has generated much controversy and concerning which there are two possible and often confused interpretations. In one sense, monogenesis is taken to mean that human language came into being just once and that all languages that now exist (or have ever existed) are (or were) altered later forms of this original language. In a more restricted sense, monogenesis is taken to mean that all *presently extant* languages derive from a single common source, but that there may well have been earlier, independently evolved languages that died out, languages spoken either by other groups of *Homo sapiens* or by earlier hominids. In any case, because we know so little about languages that might have been lost (remember that writing developed only 5,000 years ago and that even today most of the world's languages have no written form), we will concern ourselves in this book solely with the relationships among currently existing (or historically attested) languages. We are forced to leave in abeyance the intriguing question of how and when (and where) the linguistic abilities of modern humans developed, though we should note that these linguistic abilities are surprisingly uniform across the entire human species today. All normal humans learn to speak the language of the community in which they are raised.

What we have in abundance today—thanks to the efforts of linguists and anthropologists over several centuries—is information on the roughly 5,000 languages currently spoken in the world by the sole surviving subspecies of hominids, *Homo sapiens sapiens*, or modern humans. It is the origin of *these* languages, and the relationships *among* them, that form the focus of this book.

But what does it mean to say that two languages are related? It means quite simply that both languages *have evolved from a single original language*, whether recently or in the distant past. For example, we know that Rumanian, Italian, French, and Spanish are related because each is a descendant of Latin, the language spoken in Rome two millennia ago that was spread throughout much of Europe, from Portugal to Rumania, by the Roman conquests. With the collapse of the Roman empire, around 500 A.D., the various regional dialects of Latin, more or less cut off from their source, developed over time into the modern Romance languages. In the metaphor that is usually used, Latin is said to be the *mother language* and Rumanian, Sardinian, Italian, French, Catalan, Spanish, and Portuguese are *daughter languages*. A group of related languages, however small or large, is called a *language family*; in this case, Latin and its descendants are known as the Romance family.

If the question of what it means to be related is straightforward enough, how one actually *determines* whether languages are related (or more precisely how one discovers valid linguistic families like Romance) is a good deal less transparent. Because the language that gave rise to the Romance family, Latin, is abundantly attested in written records, we can in effect trace the entire history of the Romance family, by means of these written records, from its origin in Latin, through such intermediate stages as Old French and Old Spanish, down to the whole spectrum of modern Romance languages. Our problem is that Latin and the Romance languages constitute a special case; we rarely find comparable records written in the mother language of other families. What would we have done if Latin had never been written down? And what if the Romance languages themselves had never developed writing systems, so that our only knowledge of them would have been descriptions of the modern languages made by linguists? Under *these* conditions, which represent the norm for almost all of the world's languages, how would one go about discovering the Romance family? In other words, how do we discover relationships among languages that have no written history?

How Classification Proceeds

Actually, we discover relationships *not* by looking for them in a direct comparison of, say, English and Chinese, but rather by classifying languages into families, these families in turn into larger families, and so forth, in the form of the branching tree familiar from genealogical charts. The relationship of two people, or two languages, depends on their relative positions in the overall genealogical tree. Were we to adopt the naive view that the relationship of English and Chinese *could* be determined by an exhaustive comparison of just these two languages, we would probably conclude, after comparing them, that the two have next to nothing in common beyond the general characteristics that all human languages share.

The enormous diversity of human languages—English and Chinese attest it well—has certainly been an impediment toward recognizing the relationships among them, but the same is true of biology: "Historically, the extraordinary diversity of living things was an obstacle to the discovery of unifying principles about biology in general and about heredity in particular. It is not easy, after all, to see the relation between a tree and a horse" (Berg and Singer 1992:9). Nor is it easy to see the relationship between English and Chinese, but that does not mean they are unrelated, as is often supposed.

If we return now to our original example of Latin and the Romance languages, we can see why it is *classifications* we seek rather than just relationships. We have seen that Italian is related to Spanish, since both are members of the Romance family, but Italian is also related to English, not because English is a Romance language, but because the *family* to which English belongs, called Germanic, is related to the family to which Italian belongs (Romance). The classification embracing all these, usually represented in the form of a branching tree as shown in Figure 1, tells us not just that Italian is related to both Spanish and English, but that Italian is *closely* related to Spanish, one of its siblings in the Romance family, and *more distantly* related to English, the two belonging to a more ancient family called Indo-European, two of whose daughter languages were Latin and Proto-Germanic. Proto-Germanic, the mother tongue of the Germanic family, was not a written language, so its nature can only be inferred, from close examination of daughter languages like English, Dutch, German, Danish, Norwegian, and Swedish. (We cannot know, in exhaustive detail, the nature of the postulated Proto-Germanic, but we know, in part from the example of Latin, *that there had to have been such a language*.) Similarly, the only evidence for Proto-Indo-European, an unwritten language spoken at least 6,000 years ago, is its several daughter languages, which include Latin, Greek, Sanskrit, and Proto-Germanic.

Note in Figure 1 that Latin is the *mother* of the Romance languages, but a *daughter* of the Indo-European family. This suggests that Indo-European, in turn, might be a sister language of an even more ancient family. We will return to this question in Chapter 3, where we will examine some of the evidence connecting Indo-European with other families, as well as the reasons for the opposition to such evidence maintained by the majority of contemporary historical linguists.

The problem we are faced with, in seeking the origins of languages, is therefore the *classification* of the world's languages. It is classification that will tell us which languages are related, and how closely. And it is classification, at its highest levels, that will tell us whether or not all presently existing languages can be shown to share a common origin.

So how does one go about classifying languages? It is one of the goals of this book to show how this is done, but the goal is even more ambitious than that might seem, for I propose to let you, the reader, do the classifying! Now before you close this book, with a shrug of the shoulders and a lament that you were never good at foreign languages and don't really understand English grammar all that well either, let me assure you that none of that will matter. I am not going to assume that you know anything at all about language, or historical linguistics, or classification (though that would help). Human beings are very good at classifying buttons and wines and dogs, and I think you will find that you are surprisingly good at classifying languages, too, once I have shown you the process. I am asking you to classify the languages yourself because some of the conclusions we shall arrive at are considered highly controversial, and I think you will be more inclined to accept them if you come to them yourself. Then, too, I think you will learn more about classification as an active participant than you would as

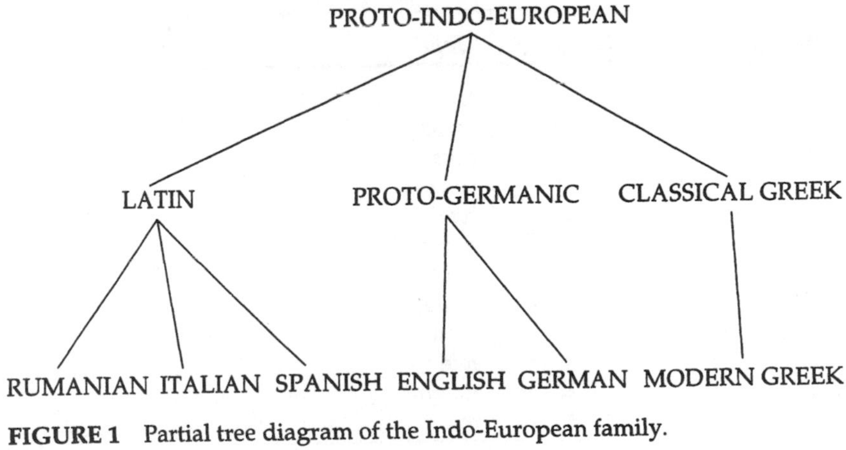

PROTO-INDO-EUROPEAN

LATIN   PROTO-GERMANIC   CLASSICAL GREEK

RUMANIAN ITALIAN SPANISH ENGLISH GERMAN MODERN GREEK

FIGURE 1 Partial tree diagram of the Indo-European family.

an innocent bystander. And perhaps you will also come to appreciate the pleasure to be had in reaching back into human prehistory by the comparison of living languages.

OK, let us proceed. The classification of languages into language families is based on discovering words in different languages that are similar in sound *and* meaning. It is not sufficient that a pair of words in two languages be similar in sounds alone, such as possessing both *p* and *r*; nor is it sufficient that two languages have words that simply have the same meaning, such as words for the color 'pink,' or words for the kinship term 'mother's older brother.' Only where both languages use, for example, the sounds *tik* to represent the meaning 'finger' is there sufficient similarity to suggest relatedness.

The best way to begin to understand how classification works is to work through a few examples. Throughout this book you will be shown tables that list words in different languages, and you will be asked, on that basis, to classify the languages into families. In these tables the languages will be identified only by letters (A, B, C, . . .), and you will not be told what the languages are until you have classified them. Table 1 lists the word for 'hand' in twelve languages. Your task is to classify these languages into language families simply on the basis of perceived similarities among these twelve forms. Since

TABLE 1   An Example

Language	Hand
A	lāmh
B	ranka
C	rēka
D	ruka
E	hænd
F	hănd
G	hant
H	mɨnə
I	mano
J	mǽ
K	mano
L	te

the *meaning* of all the forms in Table 1 is the same, you need concern yourself only with deciding which forms are similar in their constituent *sounds*. (You needn't even be concerned with the unfamiliar characters and diacritical marks that linguists and phoneticians employ to render precisely the sound of the spoken words; your guesses will usually be close enough). How many language families, then, can you identify, and what are the members of each?

If you classified these twelve languages correctly, into five families, you have successfully completed your first attempt at classification. The first of the five families consists of language A alone, since its word for 'hand' does not resemble any of the other forms listed. The second family, characterized by an *r–k* form for 'hand,' consists of languages B, C, and D. The third family, made up of languages E, F, and G, is characterized by an *h–nd* form. The fourth family, with the characteristic form *m–n*, contains languages H, I, J, and K. The fifth family, like the first, consists of a single language, L, whose characteristic form is unlike any of the others.

Each of the families in this example is characterized by a different *root* (for example, something like *hand* in the family to which languages E, F, and G belong), from which the similar modern form or forms meaning 'hand' have evolved. Such evolved forms are called *cognates*, a word that derives from Latin *cognatus* 'born together.' Thus, cognates are those words that derive from a single earlier word in a single earlier language, a word that has diversified into similar (or even dissimilar) forms in contemporary languages. (That cognates should be the focus of a book dedicated to twins is thus etymologically appropriate.)

I propose that we adopt the following conventions for representing a classification. Language *families* will be indicated by Roman numerals (I, II, III, IV, . . .); and *languages*, by capital letters (A, B, C, . . .). The classification will be expressed in the form of branching trees, one tree for each family. Thus, the proper solution to Table 1 would be the tree in Figure 2. The identification of the languages represented in Table 1 is as follows: A = Irish, B = Lithuanian, C = Polish, D = Russian, E = English, F = Danish, G = German, H = Rumanian, I = Italian,

J = French, K = Spanish, and L = Japanese. The five language families represented are known as Celtic (I), Balto-Slavic (II), Germanic (III), Romance (IV), and Japanese (V). Note that we have correctly identified the Romance family without recourse to Latin; that is, we have been able to isolate four of the languages in the Romance family independently of the written records of the mother language.

Figure 2 raises a number of interesting issues that should be explored. For example, it would appear from the figure that English (E) and Italian (I) belong to different, unrelated families. This is, however, a misreading of the figure (compare Figure 1), because classifications tell us nothing that allows us to declare that various languages are *not* related. What the classification in Figure 2 does tell us is that on the basis of the information in Table 1 we may classify these twelve languages into five distinct families. This is not a bad start for one word, but it can hardly be considered more than a beginning. When we take additional words into account, as we shall do in Chapter 1, we will confirm the classification given so blithely in Figure 2, and we will find that it can be refined in two ways. First, a comparison of several other words will show fairly quickly that families I, II, III, and IV all belong to the even more ancient family Indo-European (again, compare Figure 1). Japanese, however, will remain apart. Second, the comparison of additional vocabulary will show that the Balto-Slavic family consists of exactly two subfamilies: Baltic (Lithuanian and Latvian) and Slavic (including Russian, Polish, Czech, Slovak, Slovenian, Serbo-Croatian, Bulgarian, and others). It just so happens that the word for 'hand' is one of the characteristic traits that con-

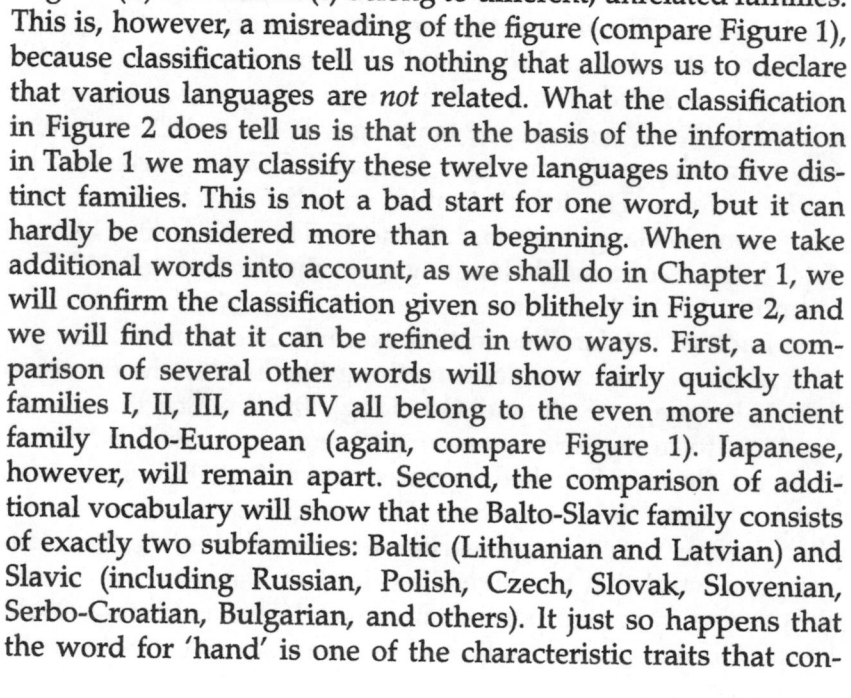
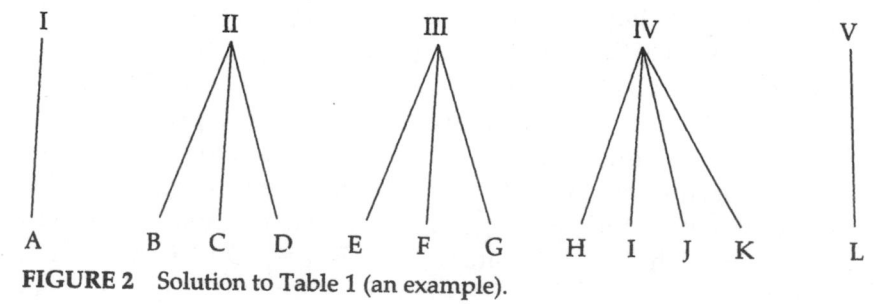

FIGURE 2   Solution to Table 1 (an example).

nects Baltic and Slavic, to the exclusion of other Indo-European languages; other words will distinguish Baltic from Slavic.

Why Classification Succeeds

Now that we have seen *how* one classifies languages, and what the meaning of the classification is, let us turn to the question of *why* this method of classification *works*. Why should a method as simple as looking for similarities in the words of different languages reveal historical connections thousands of years old? The reason this method is so successful is because it is based on the most fundamental property of human language, namely, that a word—any word in any language—is an *arbitrary* association of certain sounds with a certain meaning. The word "arbitrary" cannot be too greatly emphasized. As we saw in Table 1, different languages represent the meaning 'hand' by very different sounds: Irish *lāmh*, Lithuanian *ranka*, English *hænd*, Italian *mano*, and Japanese *te*. A little reflection should convince you that there are literally hundreds (or even thousands) of possible combinations of sounds that a language might use to represent the meaning 'hand' (English alone employs about 22 consonants and 12 vowels). So if different languages are found to use the same combination of sounds for the same meaning, it is not likely to be by chance. There are simply too many random possibilities for different sound representations (even if we ignore the vowels) for us to believe that accidental similarities occur very often. Furthermore, the longer a word is, the less likely that chance resemblances will occur. The probability of finding a word involving the same three consonants in the same order, say *malik*, with the same meaning in three different languages is much smaller than the probability of finding words with the same meaning that agree in only one consonant, say *os*, in two languages.

If one does find similar forms with the same meaning in different languages, what are all of the possible explanations for their similarity? In fact, the possible explanations for similarities among the words of different languages are the same as the possible explanations for similarities among proteins, animals, or religions. The science of classification, called *taxonomy*, is based on certain general principles, not on principles that are specific to the objects being classified. Whatever the field—animals, religions, language, whatever—similarities can be explained by just three mechanisms: convergence, borrowing, and common origin. No one has ever persuasively proposed a fourth or a fifth.

By the process of *convergence*, objects that were originally different have come to resemble each other, either accidentally or because of some motivating factor. In biology there are many fascinating cases of convergent development, such as that of dolphins (which are mammals, like us) and fish, or that of bats (also mammals) and birds. But there is a crucial distinction between biology and language, a distinction that makes convergent similarities much easier to detect in language than in biology. The convergent development of bats and birds is hardly an accidental coincidence, for if an animal is going to fly it must obey the same aerodynamic laws whatever its biological origin, whether initially a reptile (in the case of birds) or a mammal (in the case of bats). The similar bodily configurations of the two are thus motivated, in fact *dictated*, by the environment.

But as I have already emphasized, the *arbitrary nature* of the sound/meaning relationship in language guarantees that neither the environment, nor human psychology, nor anything else, other than common descent, can motivate the matching of certain sounds with certain meanings in different languages. Convergence in language is *always* accidental and the chance of its occurring is thus automatically minimized by the laws of probability noted above. (Accidental similarities do occur, but the *same* accidental resemblance cannot be expected to occur over and over.)

Actually, "always" is a bit too strong, because there *is* a small class of words where the sound/meaning relationship is not arbitrary. Such exceptions include cases of *sound symbolism*, like the widespread pattern *i* 'near (the speaker)' vs. *a* 'far (from the speaker),' or the various onomatopoeic (imitative) words like "buzz" and "murmur." The widespread kin terms *mama* 'mother' and *papa* 'father' are also generally considered sound-symbolic by most linguists. It turns out, however, that sound-symbolic words—the sole exception to the arbitrary nature of the sound/meaning relationship—constitute an exceedingly small proportion of a language's vocabulary. Because they are so anomalous, so few in number, and so vulnerable to dispute, onomatopoeic words are simply ignored when classifying languages.

The second way by which different languages may come to have similar words is when one language *borrows* a word from another language. That English, for example, has so many words that closely resemble French words is due to the fact that Middle English borrowed close to ten thousand words from Old French following the Norman conquest of England in A.D. 1066, and many of these have survived to the present day (e.g. *people, beef, crime, religion, virgin, nature, art, sport, beauty, table*). How do we distinguish similarities due to borrowing from those resulting from convergence or common origin? There are two basic techniques that are quite effective in detecting borrowed words.

First, though it is true that on occasion *any* word may be borrowed, it is equally true that in most cases only certain *kinds* of words are borrowed. The most frequent of these cases is when the name of an item is borrowed *along with the item itself,* such as the ubiquitous "coffee," "tobacco," and "television." On the other hand, such basic words as "I, you, two, who?, tooth, heart, eye, tongue, not, water," and "dead" are seldom borrowed, and are never borrowed among numerous languages covering a wide area. Thus when we find that the basic vocabulary is shared by many languages over a broad geographical expanse, we may rule out borrowing as an explanation; such mass borrowing of basic vocabulary is not known to occur in human language. When we do find similar words spread over a large geographical area, the most likely explanation is that these similarities derive from an earlier migration of people across that area. As we have seen, the similarities among the Romance languages are a consequence of the Roman conquests, which spread Latin over much of Europe; and at a greater time depth, the similarities among Indo-European languages are the result of the migration of Indo-Europeans into Europe and South Asia.

The second technique that is used to detect borrowing is to look at the distribution of the words in question in nearby languages other than those involved in the apparent borrowing. We noted above that English and French have many similar words, due to the historically documented Norman conquest of England. But would it be possible to know that English borrowed these words from French if we lacked historical records? The answer is "yes," and with little difficulty. We begin by observing that, however many similar words English and French share, it remains true that *in basic vocabulary* English resembles the other Germanic languages, and French the other Romance languages, more than either resembles the other. This by itself indicates that we are dealing with borrowing from one language family to another, but in which direction? Here the crucial clue is that the shared words tend to be characteristic of the Romance family (to which French belongs) rather than of Germanic (to which English belongs). Finally, whenever an English word does resemble one of these Romance roots, it resembles precisely the French variant (and not the Italian or whatever), which shows conclusively that English borrowed these words from French. For example, the English word "people" is very similar to French *peuple*, and much less similar to other Romance cognates of this root such as Rumanian *popor*, Italian *popolo*, Spanish *pueblo*, or Portuguese *povo*. It would thus be clear, *even in the absence of written records*, that English borrowed the word "people" from French.

If we then eliminate convergences and borrowings by the methods outlined above, the resemblances that remain must be attributed to the sole remaining explanation for such similarities, *common origin*. The perceived similarities are there today *because they have been there from the start*. What we are left with is the simple evolutionary explanation of descent with modification, the explanation that, since Darwin, has been the backbone of the biological sciences. It should be the backbone of historical linguistics as well.

In the remainder of the book we will see what can be done when common origin is given its due. In Chapter 1 you will be asked to classify languages that are found predominantly in Europe, and in Chapter 2 you will be presented with tables of languages from Africa, Asia, and the Americas. For each table, in both chapters, you will be asked to group the languages into language families on the basis of the evidence contained in the table. You will find that the same methods of classification that work so well on European languages are equally applicable to languages from any other part of the world. In Chapter 3 we will turn to the classification, not of languages, but of language families, some of which you will have already discovered in Chapters 1 and 2, and you will find that the same principles used to classify languages can be used equally well to classify language families into larger, and more ancient, families. Opposition to the idea that such broader classifications *can* be constructed will also be discussed. Chapter 4 pursues a similar theme, the comparison of New World families and the attempt to establish more comprehensive classifications of Native American languages. Once again, opposition from the experts is discussed.

In Chapter 5 you will be asked to classify language families from around the world, and will inevitably suspect that the very wide distribution of certain cognates can only be explained by concluding that all the world's language families must derive from a common source. In Chapter 6 we will make a final attempt to reconcile the abundant evidence for the various ancient families identified in Chapters 3, 4, and 5 with the almost irrational hostility displayed toward these higher-level families by traditional historical linguists. In Chapter 7 we will examine the recently discovered correlations between linguistic and biological classifications. We will see that classifications based on human genes—constructed independently of the work of linguists—correspond remarkably well with the linguistic classifications we have worked out in the earlier chapters solely on the basis of language, and we will see why there should be such a correlation. Finally, in Chapter 8, we will consider these linguistic and biological findings in a broader context, one that includes archaeological evidence as well, in an attempt to develop a general picture of when and where modern humans arose and how they spread to the farthest corners of the earth. The book concludes with an Epilogue that discusses the work of traditional historical linguistics, work that the traditionalists argue must precede classification, but that in fact *cannot begin* until the preliminary task of classification has been accomplished.

1

Language and History

Voices from the Past

Inasmuch as written language, so far as anyone knows, is only about 5,000 years old—and spoken language by itself leaves no historical trace at all—one might imagine that language would have little to tell us about human prehistory. But in fact it can tell us a great deal, not only about languages that existed long before the invention of writing, but also about the prehistorical migrations that led to the present distribution of the world's languages. This book will explore these two themes in some detail.

In a nutshell, we are able to reach back into prehistorical times and reconstruct portions of languages that existed at that time by extrapolating backward on the basis of contemporary languages and our knowledge of how languages change over time. In the Prologue we saw that similar words in different languages are usually the result of divergent evolution from a single earlier form in a single earlier language. For example, if we compare the word for 'mouse' in various European languages we will be struck by the similarity of the form in many of them: English "mouse," Swedish *mus*, German *Maus*, Dutch *muis,* Latin *mūs,* (Classical) Greek *mûs,* Russian *myš',* Polish *mysz,* Serbo-Croatian *miš.* It is a safe bet that all of these languages (and others we could mention) did not independently invent such similar forms for the name of this animal. Our first conclusion, then, is that all of these similar words for 'mouse' have evolved from a single earlier form, which was the word for 'mouse' in a single earlier language. In this case the hypothetical earlier language—about which nothing is known except the indirect evidence of its daughter families and languages— is called Proto-Indo-European.

That all of these forms are probably related, and thus provide evidence for the validity of the Indo-European family (words for 'mouse' even in neighboring Asia and Africa take quite different forms) is obvious to anyone. You don't need a Ph.D. in linguistics to reach that conclusion, just common sense. Furthermore, we can go beyond this initial conclusion—that the forms are related—to build a hypothesis about the exact phonetic form that this word had in the original Proto-Indo-European language. The problem is this: if you could somehow go back in time and listen in on a group of people speaking Proto-Indo-European around a campfire at night, and if a mouse suddenly ran through the light of the fire, what would the people have called it? Since the modern descendants of this word, several of which are enumerated above, all begin with an *m-* and end with *-s* (or some *s*-like sound), common sense, once again, tells us that the word in Proto-Indo-European also probably began with *m-* and ended with *-s.* But common sense does not tell us what the vowel was in the Proto-Indo-European word. To figure this out, you do need some advanced training, the nature of which is discussed further in the Epilogue. Suffice it for now to report that specialists who study this family—they have been at it for 200 years—believe the original Proto-Indo-European word for 'mouse' was **mūs.* The * indicates that the form is a hypothetical reconstruction, not attested in any written source; the ˉ over the *u* indicates that the vowel was pronounced with extra length, something like *muus,* as in modern English "moose."

In this book we will concern ourselves very little with reconstructing precise forms of earlier languages. Rather we shall be satisfied with merely identifying families of languages. We will see, however, that the identification of such language families, at increasingly deeper time depths, can lead to a number of surprising discoveries about the origin and dispersal of modern humans. Let us then return to the main subject of this book, the identification of language families by means of language classification.

To be honest, the simple example in the Prologue (how to classify languages on the basis of the word for 'hand') was ridiculously easy. One could scarcely go wrong. But can it really be that easy to classify languages on the basis of *many* words? Wouldn't the addition of more words lead to inconsistent or mutually contradicting patterns? Let's find out.

European Languages

Table 2 gives the forms of 13 words in nine European languages, 117 words together. Once again your task is to classify these nine languages into families (and subfamilies, if necessary), as indicated in the Prologue. I'll assist you with a few hints, but you could probably do as well without them. (If you're the intrepid sort, you're welcome to turn immediately to Table 2, but if you feel you need those hints, read on.)

As an initial strategy, try placing the most similar forms together to form very obvious families, and then compare these obvious families with each other to find less obvious families. For example, the word for 'two' in languages E and F is the same (*duo*), so at least with regard to this word you *must* group E and F together. The same considerations would apply for the words for 'me' and 'you' in languages C (*mám* and *tuvám*) and D (*mǫm* and *tuvəm*), which are virtually identical.

You will see that there are some funny-looking symbols in these words, symbols with which you probably are not familiar, though the sounds they represent are not uncommon. English has two *th* sounds, which linguists represent with the symbols θ and ð. The symbol θ represents the *th* sound in such English words as *think*, *three*, *both*, and *cloth*. The symbol ð is used to

TABLE 2 European Languages

Language	Two	Three	Me	You	Who?	Not	Mother	Father	Tooth	Heart	Foot	Mouse	He Carries
A	ʔiθn-	θalaθ-	-ni	-ka	man	lā	ʔumm-	abū	sinn	lubb	rijl-	fār	yaḥmil-
B	šn-	šaloš	-ni	-ka	mi	lo	ʔem	aβ	šen	leβ	regel	ʕak̠ḇɔr	nošeh
C	duvá	tráyas	mám	tuvám	kás	ná	mātár-	pitár-	dant-	hṛd-	pád	muṣ-	bhárati
D	duva	θrayō	mąm	tuvąm	čiš	naē-	mātar-	pitar-	dantan-	zərəd	paiðya		baraiti
E	duo	treîs	eme	sú	tís	ou(k)	mātēr	pater	odṓn	kardiā	pod-	mûs	phérei
F	duo	trēs	mē	tū	kwis	ne-	mātēr	pater	dent-	kord-	ped-	mūs	fert
G	twai	θreis	mik	θu	hwas	ni	aiθei	faðar	tunθus	hairtō	fōt		baíriθ
H	dó	trí	-m	tú	kā	ní-	māθir	aθir	dēt	kride	traig	lux	berid
I	iki	üč	ben-i	sen	kim	deyil	anne	baba	diš	kalp	ayak	sičan	tašïyor

represent the *th* sound in English words like *this*, *there*, either, and clo*the*. The symbols š and č are used to represent the sounds written *sh* and *ch* in English: *she* and pu*sh* have š, while *church* begins and ends with č. There are a few other symbols in Table 2 that are probably unfamiliar to you, but we won't worry about them (they are the symbols used in *phonetics*, not in the languages themselves). You should be able to classify these languages without knowing precisely what each symbol stands for, though of course a knowledge of what all the symbols mean, and which sounds are *likely* to change into which other sounds, would be helpful in classifying languages. Such information can be found in any introductory textbook of phonetics (for example, Abercrombie 1967, Ladefoged 1982), the field of linguistics that studies the sounds used by human languages, how they are used, and how they change over time.

Before you attempt to classify the languages in Table 2, one final observation is warranted. Notice that where we would expect the word for 'mouse' in languages D and G, there is a blank. The fact is we don't know the word for 'mouse' in these languages. In the world of linguistics we often have to put up with such partial information and do our best with what we have. As you will find out, such gaps do not prevent us from classifying languages.

If you arrived at a solution similar to that given in Figure 3, you should congratulate yourself, for two reasons. First, there are over 20,000 mathematically possible classifications of these nine languages, so your selection of the single correct one was unlikely to occur by accident. You should have been able to distinguish the three main families shown in the figure with little difficulty. As the solution shows, however, a more precise classification would group C and D together as a node intermediate between the highest level (II) and the two languages C and D. What this means historically is that C and D did not diverge from one another for some time after language II started to break up. It is because they diverged from each other later than they diverged from languages E, F, G, and H that they resemble each other more closely than they do these other languages. If you didn't group C and D together as an intermediate node, don't worry about it. This is a minor detail that would become obvious with more data and more experience. However, if you did not determine that three main families are involved, you don't get a passing grade on this test.

Second, if you correctly classified these nine languages into three basic families (I, II, and III) as indicated in Figure 3, you have discovered the same classification that Sir William Jones first noted in 1786, an event that is generally regarded as the beginning of comparative linguistics. But before we give Jones his due credit, let's examine why the classification given in Figure 3 is the correct one.

If we compare the words for 'two' in the first column of Table 2, we would immediately group C (*duvá*) and D (*duva*) together, and E (*duo*) and F (*duo*) together. Both of these groups appear to be related to each other and also to H (*dó*), since in all cases the form begins with *d-* and is followed by *u* or *o*. Language G (*twai*) should also be added to this large group, but this is not obvious unless you know that *t* and *d* are very similar sounds, as are *u* and *w*. You couldn't be expected to know that, so it's alright if you left G out of the comparison. On the other hand, the forms in languages A (*ʔiθn-*), B (*šn-*), and I (*iki*) resemble neither each other nor the forms in the one large group we have thus far identified. Thus on the basis of the word for 'two' alone we would classify the languages into four families: A ‖ B ‖ CDEFGH ‖ I, where ‖ separates families.

When we turn to the second column, the word for 'three,' we note that the forms in A (*θalāθ-*) and B (*šaloš*) are very similar, except that A has *θ* where B has *š*. If you know that *θ* and

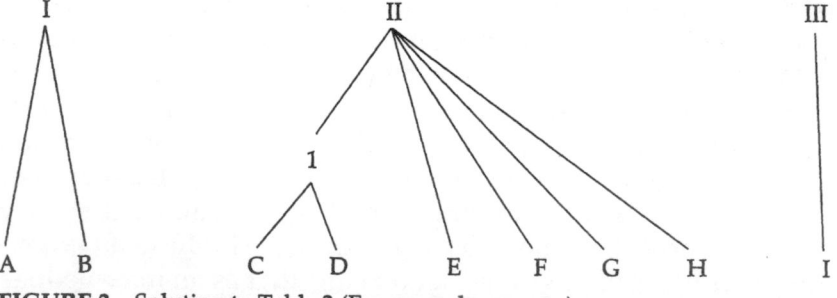

FIGURE 3   Solution to Table 2 (European languages).

š are similar sounds, one would not hesitate to group A and B together. But even if you didn't know this, it would still be a good bet that the word for 'three' would not be this similar in two different languages by chance. If one now glances back at the words for 'two' in languages A (*ʔiθn-*) and B (*šn-*), which at first appeared to have nothing in common, we observe the same correspondence, θ in language A corresponds to š in language B. Taking this into account, it appears in retrospect that perhaps the words for 'two' in A and B *are* cognate after all, that is, both derive from the same source. If the word in language A consists of two parts, *ʔi-θn-* (say, a prefix *ʔi-* followed by the root *-θn-*), then the second part corresponds exactly to the form in B according to the θ = š equation. Correspondences like this one are known in the technical literature as *sound correspondences*. You will note such correspondences from time to time in the various tables, and we will discuss them further in the Epilogue.

We are pleased to find that the large grouping identified on the basis of 'two' has an equally distinctive word for 'three,' beginning with *tr-* and often ending in *-s* (C: *tráyas*, D: *θrāyō*, E: *treîs*, F: *trēs*, G: *θreis*, H: *trí*). And once again the form in language I (*üč*) appears dissimilar to all the other forms. If we now revise the earlier classification we concocted on the basis of 'two,' then taking into account the information supplied by 'three,' we would be inclined to reduce our original classification to just three families: AB ‖ CDEFGH ‖ I. We have, in fact, on the basis of just two words, arrived at precisely the classification into three basic families that is accepted as valid by all experts.

When we examine the third column, the word for 'me,' we find a distribution of forms that fully supports our previous conclusions. The first family, involving A (*-ni*) and B (*-ni*), has identical forms. The second family, C–H, shows various forms all involving *m* (C: (*mám*, D: *mąm*, E: *eme*, F: *mē*, G: *mik*, H: *-m*). The word in language I (*ben-i*) differs from all the other forms. Thus taking into account the information in the third column, the classification is the same as before: AB ‖ CDEFGH ‖ I.

When we turn to other columns we find this three-way classification of the nine languages supported over and over. Rather than confusing the classification, each additional word we take into account confirms again and again that our early conclusions were fully justified. In addition to the evidence of the first three columns, further perusal of Table 2 leads to the conclusion that the first family, A and B, is also defined by characteristic words for 'you' (-*ka*), 'who?' (*m*-), 'not' (*l*-), 'mother' (*ʔ–m*-), 'tooth' (*s–n*), 'heart' (*l–b*), and 'foot' (*r–g–l*, where *g* has become *j* in A).

The additional evidence for the second family, C–H, is no less impressive: 'you' (*tu*), 'not' (*n*-), 'mother' (*mater*), 'father' (*pater*), 'tooth' (*dent*), 'heart' (*k–r–d*), 'foot' (*p–d*), 'mouse' (*mus*), and 'he carries' (*b–r–t*).

The final language, I, exhibits almost no similarities with the others. The word for 'who?' (*kim*) does begin with the consonant *k*-, as in the second family, but the final consonant is different and the chances of a random resemblance of a single consonant in two languages are fairly large, since most languages have only ten to twenty different consonants. Similarly, the word for 'father,' based on the consonant *b*, resembles somewhat the forms of the first family, but again the resemblance of a single consonant is not probative. Once again, I emphasize that this does not mean that language I is "unrelated" to the other eight languages, for classifications tell us nothing about "unrelatedness." They tell us rather what languages can be *shown* to be *related*, and how, on the basis of the available evidence. And on the basis of the data in Table 2 language I should be classified as a family consisting of one language, since—as far as our example takes us—there are virtually no visible similarities between I and the other languages.

You may also have asked yourself how language H can belong to the large group characterized by the word *mus* 'mouse,' when its word for 'mouse,' *lux*, looks totally different. How can H be a member of this putative family and have such a radically different word for 'mouse'? Very simply. There is no reason to expect that every language in a family will have preserved every word in the proto-language. In fact, we know that in the real world various words are replaced or lost in various languages all the time, and the reflection of the ancient store of words in the modern languages is always imperfect. But the reflection here is clear enough to allow us to perceive easily that the nine languages in Table 2 fall naturally into just three families.

The languages that I chose for your first test are as follows: A = Arabic, B = Hebrew, C = Sanskrit, D = Avestan, E = Classical Greek, F = Latin, G = Gothic, H = Old Irish, and I = Turkish. Before you protest that Arabic, Hebrew, Sanskrit, Avestan, and Turkish are not European languages, and should not have been included in a table of European languages, I admit that I deliberately led you astray. I wanted you to classify these languages strictly on the basis of the linguistic evidence found in them, without being prejudiced by such irrelevant information as where a language is spoken, the skin color of its speakers, or the mode of subsistence of the speakers. Let this be a warning that some of the other tables may well contain "ringers" too, that is, languages that are not actually spoken in the area supposedly being studied. The lesson you should draw from my deception is that linguistic boundaries often transcend both geographical boundaries (for example, Africa, Europe, Asia) and political boundaries (for example, Canada, United States, Mexico).

Sanskrit, a language spoken in northern India during the first millennium B.C., is still used in the Hindu religion in much the way Latin was used by the Catholic church until recently. And just as Latin gave rise to the modern Romance languages, the language that was originally Sanskrit has evolved over three millennia into several dozen distinct languages, including Hindi, Bengali, Gujarati, and Punjabi—all spoken in northern India—and Nepali, spoken in Nepal. In a similar fashion, Avestan, the sacred language of the ancient Persians, has given rise to the modern Iranian languages, including Farsi and Kurdish. Gothic is the language of the oldest Germanic text, a translation of the Bible made in the middle of the fourth century A.D. in what is today northern Bulgaria.

The first family you identified (A and B) is known as the Semitic family. Though Arabic and Hebrew are probably the two best-known Semitic languages today, there are altogether some twenty extant Semitic languages, in addition to such important extinct languages as Akkadian, Phoenician, and Geez. Other Semitic languages still spoken include Amharic, the national language of Ethiopia, and Tigrinya, the national language of the newly independent country Eritrea.

The second family (C–H) is the Indo-European family, which contains all of the languages presently spoken in Europe, with very few exceptions (for example, Basque, Hungarian, Finnish, Estonian). The Indo-European languages also extend into Asia, running through Iran, Afghanistan, and Pakistan into India.

Turkish (I) is one member of a family called Turkic, which includes about 30 other languages (for example, Uzbek, Kazakh, Azerbaijani, Yakut) extending from Turkey across Asia as far as northeastern Siberia. The geographic distribution of these three families is shown in Map 1.

I chose these languages for your first test not at random but rather because it was precisely these languages that Sir William Jones first classified, in just the manner we have, at the inception of historical linguistics. Jones's recognition of the

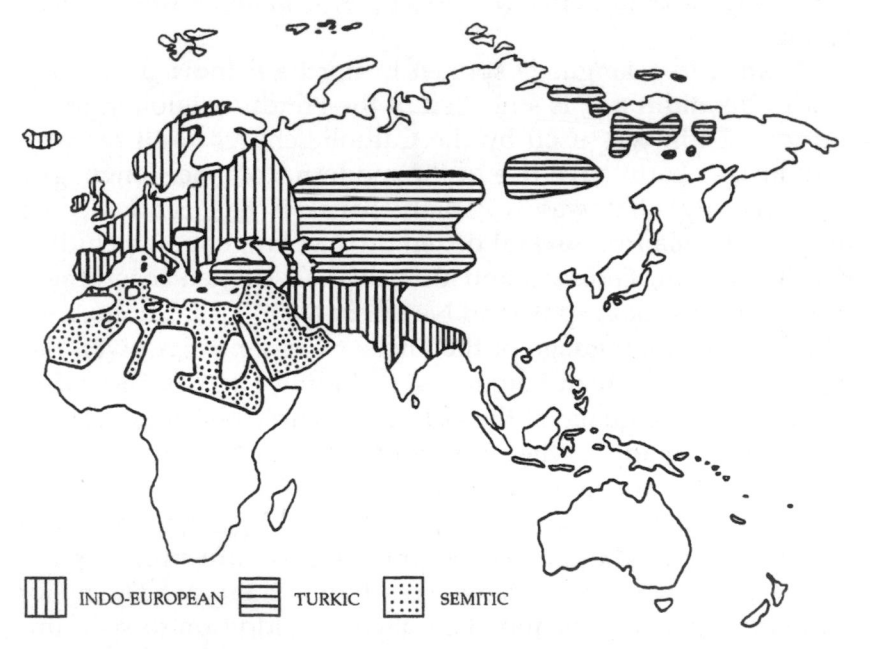

MAP 1   The Indo-European, Turkic, and Semitic Families.

Indo-European family in his *Third Discourse to the Asiatic Society* (Calcutta), in 1786, has been called

> One of the most quoted formulations among all scholarly formulations in all disciplines. In the history of ideas it stands as one of the great conceptions that attempt to explain human beings and their intellectual–cultural advances. In some ways it ultimately separated language from religion as clearly as Darwin later separated science from religion. It moved language study away from mythology, speculation, and intuition, and toward the sciences. (Cannon 1990: 360)

Jones's postulation of an Indo-European family was as follows:

> The *Sanscrit* language, whatever be its antiquity, is of a wonderful structure; more perfect than the *Greek*; more copious than the *Latin*, and more exquisitely refined than either, yet bearing to both of them a stronger affinity, both in the roots of verbs and in the forms of grammar, than could possibly have been produced by accident; so strong indeed, that no philologer could examine them all three, without believing them to have sprung from some common source, which, perhaps, no longer exists; there is similar reason, though not quite so forcible, for supposing that both the *Gothick* and the *Celtick*, though blended with a very different idiom, had the same origin with the *Sanscrit*, and the old *Persian* [= Avestan] might be added to the same family.

It was not by accident that Jones chose these particular languages to compare. In addition to serving as a Supreme Court justice in India, Jones had a lifelong fascination with language and was reputed to have "mastered" some 28 languages. Of these he knew Latin, Classical Greek, Persian, Sanskrit, and Arabic well, and with the aid of a dictionary could read Hebrew, Turkish, Hindi, Bengali, German, and Spanish, among others. Still other languages he had studied more briefly (Tibetan, Chinese, Japanese, Russian, Coptic, and Amharic). From his extensive linguistic studies Jones had realized that Arabic, Hebrew, Chaldean (also called Akkadian), and Amharic (which Jones referred to as Ethiopic) belonged to the same family, now called Semitic. And he knew that Turkish was a member of neither the Indo-European nor Semitic families. So when Jones outlined the membership of the Indo-European family in 1786, he excluded such languages as Arabic, Hebrew, and Turkish not because he hadn't looked at them, but rather because he *had* looked at them and had seen at a glance—just as you saw in Table 2—that these languages were totally different.

We would not be giving Jones his due credit, however, if we were merely to mention that he noted similarities among Indo-European languages. His crowning achievement was not just that he saw these similarities, but that he *explained* them. And the evolutionary explanation he gave—descent with modification from a common ancestor—was the one Darwin would give 72 years later for biology (with the addition of natural selection, which does not apply in language).

Even before Jones, resemblances among languages had been recognized, say between Classical Greek and Latin, but the explanation was that one language had changed into the other; in this case Greek was thought to have given rise to Latin, as described in the *Aeneid*. When it was recognized that Sanskrit shared many words with both Greek and Latin, the hypothesis was revised: perhaps Sanskrit had given rise to Classical Greek in the same manner that Classical Greek later gave rise to Latin. This was an evolutionary explanation in a static framework; there was no sense of historical depth, no sense that the relationships among these languages were more complex than simply one language's giving rise to another. In very similar fashion, scholars of the day were attempting to derive *all* languages from one language, with Hebrew the favored choice (though one Dutch scholar held out resolutely, and patriotically, for Dutch). Jones realized, however, that the mother language of Latin, Classical Greek, and Sanskrit no longer existed, and that the similarities among them were due to their having each inherited these words *independently* from Proto-Indo-European. Today, over a century after Darwin, such a conception seems natural and obvious, but to the static mode of thinking of the eighteenth century it was revolutionary.

To better understand what kind of evidence led Jones to his discovery of the Indo-European family, let us examine in slightly more detail one of the words that Jones recognized as being of Indo-European origin, one that you too identified in Table 2, namely, the word for 'he carries,' which takes the form b–r–t. You were able to group the words for 'he carries' together on the basis of their overall resemblance in form, but Jones knew that the resemblance was even deeper, in that the final -*t* was the marker of the third person (*he*) and the initial portion of the word (*b–r*) was the verb root (*carry*). (The English verb 'bear' is a direct descendant of this root.) It was these kinds of facts that Jones was referring to when he mentioned a strong affinity "in the roots of verbs and in the forms of grammar" among the various Indo-European languages. Furthermore, just as -*t* marked the third-person singular 'he,' first-person 'I' was represented by the ending -*m* and second-person 'you' by the ending -*s*. There was thus a complete verbal paradigm, reflected in various degrees in various languages, whereby suffixes were added to the verbal root to express the first three persons. In Sanskrit the three forms were *bhárā-mi* 'I carry,' *bhára-si* 'you carry,' *bhára-ti* 'he carries.'

Why Languages Change

We have seen in this chapter that it is possible to classify languages into language families on the basis of similarities in words, the assumption being that over time a single original word can change in various ways, through both phonetic and semantic shifts, in various daughter languages. The question we haven't yet touched upon, however, is why languages change at all. Our first reaction might well be that this is the wrong question to ask. After all, everything in the natural world is constantly changing, from the weather to fashion, so shouldn't we expect language too to be in a constant state of flux? The reply to this flip response is "Of course," but that doesn't really answer the question of why languages change. In fact, it has long been clear that there is no single, simple reason why language changes; rather, there are a whole series of reasons—which interact in incredibly complex ways—to produce the linguistic variation that we perceive in the world's language families.

Though it is a point that is seldom appreciated, linguists have learned which linguistic changes are normal, or usual, and which are abnormal, or nonexistent, *largely from the process of classifying the world's languages.* We know what linguistic changes are likely to occur by comparing real languages, as you have done and will do in this book, and as you classify the languages in the various tables, you will come to sense what linguistic change is really like. In the Epilogue we will examine certain aspects of linguistic change in more detail, but such considerations are really more appropriate after we have some first-hand contact with real languages. For now, we will examine briefly a few of the general factors that are responsible for language change.

One of the most important of these factors is a general human tendency to make things simpler, which is variously described as ease of articulation or human laziness. Let us consider an example. In many languages around the world we find that [p,t,k] have changed into [b,d,g], respectively, when they occur between vowels. Thus, language A might have *aba* 'fish,' *uda* 'walk,' and *paga* 'tree,' while the closely related languages B, C, and D all have *apa, uta,* and *paka* for the same three words. But why should [p,t,k] tend to become [b,d,g] between vowels? The answer is that vowels are pronounced with the vocal cords vibrating, and so are the consonants [b,d,g]. For [p,t,k], however, the vocal cords do not vibrate; in fact it is precisely the vibration of the vocal cords that distinguishes *p* from *b*, *t* from *d*, and *k* from *g*. So to pronounce, say, *aba* the speaker needs only to turn the vocal cords on at the start of the word, pronounce *a*, then *b*, then *a*, and then turn them off. To pronounce *apa*, however, the speaker must first turn the vocal cords on, pronounce *a*, then turn the vocal cords off and pronounce *p*, then turn the vocal cords back on and pronounce *a*, and, finally, turn them off, at the end of the word. In other words the vocal cords must be turned on and off twice to pronounce *apa*, but only once for *aba*. It is in this sense that *aba* is easier to say than *apa*. Changes like this can take place almost imperceptibly in a language. In fact, if you are a speaker of standard American English, the odds are that you pronounce 'water' as [wadr] and would consider a pronunciation of [watr] foreign (brackets indicate that a word is being written in phonetic symbols rather than in the usual orthography).

Another cause of language change is that people apparently *like* a certain amount of change, for whatever underlying psychological reasons. One can only marvel at the rapidity with which school-age adolescents adopt and then drop new words, sometimes in imitation of their peers, other times on the basis of a character in a popular TV show. Words for expressing approval of something seem particularly susceptible to this process, as the succession 'neat' (1950's), 'cool' (1960's), 'bad' (1970's), 'rad' (1980's), and 'awesome' (1990's) indicates. Of course all of these words were always in the language ('rad' is a shortening of 'radical'), so what changed was only the context in which they were used.

Sometimes an entirely new word develops in a language. For example, the Proto-Indo-Europeans had a word for 'dog,' **kwon-*, which survives in modern English as 'hound.' About a thousand years ago, during the stage of the language known as Old English, a new word appeared, spelled originally *docga*, which eventually came to replace the original word. Today, 'dog' is the normal English term and 'hound' has assumed a more specialized meaning of 'hunting dog.' Where did this new word for 'dog' come from? No one knows. We can follow in historical texts its first attestation, its subsequent rivalry with 'hound,' and its ultimate victory as the general English word for 'dog,' but we are not likely ever to know how this particular word came into being. The Spanish word for 'dog,' *perro*, which replaced the original Latin form *cane(m)*, is also of unknown origin.

These brief comments on linguistic change are intended simply to illustrate a few of the many aspects of linguistic change, a topic that is discussed in depth in any standard textbook on historical linguistics (for example, Hock 1986, Anttila 1989). Still we have not really answered the question why languages change. It is all well and good that voiceless consonants like [p,t,k] tend to change into the voiced consonants [b,d,g] when they occur between vowels—this is certainly useful information to have when comparing languages—but there are many languages in which [p,t,k] show no signs of changing between vowels, even over long periods of time. Thus, if a change is going to take place we are likely to know what kind of a change it will be, but predicting when, or even if, one of these normal sound changes will actually take place is as impossible as predicting next month's weather. Or, in the case of 'dog,' why should a word that had persisted for 5,000 years suddenly be replaced by a new word of unknown origin? And why should this happen in English and Spanish, rather than in German (which retains the normal Germanic word *Hund* 'dog') or in Italian (which retains the Latin word *cane* 'dog')? These kinds of questions we cannot answer. We *can* understand why various types of linguistic change have taken place, especially when they occur across whole ranges of words, and we shall explore this topic further in the Epilogue, but we cannot predict how specific languages *will* change in the future.

2

Language Families

What is Known

We have seen how the comparison of even a few words can lead to the grouping of certain languages, on the basis of fairly obvious similarities; such a group of related languages is called a language family. In Chapter 1 we identified the Indo-European family, which includes most of the languages of Europe and extends into southwestern Asia as far as India. Over the past five centuries, of course, Indo-European languages have been widely dispersed around the world, following the voyages of exploration and conquest. English has largely supplanted the native languages in North America, New Zealand, Australia, and various smaller localities around the world; Spanish has replaced the indigenous languages of Central and South America and some of the larger Caribbean islands; Portuguese has been spread to Brazil and parts of Africa; French was transplanted to parts of North America and the Caribbean, including Quebec, Louisiana, and Haiti, and to parts of Africa; and Russian has expanded eastward through Asia as far as the Pacific coast. But when we speak of the distribution of languages and language families in this book, it should be understood that we are referring to the pre-Columbian distribution, not the modern one.

We also identified the Semitic family of the Middle East and North Africa, and we saw that the Turkish language belongs to neither of these two families. Rather, Turkish belongs to the Turkic family, as an examination of further Turkic languages (for example, Azerbaijani, Uzbek, Kazakh) would quickly reveal.

In the present chapter you will be asked to classify languages—to identify language families—from other parts of the world. You will be presented with tables of languages from Africa, Asia, and the Americas, and you will be asked to classify these languages into families, just as you did with European languages in the previous chapter. We saw why Sir William Jones's recognition of the Indo-European family on the basis of similar words in different languages was so revolutionary in its implications. But could this simple method work as well elsewhere in the world? Some scholars have doubted it. After all, the Indo-European family is privileged to have ancient written records dating back thousands of years, in some of its languages, while elsewhere in the world it is more often the case that there are *no* written records at all. With that in mind, let us, without further ado, take a look at some African languages.

African Languages

In this section you will be presented with a table that gives twelve words in twelve African languages, and you will be asked to group these twelve languages into the correct families, just as you did in the previous chapter. Later sections will present similar tables for Asian languages and Native American languages. By actually working through these tables yourself, rather than simply reading my explanation of them, you will come to understand what classification is really like. Consider, then, the data given in Table 3.

You may analyze this table any way you see fit, but the way I recommend is to go through the table one word at a time

TABLE 3 African Languages

Language	I/Me	You	Four	Tongue	Squeeze	Speak	Drink	Blow	Year	Eye	Sun	Meat
A	mi	i	!nani	theri	tsam	okx'ui	k''ã	čũ̄	kuri	/gã	/am	!hã
B	am	aŋgo	nei	yeme	kambe	ambo	nyɔ	pɛp	mbu	isɔ	oɓa	nyama
C	yɛn	yin	nguan	liep	nyač̌	jam	dek	koth	ruon	nyin	akɔl	riŋo
D	ami	akhu	ne	limi	kham	amb	phuza	phepheth	nyaka	so	langa	inyama
E	ni	kai	fuɗu	haršě	matsa	faɗa	šã	būsa	sěkara	idõ	rana	nama
F	ke	tsa		dam	kxao	kxoi	kxa	gom	kuri	!kai	/am	/ka
G	ame	ku	kwala	limi	kam	tana	nyw	pepe	lima	iso	kumbi	situ
H	ane	inye	añgwan	ñgelyep	iny	mwa	ie	kũt	keny	koñg	asis	peny
I	ti	tsa	haka	nami	tsam	kx'ui	kx'a	igom	kuri	mũs	/am	kx'o
J	mimi	ako	ñne	limi	kamu	amb	nyw	pepe	aka	čõ	jua	nyama
K			fhwaɗi	lisi	matsu'ɔ'i	puwo'i	sawo'i	pintu	soni	idi	futi	lo
L	nanu	inyi	õnguan	ngejep		iro	mat	kut	arin	ongu	olong	kiriŋo

and for each word mark down what appear to be the obvious groups. Put the leftover languages, those that don't seem to group with anything, off to the right. If a language looks as if it might belong to a group, but you are not completely persuaded, you might put parentheses around the language to indicate a certain amount of doubt. Following these conventions, my analysis of the African table takes the form given in Table 4.

Beginning with the first column, the word for 'I, me,' we see that there is a group of forms with the consonant *m* (A: *mi*, B: *am*, D: *ami*, G: *ame*, J: *mimi*) and another with the consonant *n* (C: *γεn*, E: *ni*, H: *ane*, L: *nanu*). There are also two languages with completely distinct forms (F: *ke*, I: *ti*) and one language, K, whose first-person pronoun was not given in the source of these data.

In the second column, the pronoun 'you,' the forms for languages D (*akhu*), G (*ku*), and J (*ako*) are very similar, while B (*aŋgo*) and E (*kai*) are somewhat similar to these forms and could conceivably be related to them. C (*yin*), H (*inye*), and L (*inyi*) also seem to form a group by themselves, as do F (*tsa*) and I (*tsa*). Language A (*i*) is unlike any of the others, and the information is again lacking for language K.

When we examine the third word, the number 'four,' we

TABLE 4   Analysis of Table 3

Word	Groups				Leftovers
I/me	ABDGJ	CEHL			F,I,K
you	(B)D(E)GJ	CHL		FI	A,K
four	(A)BDJ	CHL	EK		F,G,I
tongue	(B)DGJ	CHL			A,E,F,I,K
squeeze	BDGJ	(C)(H)	EK	AI	F,L
speak	BGJ		E(K)	AFI	C,D,H,K,L
drink	BGJ		E(K)	AFI	C,D,H,L
blow	BDGJ	CHL		FI	A,E,K
year	DJ	CL		AFI	B,E,G,H,K
eye	BDG(J)	(H)(L)	EK		A,C,F,I
sun		(C)(L)		AFI	B,D,E,G,H,J,K
meat	BDEJ	CL			A,F,G,H,I,K

see three distinct groups: (1) B (*nei*), D (*ne*), J (*ñne*), and perhaps A (*!nani*); (2) C (*nguan*), H (*añgwan*), and L (*õnguan*); (3) E (*fuɗu*) and K (*fhwaɗi*). Data for F are lacking, and G (*kwala*) and I (*haka*) are leftovers. After just three words, we already begin to see an outline of a classification into four groups.

The final nine words show, however, that this preliminary classification is only partly correct. The words for 'squeeze, speak, drink, year,' and 'sun' all indicate that A belongs with the FI group. Note, for example, that the word for 'squeeze' in A (*tsam*) is identical to the same word in I (*tsam*), while the word for 'speak' in A (*okx'ui*) strongly resembles the same word in both F (*kxoi*) and I (*kx'ui*).

Furthermore, when the final nine words are taken into account, the position of E becomes clearer. The first three words suggested (unhelpfully) that E had fallen in with three different groups, but the remainder of the data in Table 4 shows that E is to be grouped with K, as the words for the number 'four' suggested (E: *fuɗu*, K: *fhwaɗi*). For example, the word for 'squeeze' in language E is *matsa*, which bears more than a striking resemblance to the same word in language K (*matsu'o'i*), and the words for 'eye' in E (*idõ*) and K (*idi*) are also similar.

Weighing all the evidence in Table 3, as analyzed in Table 4, it appears that there are four basic groups: BDGJ ‖ CHL ‖ EK ‖ AFI. Finally, within the BDGJ group there are hints that language B stands somewhat apart from D, G, and J, as seen in the words for 'you' (B: *aŋgo* vs. D: *akhu*, G: *ku*, J: *ako*) and 'tongue' (B: *yemɛ* vs. *limi* in D, G, and J). Further evidence would quickly confirm the notion that languages D, G, and J

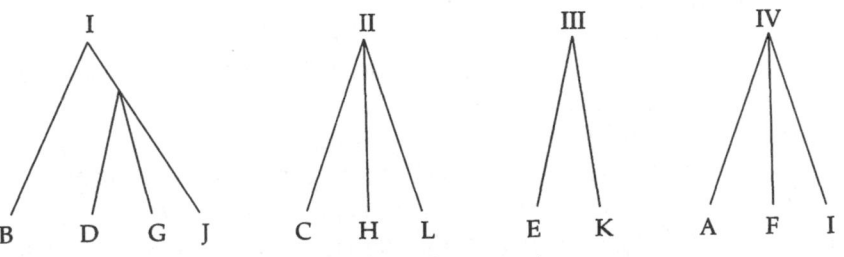

I   II   III   IV

B   D   G   J   C   H   L   E   K   A   F   I

FIGURE 4 Solution to Table 3 (African languages).

are closer to each other than any of them is to B. The solution to Table 3 is shown in Figure 4.

The evidence in the tables of this chapter can, of course, be interpreted to different degrees of thoroughness according to the reader's linguistic knowledge. At one level of interpretation—the level of most readers of this book—similar words can be identified and grouped impressionistically, on the basis of the most obvious similarities among perceived cognates, without either a detailed knowledge of what all the phonetic symbols sound like or any specialized knowledge of what sounds are likely to change into which other sounds. One could hardly fail to notice that the word for 'tongue' is identical (*limi*) in languages D, G, and J, and is somewhat similar in language B (*yemɛ*). The cognates are sufficiently similar (which is to say, obvious) at this basic level that they allow one to determine the classification of the proper linguistic families even without any specialized knowledge of the languages.

At another level of linguistic knowledge—where one knows all the phonetic symbols and has a general understanding of which sound changes are common—it is possible to recognize additional cognates, that is, to identify similarities that are not obvious. In this case, however, these additional cognates will merely confirm the classification arrived at on the basis of the most obvious similarities. For example, the reader who has no training in linguistics might well not have suspected that the word for 'tongue' in language B, *yemɛ*, is related to the words for 'tongue' in languages D, G, and J, *limi* in all three cases. To a linguist, however, such a relationship would seem highly probable since *l*'s often turn into *y*'s in linguistic evolution. For example, Spanish *calle* 'street' is pronounced [kaye] (brackets indicate the word is being written in phonetic symbols rather than in the usual orthography), and in French *papillon* 'butterfly' the *-ll-* is pronounced like a *y*. In addition, because the vowel *i* is very similar to the vowels *e* and *ɛ*, this difference, too, in the word *yemɛ*, is of little importance. A linguist would most likely assume that the 'tongue' word in language B has undergone three simple sound changes, *limi* > *yimi* > *yeme* > *yemɛ*, and thus the form in language B is much closer to that in languages D, G, and J than the nonspecialist might think.

There is yet a third level of cognates whose relationships are even more obscure than are those in the case of *yemε*. To detect these cognates one must have not just a *general* knowledge of phonetics, but also a *specialized* knowledge of the family in question, in particular the family-specific sound correspondences, which we will discuss more fully in the Epilogue. Obviously, these obscure cognates play no role in the *discovery* of language families, for the simple reason that these obscure cognates become apparent as a result of sound correspondences in a family *that has already been recognized*. A classic example of such a cognate is the Armenian word for 'two,' which is *erku*. Even though it is a single language, Armenian constitutes a separate branch of the Indo-European family, comparable to the Slavic, Germanic, or Romance branches of that family. It turns out that Armenian *erku* is cognate with the other Indo-European words for 'two' given in the first column of Table 2; that is, Armenian *erku* shares a common origin with Latin *duo*, Greek *duo*, Avestan *duva*, and Old Irish *do*. Despite its dissimilar form, linguists have been able to unravel the sequence of sound changes that led from the original Proto-Indo-European form **dwo* (the asterisk means that this form is the hypothetical reconstructed ancestor from which all the modern Indo-European forms for 'two' have derived) to modern Armenian *erku*. This cognacy of Armenian *erku* with the other Indo-European forms was not recognized, however, for almost 100 years after Jones identified the Indo-European family, and—most significantly— *it never played any role whatsoever* in the classification of Indo-European languages.

We will not generally be concerned with obscure cognates like *erku* in this book, though such nontransparent cognates do exist in some of the tables. In the initial stages of classification it is the *obvious* similarities that count; refinements and extensions proceed from that base. But it will be helpful in analyzing subsequent tables if you are able to recognize more of the second-level cognates, so, toward that end, we will do well to see which sounds are similar and may, therefore, correspond among cognate words. The vowels *i, e, ε* are similar to each other, as are *u, o, ɔ*. The consonants, which are more numerous, present greater complexity, but we may begin by recognizing the following three groups of closely related sounds that may correlate in cognate forms: (1) *p, ph, f, b, ɓ, β,* (2) *t, th, d, ɗ, ð,* and (3) *k, kh, x, g, γ.* The first group comprises consonants that are all pronounced with the lips; the second group contains consonants pronounced with the tip of the tongue; and the third group consists of consonants pronounced with the back of the tongue.

In looking for cognates in the tables it is important not to be too concerned by differences *within* one of these three consonant groups, but differences *between* the groups, such as *b* in one language and *x* in another, will usually rule out the possibility of cognacy. For example, in the word for 'blow' in Table 3, language D (*phepheth*) shows *ph* where languages B (*pɛp*), G (*pepe*), and J (*pepe*) have *p*. Since both *ph* and *p* belong to the first group of related sounds listed above, this difference is of little importance, and it is fair to assume that all four forms are probably cognate. Moreover, if we look at the word for 'squeeze' in these same languages we see that language D (*kham*) has *kh* where B (*kambe*), G (*kam*), and J (*kamu*) show *k*. This difference too should not trouble us, since both *kh* and *k* belong to the third group of similar consonants. A consideration of additional words would reveal that this difference between language D, on the one hand, and languages B, G, and J, on the other, is in fact a regular, predictable difference. Compare also, for example, the word for 'you' in language D (*akhu*) with the corresponding word in languages G (*ku*) and J (*ako*). In its most general form the rule that describes this predictable difference would state that *ph, th, kh* in language D correspond to *p, t, k* in languages B, G, and J. Thus, rather than constituting an anomaly to be explained, this difference represents a regular sound correspondence of the kind we discussed with regard to Arabic *θ* and Hebrew *š* in the last chapter, a kind we shall discuss in more depth in the Epilogue.

Before we move on to consider Asian languages, let me identify the twelve African languages in Table 3, and the families into which they should be classified. Languages B (Duala), D (Zulu), G (Mbundu), and J (Swahili) belong to the Bantu family of languages that covers most of the southern half of Africa. Despite their enormous geographical distribution, all Bantu languages are very similar, as you saw in Table 3, even though the four Bantu languages chosen for this exercise were taken from the geograpically most distant regions of Bantu territory, Duala and Mbundu from West Africa, Swahili from East Africa, and Zulu from South Africa. How can languages spoken so far apart be so similar? The answer is quite simple. The Bantu family of languages, which number several hundred, represent the modern reflection of the Bantu migration that began near southeastern Nigeria around 2,300 years ago and rapidly spread southward and eastward across southern Africa. The Bantu languages are so similar for the same reason the Romance languages Portuguese and Rumanian are so similar: a relatively recent and rapid expansion from a single original homeland, West Africa for Bantu and Italy for the Romance family. In Chapter 8 we will see how the evidence from linguistics, genetics, and archaeology can be aggregated to form a general, and well-supported, theory of how and when the Bantu family spread through southern Africa.

Languages A (!Kung), F (G//ana), and I (Nama, better known as Hottentot, which is a pejorative name to be avoided) belong to the Khoisan family, which is renowned for its abundance of click consonants. Many languages, including English, use clicks as interjections. In English, for example, the dental click [/k] is written as 'tsk, tsk' and expresses mild disapproval. A lateral click, [//k], is used by English-speakers to urge on horses or to call cats and dogs, while a retroflex click [!k] is sometimes used to imitate the popping of a cork out of a bottle. In Khoisan languages, however, clicks are used not in this imitative fashion, but as ordinary consonants that combine with other sounds to form words.

Clicks are also used in Zulu and Xhosa, two Bantu languages that have borrowed the clicks from the surrounding Khoisan languages. It was almost certainly at the expense of these Khoisan peoples that the Bantu expansion spread through southern Africa, as the isolation of two Khoisan languages in East Africa (Hadza and Sandawe) seems to suggest. The ability of the Bantu people to spread so quickly through territory already occupied by others reflected two advantages they held over the Khoisan people. First, the Bantu were agriculturalists, and could thus support a much larger population than the hunting-and-gathering Khoisan, whose numbers were severely limited by their mode of subsistence. Second, the Bantu possessed, across at least part of their expansion, an advanced metal technology that provided them with superior weapons.

Languages E (Hausa) and K (Bole) belong to the Chadic family, a group of over a hundred languages found in central Africa. Hausa is one of the most widespread African languages, with speakers numbering in the millions, whereas Bole had only 32,000 speakers at last count (in 1952, the latest date for which numbers are available). Were we to examine further the Chadic family, we would soon see that the Semitic family (which, as we saw in Chapter 1, includes Arabic and Hebrew) shares many fundamental cognates with the Chadic family. These families are, in fact, recognized today as branches of an even more ancient family known as Afro-Asiatic, which we shall meet again in Chapter 5.

Finally, languages C (Dinka), H (Nandi), and L (Maasai) are members of the Nilotic family of East Africa. The Nilotic group is but a subbranch of an even larger family, Nilo-Saharan, which will also be discussed in Chapter 5. The distribution of these four families—Bantu, Khoisan, Chadic, and Nilotic—is shown in Map 2.

Asian Languages

Having already classified European and African languages, we can move on to the Asian languages with confidence. Relying once again on common sense, we will find our task no more difficult than before. As we examine the Asian languages, bear in mind that we are not obliged to arrive at a *final* conclusion on the basis of one table. Rather, we shall simply draw whatever conclusions seem likely.

Before examining the table, however, a few more hints are in order, concerning which sounds are similar and are thus likely to be found in cognate words. The sounds Λ and $ł$ are varieties of *l*, and all *l*-sounds may be compared with one another. Furthermore, *r*'s and *l*'s are similar to one another, and often interchange in cognate forms, not just in Asia but around the world. Note, for example, that the Amste*l* river flows through Amste*r*dam. The symbol *η* represents the sound written *ng* in English words like 'sing' (since some linguistic descriptions use *ng* for *η*, the two may be considered equivalent). We are now ready to tackle the twelve Asian languages listed in Table 5, proceeding word by word as before.

This time I won't be providing an analysis sheet for the table, partly as an encouragement for you to construct one your-

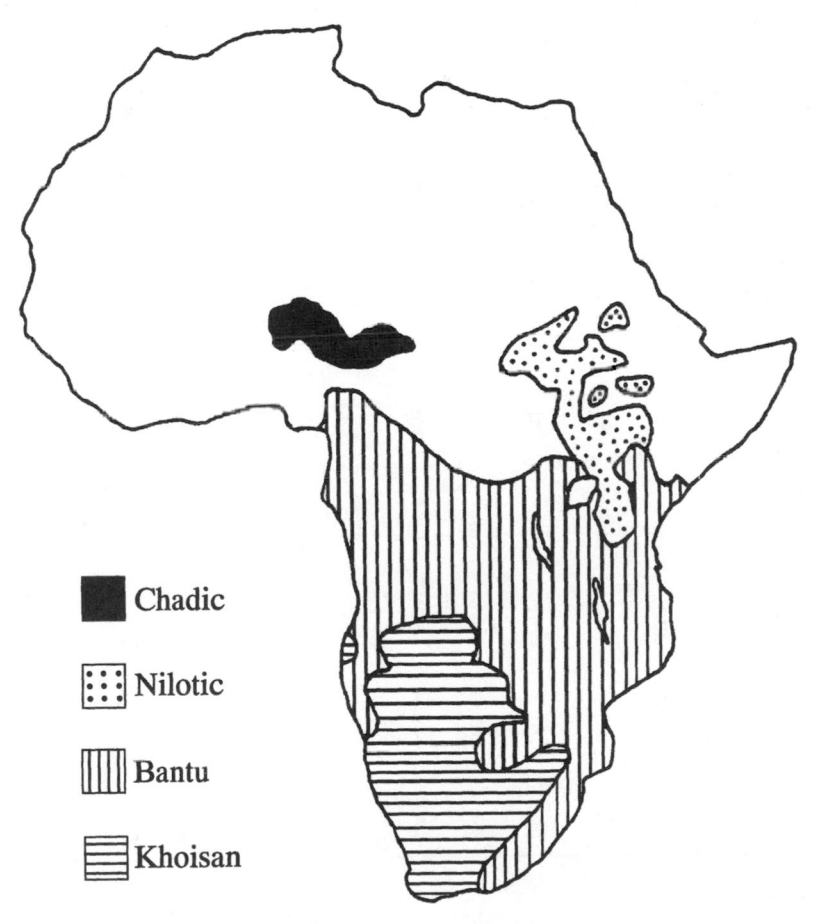

MAP 2 The Chadic, Nilotic, Bantu, and Khoisan families.

TABLE 5 Asian Languages

Language	Two	Three	Bird	Eye	Give	Blood	Water	Stone	Name	Snow	Who	Say
A	tkit	yaloi	nonda	aŋǰĕ	kei	čimeŋ	lauye	šeul	niu	erimeŋ	kin	mon
B	in	dɔʔŋ	dūm	dĕš	qʌdəm	šúʎ	ũʎ	tiʔš	i	tĭk	ana	sagabet
C	ñũ	sum	bya	mig	sɓyin	ťħaa	čʰũ	to	miŋ	qhaɲ	sũ	smra
D	ñi	pu	noŋ	mua	pu	ntšħaŋ	ʔoŋ	ywi	meŋ	npaŋ	tu	hai
E	irä	musi	xăxũr	xan	tir	ditar	dir	xal	pin	barf	dĕr	pănĭng
F	kahte	koɦme	lintu	silmä	anta	veni	vete	kivi	nimi	lumi	ken	sanoa
G	hnats	sum	pya	myak	pe	swe	re	kyauk	maɲ	hninge	bhay su	mrwak
H	iru	mũŋu	kokku	kaɳ	tăr	neyttŏr	nĭr	kal	pĕr		ēvaṉ	paɳi
I	ina	tõŋa	tũma	tiš	hipenaŋ	šur	ũl	šĭš	ix	thĭk	ašĭx	dačagaraŋ
J	ñi	pua	nɔʔ	mwei	pun	dzyaam	wam	gyou	meŋ	bwon		kɔŋ
K	kĕt	hãrma	lũd	sem	ad	vĕr	vize	kŏve	nĕv	lom	ki	mon-d
L	njidh	səm	tiog	mjɔkw	pjid	χiwet	šwi	χiagw	myẽŋ	htin		gywat

self. I will, however, discuss the table in general terms, but you should read further only after you have finished classifying the languages in Table 5.

The first column in the table gives the word for 'two.' One may discern three basic forms, one with *k–t* (AFK), one with *ir–* (EH), and a large third group characterized by some variety of *-n-* (BCDGIJL). For the moment, let's not try to subdivide this large group, but we should note that the forms in languages D and J, *ñi* are identical. As a first step, then, we can set up three families: AFK ‖ BCDGIJL ‖ EH.

You may have noticed that language A has an initial *t-* before the *k–t* form. Human languages often add *prefixes* or *suffixes* to roots to modulate their meaning; in English, for example, the word 'revisited' consists of the prefix *re-*, the root *visit*, and the suffix *-ed*. Analogously, we assume, in the case of the word for 'two' in language A, that the initial *t-* is some kind of prefix that has been added to the root *kit*. In other cases, such as the word for 'say' in language K (*mon-d*; the hyphen means that *-d* is a suffix, not part of the root), a suffix has been added to a root. In even more difficult cases a root might be both preceded by a prefix *and* followed by a suffix (prefixes and suffixes are jointly called affixes). In the examples I cite in the various tables in this book I have sometimes eliminated extraneous suffixes and prefixes so that we can compare only the roots themselves. I have not always done so, however, and you should be alert to this possibility as we work through the tables.

The second column of Table 5 gives the word for 'three.' Several roots seem clear, while others are only possible. Beginning with the obvious, languages C (*sum*), G (*sum*), and L (*səm*) show a *s–m* form; D (*pu*) and J (*pua*) share a *pu–* form; and B (*dɔʔŋ*) and I (*tōŋa*) both have a *toŋ* form (remember that *t* and *d* are similar sounds). Less likely possibilities would be a root *mu*-connecting E (*musi*) and H (*mūṇu*), which have nonetheless totally dissimilar endings, and a root *k–lm*-connecting F (*kolme*) and K (*hārma*). Both of these less-likely possibilities turn out to be correct (though confirming that requires a more thorough study of these languages than one brief table can supply), as are the three obvious roots. Language A (*yaloi*) has a form unlike any other, and thus provides no information for the overall classification. But as we saw in the case of the word for 'two,' there is already a presumption that language A is to be grouped with languages F and K; the lack of confirmation of this hypothesis in the word for 'three' does not affect our earlier conclusion. It is the *positive* evidence—in the form of similar words—that leads to the classification; negative evidence plays no role and should be ignored. As a second approximation of the classification of these dozen languages we will posit five families: AFK ∥ BI ∥ CGL ∥ DJ ∥ EH (our first-pass family BCDGIJL has become three).

When we go on to the third word, 'bird,' we find obvious support for both the BI group (*dūm* and *tūma*, respectively; note that, as in the word for 'three,' *d-* in language B corresponds to *t-* in language I) and the CG group (*bya* and *pya*, respectively, though language L shows a different form). There is also a reasonable chance that E (*xāxūr*) and H (*kokku*) go together, as do D (*noŋ*) and J (*nɔʔ*). The problem with the EH group is that *x* in the E word corresponds to *k* in the H word. But finding this same pattern in the words for 'eye' (*xan* in E and *kan* in H) and 'stone' (*xal* in E and *kal* in H) encourages us to accept our putative connection of the words for 'bird' in these two languages.

Finally, three forms for 'bird' show a vague similarity that would probably escape the attention of those without linguistic training. The forms in question are found in languages A (*nonda*), F (*lintu*), and K (*lūd*). One way of relating these modern forms to a single ancestral one would be to assume that they all derive from **l–nt-* (the * indicates a hypothetical earlier form). This basic form survives intact in language F (at least with regard to the consonants). To arrive at the K form we would suppose the following evolution: **l–nt-* > **l–nd-* > *l–d*. Such changes are common in human languages. Bumping into the same correspondence in the word for 'give' (*anta* in F and *ad* in K) should convince us that we are on the right track. But notice now that the A form for 'bird' (*nonda*) is similar to the hypothetical intermediate form given above, **l–nd-*, the only difference being that the initial *l-* has changed to *n-* under the influence of the *-n-* later in the word. These kinds of changes, where one consonant influences another elsewhere in the word, are not uncommon, but they are sporadic in their occurrence, affecting individual words rather than sequences of sounds. (We will return to this difference between regular phonetic sound changes and irregular sporadic changes, seemingly attested by language A, in the Epilogue.) In the present case, we can see that there is at least a plausible scenario for relating all three forms. It is thus possible that all of the language data we have for 'bird' (except for *tiog* in language L) supports the five-fold classification proposed above, and, in fact, all of the putative cognates suggested above are today considered correct by linguistic specialists.

Examination of the final nine words corroborates this five-way classification in many ways. (Do not be deceived by the *s*-prefix in the language C word for 'say,' and do not overlook the *d/n* correspondence exhibited by languages E and H in the words for 'blood' and 'water.') There is, however, one problem. The word for 'name' is virtually identical in both the DJ group (*meŋ* in both languages) and the CGL group (*miŋ, mań,* and *myĕng,* respectively); the word for 'name' is thus *meŋ* (or something similar) in all five languages of these two groups. How should we explain this striking similarity? Perhaps it is a remnant of an even earlier group, of which DJ and CGL are two branches. Or perhaps the word has been borrowed from one group by the other. But the fact that this word belongs to the fundamental vocabulary—words like pronouns, body parts, and natural phenomena—makes that less likely. Possibly we have here an accidental resemblance, but the fact that it exists in all five languages makes *this* unlikely, too. For the moment it seems best to stick with the conservative five-way classification, but we must bear in mind that the words for 'two' (all based on *n*-) and 'name,' both of which are known to be highly stable over time, suggest that these two groups may fall together at the next level of classification, where we will be comparing language families with one another.

Finally, within the AFK group, languages F and K appear closer to each other than either is to A. Thus we should divide this group into two subbranches, one with A by itself, the other containing F and K. The correct solution to Table 5 is shown in Figure 5.

One of the reasons I have been identifying languages by

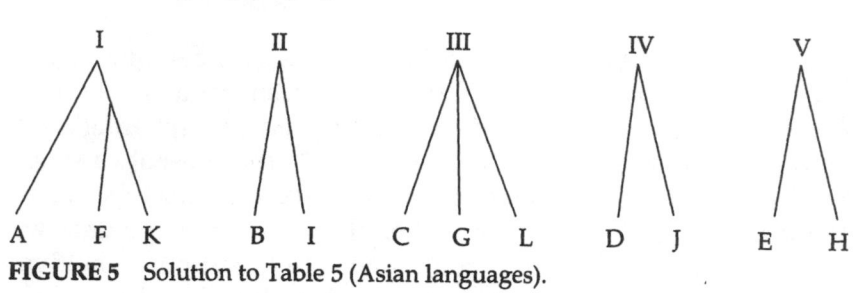

FIGURE 5   Solution to Table 5 (Asian languages).

letters in this book, rather than by their real names, is to prevent you from being prejudiced by expectations you might have if you knew the identities of the languages being classified. For example, if you knew that language A (Yukaghir) was spoken in northeastern Siberia, by people who look like other Asian Mongoloids, you would probably not have expected their language to show similarities with languages F (Finnish) and K (Hungarian), both of which are spoken by European peoples who live more than 5,000 miles to the west and who, in appearance, are indistinguishable from the other Caucasoid populations of Europe. Yet despite racial differences and the enormous geographical distance separating these peoples, their languages betray a common origin. Could it be that these apparent similarities are just accidental, and that we are fooling ourselves into thinking these languages truly have anything in common? If we consider the first- and second-person pronouns in these three languages, shown in Table 6, the answer is a resounding no. In this table all of the forms in each column are cognate, even the slightly deviant Hungarian form for 'I,' which has lost the initial *m-*, and the second-person-singular Finnish

TABLE 6   **Uralic Prounouns**

Language	*I*	*You (Sg.)*	*We*	*You (Pl.)*
Finnish	minä	sinä	me	te
Hungarian	ēn	të	mi	ti
Yukaghir	met	tet	mit	tit

form, in which the initial *t*- has been weakened to *s*- under the influence of the following vowel.

These pronominal similarities, no less than the lexical ones in Table 5, provide strong evidence of a common origin for these three languages. The claims by some experts that Yukaghir has never been shown to be related to any other language must be attributed to a reliance on nonlinguistic considerations such as race. The linguistic evidence, of which we have seen but a small portion, could hardly be clearer. The explanation for this unusual distribution once again involves migrations. Both the Hungarians and the Finns are known to have migrated to their present locations in Europe within historical times, from an original homeland in the Ural Mountains. Presumably the Yukaghir migrated eastward to their present location from this same homeland. Yet a third branch of this family, speaking Samoyed languages, remained near the original homeland. This language family, appropriately known as the Uralic family, covers much of northern Eurasia.

The identities of the rest of the languages in Table 5 are as follows. Languages B (Ket) and I (Kott) are two members of the Yeniseian family spoken in central Siberia; Ket is the sole surviving language in this family, but a few others (like Kott) are known from historical documents. Languages C (Tibetan), G (Burmese), and L (Chinese) belong to the Sino-Tibetan family, which includes several hundred other, less well-known languages spoken throughout Southeast Asia. The Chinese citations in the table represent Archaic Chinese, the ancestor of all the modern Chinese languages, which is believed to have been spoken about 1,000 B.C. Languages D (Miao, or Hmong) and J (Yao, or Mien) comprise the two branches of the Miao-Yao family. Each of these two languages has a number of distinct dialects, and the peoples speaking them are scattered across Southeast Asia in small pockets surrounded by other languages. Finally, languages E (Brahui) and H (Tamil) belong to the Dravidian family, which is found primarily in southern India. Brahui, however, the most divergent language in the family, is spoken in Pakistan, and appears to attest to an earlier, more widespread, distribution of the Dravidian family, before it was overrun by speakers of various Indo-European languages who

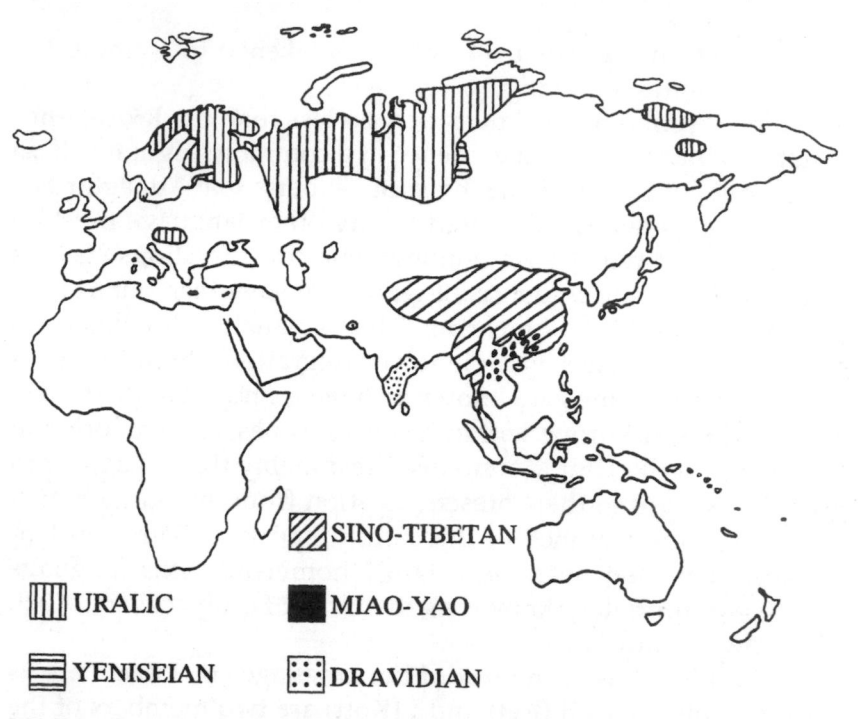

MAP 3   The Uralic, Yeniseian, Sino-Tibetan, Miao-Yao, and Dravidian families.

now occupy most of Pakistan and northern India. Except for Brahui, the Dravidian languages are all very similar to one another. The general distribution of these three families is shown in Map 3.

Native American Languages

Having just seen that the techniques of comparative linguistics work equally well on European, African, and Asian languages, we should have no fear in tackling the classification of Native American languages, and, indeed, these languages pose no special problems.

Before proceeding to Table 7, which gives twelve words in twelve languages from North and South America, I shall provide a few more hints that will help in classifying these languages. First, we should bear in mind that the vowel *u* is similar to the consonant *w*, and in the same way the vowel *i* is similar to the consonant *y*. Second, this table includes several forms where a prefix precedes the root. It is interesting to note that such prefixes sometimes seem to indicate that the following forms are nouns (notice the nouns in language E). In many Native American languages, nouns that represent body parts can be cited only with a personal pronoun prefixed to the root. Thus, for example, the form in language G for 'mouth,' *ntun*, really means 'my mouth,' with the pronoun *n-* 'my' preceding the root *-tun* 'mouth.' We should keep this analysis in mind as we classify the words in Table 7.

Once again, I won't bother to prepare a full analysis of the table. I *will* give a brief discussion of the evidence provided, though once again you are advised to tackle the classification on your own first.

If we consider the first column, the word for 'I' or 'my,' we can discern three clear groupings. First, languages D (*wiiŋa*) and J (*uaŋa*) show the form *w–ŋa*. Second, languages E (*si*) and K (*ši*) share the form *si*. (Because the sound *š* is the sound that we write as *sh* in English, the pronoun 'I' in language K presumably sounds very much like the English word 'she.') The similarity between *si* (in language E) and *ši* (in language K) not only is visually striking, but is seen even in the fluctuating pronunciation of English 'racist,' pronounced by some as *rasist*, by others as *rashist* (note, however, that 'racial' is uniformly pronounced with *sh*.) Apart from these two clear-cut groups, there seems to be a third group based on the consonant *n*: ABCGHIL (*niisto, no, naha, nin, ahnih, n-, niin*, respectively; we are assuming that *ah-* in *ahnih* is some kind of prefix in language H). Because each of these *n-* pronouns ends in somewhat different fashion (except for G: *nin* and L: *niin*), let us for the moment consider it one large group, to be subdivided by later evidence. Language F (*de*) is unlike any of the others, and we must leave it aside for the moment. On the basis of this first word our classification is: DJ ‖ EK ‖ ABCGHIL ‖ F.

The second-person pronoun provides the resolution that the first-person pronoun did not. First, it confirms the correctness of the DJ (*elpet* and *illit*) and EK (*nyun* and *ni*) groups (if

TABLE 7 Native American Languages

Language	I/My	You (Sg.)	Mouth	Liver	Leaf	Foot	Leg	Tooth	Hand	Dead	Blood	Water
A	niisto	kiisto	oyi	kinakin	niip	mohkat	mohkat	mohpiikin	mo?tsis	i?ni	aaapan	aohkii
B	no	pʰu	noomu	opaanu	apanu	hii?pu	hii?	one	kapʰi	kainee-ǰu	iidu	hooni
C	naha	mu-	tēn	eltapač	iswa	(i)kši	mets	tan	mah	miki	es	ā
D	wiiŋa	elpet	qaneq	tenguk	čuyaq	it?gaq	ipik	keggun	aaggaq	tuqu	auk	emeq
E	si	nyun	?uẓe	?uzut	?ut'an	?uke	?ukečun	?uɢoo	?ula	datsah	?uṣkai?	too
F	de	bi	ima	bana	bana	kotʰi	dana	ari	kʰabo	odon	itʰi	oniabo
G	niŋ	gıl	ntun	usgun	nipi	ngat	ngajign	nipit	npitn	nepg	mal'tew	samgwan
H	ahnih	m-	čini	nemaǰ	hahhag	tad	kahio	tam	mahwua	muhki	ih?id	šuhdagi
I	n-	pitˣa	nama	hopna	-pna	xit'i	ksuxe·	yhi	myo	hipna	hraha	honi
J	uaŋa	illit	qaneq	tinguk		isigak	niu	kigut	assak	toquvoq	aak	imaq
K	ši	ni	?azee?	?azid	?at'āā?	?akee?	?ačaad	?awoo?	?ala?	daastsaah	diɬ	to
L	niin	gün	ndoon	nkon	niibiiš	nzid	nkaad	niibid	nninǰ	nbod	mskwi	nbi

we recognize that the J form, *illit*, is related to the D form by a series of changes such as *elpet* > *ellet* > *illit*). Second, it resolves the large third group into three subgroups, one with a form based on *ki-* or *gi-* (A: *kiisto*, G: *gìl*, and L: *giin*), another based on *m-* (C: *mu-* and H: *m-*), and a third based on *p-* or *b-* (B: *pʰu*, F: *bi*, and I *pitˠa*). If this analysis of the first two pronouns is correct, then the twelve Native American languages are to be classified into five distinct families, DJ ‖ EK ‖ AGL ‖ CH ‖ BFI, with the possibility that three of these families (the last three) are closer to each other than they are to the other two.

The remainder of Table 7 offers considerable additional evidence that this five-way classification is the correct one. On my analysis sheet, the DJ group is supported in an obvious way by no less than eight of the twelve words, while the EK group is similarly so supported no less than ten times. These two groups, at least, would appear to be in the category of the obvious. The other three groups are somewhat less well supported, but still each group may nonetheless be distinguished from the others.

The AGL group is clearly supported by the forms for 'you' (enumerated above) and 'leaf' (A: *niip*, G: *nipi*, and L: *niibiiš*), and somewhat less clearly supported in the forms for 'mouth, liver, foot, leg,' and 'dead.' There is one piece of evidence, the words for 'foot' and 'leg' in these three languages, that virtually guarantees the validity of the AGL group. Language A has *mo-hkat*, which means both 'foot' and 'leg.' Though perhaps unexpected from an English-speaker's perspective, languages that have a single word for 'foot' and 'leg' (or for 'hand' and 'arm') are not unusual. And inasmuch as the words for 'tooth' (*mo-hpiikin*) and 'hand' (*moʔtsis*) in this language also start with *mo-*, perhaps these initial segments are a prefix attached to body parts. If the root in language A is really *-hkat*, then this invites comparison with the language G word for 'foot,' *ngat*, which should more properly be analyzed as *n-gat* 'my foot,' as well as with the language L word for 'leg,' *nkaad*, which should be analyzed as *n-kaad* 'my leg.' It thus seems clear that the word which means both 'foot' and 'leg' in language A (*mo-hkat*) is related to the G word for 'foot' (*n-gat*) and to the L word for 'leg' (*n-kaad*). That such a pattern of similarity could have arisen by accident seems most unlikely.

The CH group is supported by the words for 'you, mouth, hand, dead' and possibly by 'tooth.' You may have overlooked the similarity between the C (*tēn*) and H (*čini*) words for 'mouth' because it involves a type of sound shift not mentioned yet. It is common in many languages for the vowel *i* to affect the character of a preceding *t* (or *k*) by turning it into the sound *č*, which is the sound we write as *ch* in English (for example, *church*). In the present instance one suspects that the H word for 'mouth,' *čini*, has developed from an earlier **tini*. Such a form would be sufficiently similar to the corresponding form in language C (*tēn*) for us to assume that the two are probably cognate.

The final group, BFI, is clearly supported by all three languages in the words for 'you, liver, leaf,' and 'water' (provided we assume that the root **pana* 'leaf, liver' has been truncated to *-pna* in language I). Note that the words for 'liver' and 'leaf' appear to be the same in all three languages; apparently this group applied the word for 'leaf' to the 'liver' because it saw the liver as looking something like a leaf. In addition, at least two of the three languages are connected by the words for 'mouth, hand,' and 'blood.' Actually, a more sophisticated analysis of these languages would show that the F word for 'mouth' (*ima*) is related to the B (*noomu*) and I (*nama*) words for 'mouth.' Note finally that the H word for 'blood' (*ɨhʔɨd*) is similar to the B (*iidu*) and F (*ɨtʰɨ*) words for 'blood,' even though H belongs to a different subgroup. As with the first-person pronoun, this may be an indication that these two groups shared a common origin at some more distant time in the past. For the present, we will be content to classify these twelve languages into the five families shown in Figure 6, but in Chapter 4 we shall see that these early clues of deeper relationships turn out to be correct.

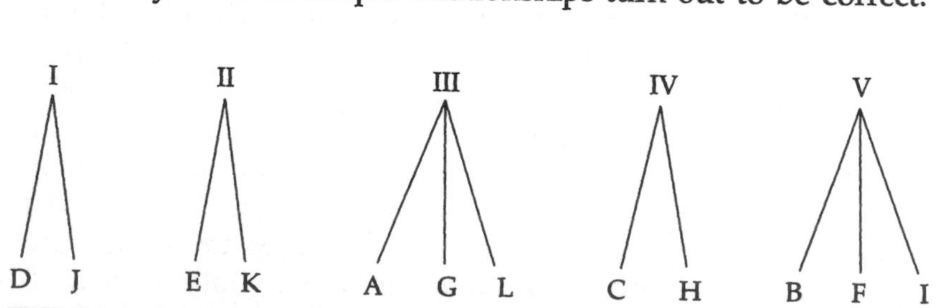

FIGURE 6   Solution to Table 7 (Native American languages).

Languages D (Yupik) and J (Greenlandic) are two Eskimo languages within the Eskimo-Aleut family. Despite the fact that Yupik is spoken in southwestern Alaska, whereas Greenlandic is spoken 6,000 miles to the east in Greenland, the similarity of these two languages is overwhelming. Once again, a fairly recent migration, in this case from Alaska across northern Canada to Greenland, is responsible for the striking similarity of geographically distant languages.

Languages E (Carrier) and K (Navajo) belong to the Athabaskan family, most of whose languages are found in Alaska and western Canada. Navajo, however, is an outlier found in the American Southwest. The Algonquian family, which stretches from Montana across the Great Plains to the Eastern Seaboard, is represented here by three languages, A (Blackfoot), G (Micmac), and L (Ojibwa). Languages C (Pipil) and H (Papago) are members of the Uto-Aztecan family, which extends from the Great Basin (Nevada, Utah) through Mexico into El Salvador. Finally, languages B (Resigaro), F (Arawak), and I (Piro) belong to the Arawakan family of South America. The general location of these five American families is shown in Map 4.

We have found in this chapter that the same techniques of comparative linguistics that led originally to the discovery of the Indo-European family, 200 years ago, can be used to classify languages into families anywhere in the world. It would be easy to provide tables that would demonstrate the same conclusion for languages in Oceania or Australia, but I think we can dispense with them. My aim in this book is not to provide all of the voluminous evidence that one might bring to bear on these questions—hundreds of volumes would be needed—but rather to lead the reader briefly through the line of argumentation that leads to the conclusion that all extant languages share a common origin. Our first task in this demonstration has been to show that languages anywhere on earth can be classified into fairly obvious families on the basis of lexical and grammatical similarities. I believe we have accomplished that task. Our next step, which will provide the focus of Chapters 3 and 4, will be to compare these obvious families with one another in an attempt to find larger, more ancient families. That is, we will attempt to go beyond the obvious. Notice in particular, at this next stage, that we will be using the same techniques that worked so nicely in the initial stage; that is, we will look for similar words shared by different *families*, just as we have looked for similar words shared by different *languages* up to this point.

MAP 4 The Eskimo-Aleut, Athabaskan, Algonquian, Uto-Aztecan, and Arawakan families.

I close this chapter with a map (Map 5) showing the location of all of the languages we have classified so far—all of the languages given in the seven tables we have examined. Now that we have successfully completed a worldwide tour of language families, it is interesting to see exactly where each of these languages is (or was) spoken.

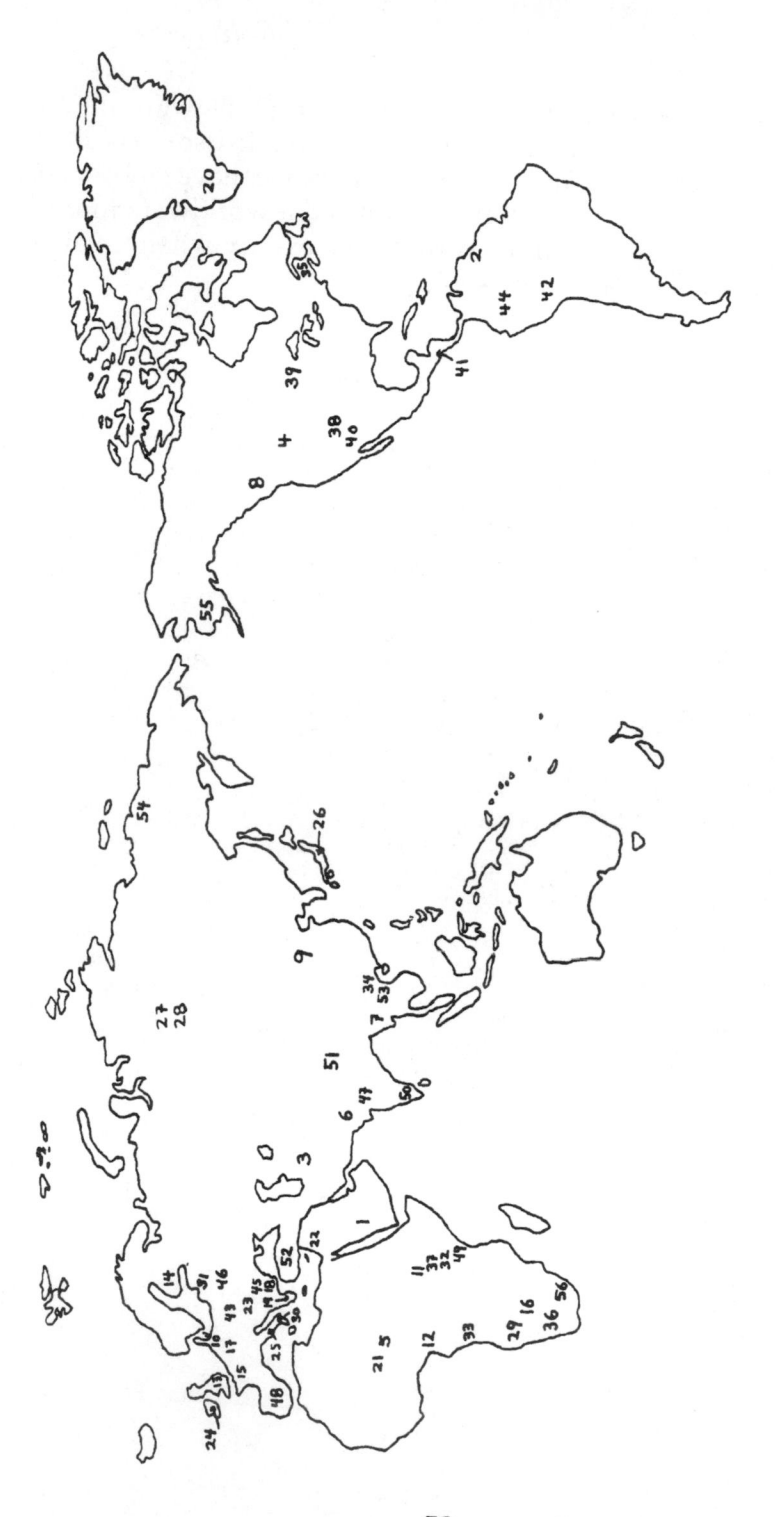

MAP 5 Location of all languages classified in the Prologue and Chapters 1 and 2.

1. Arabic
2. Arawak
3. Avestan
4. Blackfoot
5. Bole
6. Brahui
7. Burmese
8. Carrier
9. Chinese
10. Danish
11. Dinka
12. Duala
13. English
14. Finnish

15. French
16. G//ana
17. German
18. Gothic
19. Greek
20. Greenlandic
21. Hausa
22. Hebrew
23. Hungarian
24. Irish
25. Italian
26. Japanese
27. Ket
28. Kott

29. !Kung
30. Latin
31. Lithuanian
32. Maasai
33. Mbundu
34. Miao
35. Micmac
36. Nama
37. Nandi
38. Navajo
39. Ojibwa
40. Papago
41. Pipil
42. Piro

43. Polish
44. Resígaro
45. Rumanian
46. Russian
47. Sanskrit
48. Spanish
49. Swahili
50. Tamil
51. Tibetan
52. Turkish
53. Yao
54. Yukaghir
55. Yupik
56. Zulu

3

Controversy

What Is Debated

In Chapter 1 we saw how similarities among languages led Sir William Jones to posit a common origin for a group of languages that stretches from Europe to India, a group that later came to be called the Indo-European family. His suggestion of an evolutionary explanation to account for linguistic resemblances was a milestone not only in the scientific study of language, but even in the study of modern humans. In Chapter 2 we applied these same techniques of comparison to languages elsewhere in the world to identify additional families of languages, each of which must be presumed to have evolved from a single, earlier ancestral language. I could have given additional tables involving languages spoken elsewhere, but I think by now you will have concluded, correctly, that these methods will work anywhere. For wherever one goes in the world, the comparison of basic vocabulary in a number of languages inevitably—and quickly—leads to the recognition of certain language families, families that are so obvious that even a person without linguistic training can pick them out fairly easily on the basis of relatively few words. Furthermore, every family you have identified up to now is accepted as a valid family by all specialists. There is simply no doubt that Chadic, Uralic, Algonquian, etc., are all valid families: there is no disagreement about precisely what languages should be included in each, though there may be some disagreement about how the languages *within* each should be classified, that is, how the languages within each are related *to each other*.

How many such obvious families would we find if we were to carefully survey the rest of the world in the same manner? The answer is speculative (and depends on how one defines "obvious"), but my guess would be on the order of 300 to 400. What this means is that these simple procedures would quickly reduce the world's linguistic diversity from roughly 5,000 languages to 300-odd families, a rather significant simplification. Some of these families (for example Bantu) contain hundreds of languages, whereas others might consist of a single language. The Basque language of northern Spain and southern France is a well-known language *isolate*, that is, a language with no close relatives. It is thus a family consisting of one language. (This is not to say that it has no relatives, but rather that it has no *close* relatives of the kind we have been dealing with up to now.)

Families of Families

At this point it may have crossed your mind that if we can simplify the world's linguistic diversity so quickly and so easily on the basis of a few words, we should move on to a comparison of these obvious language families *with each other*, to see if they do not aggregate into more comprehensive families, deriving from a deeper time depth, and in so doing perhaps reduce the world's linguistic diversity even further. Already in the Native American table we have seen hints that the five families we identified there are not all equally distinct, since three of them seemed perhaps somewhat closer to each other than to either of the other two.

Furthermore, the comparison of language families with

one another is really no different from the comparison of languages themselves. In fact, since each language family derives from a single earlier language, comparing the Indo-European family with the Uralic family amounts to the same thing as comparing the Proto-Indo-European language with the Proto-Uralic language. That is, we are simply classifying languages that existed at some earlier point in the past. Whether these proto-languages all existed at precisely the same time is not crucial, and no one has ever objected to comparing, say, the Anatolian branch of Indo-European, which died out over three millennia ago, with the Albanian branch, which is attested only from the fifteenth century A.D on.

In comparing language families there are a number of inconveniences that must be overcome. When we compared languages we used a dictionary for each language compared. Unfortunately, the dictionaries for language *families* are of a rather disparate sort, which complicates comparisons at that level. Some language families, such as Indo-European and Uralic, have excellent etymological dictionaries, each one a dictionary of the roots that characterize the family, supplying a *reconstruction* of each root and a full citation of all the modern forms deriving from that root. In such cases we can simply use the reconstruction of a word to represent the family, so that Proto-Indo-European **dwo* 'two' would stand for all of the various Indo-European forms given in the first column of Table 2. For other families, such as Dravidian, there are also excellent dictionaries, but without reconstructions of what each root originally looked like. Rather, there is simply a list of the words in various modern languages that are presumed to be cognate, that is, presumed to share a common origin, but the more arduous task of specifying the exact form of each original root is not attempted. Lacking a reconstruction for a set of cognates, we must simply choose one of the modern forms that seems to represent best the sound and meaning of the root. Finally, it should be noted that the dictionaries of various families differ considerably in the number of recognized roots. Whereas Indo-European and Uralic have over 2,000 recognized roots, and Dravidian over 5,000, for many families the number is only several hundred. It would be nice if we had a complete dictionary, with reconstructions, for each of the families we want to work with; but even if these were available, we would find that the ancient families simply have fewer roots than do the obvious families we have dealt with up to this point. And in any event, the reality of the linguistic literature—considering that such basic work has been woefully neglected during this century (for reasons we shall touch on later)—is that the materials we have for various parts of the world are quite heterogeneous, not only in extent and character but also in rigor. Thus, as in any historical science, we must make do with the evidence at hand.

There is one other modification we must make in the rules we've been employing up to this point. In the tables in Chapter 2 the form of a word used in a given language had a single meaning. Thus, while we allowed the *sounds* to change (in certain predictable ways) in related words, we kept the meaning unchanged, so as not to muddy the process. In reality, of course, meanings can change just as easily and as often as sounds do, and we were able to get away with such unrealistic simplifications, in the tables, simply because we were dealing with obvious groupings. In comparing language families now, we will be permitting simple semantic shifts, just as we have accepted simple phonetic shifts up to this point. This should not be construed as an extension of the rules, for in fact the same rules were in effect at the "obvious" level. We just didn't bother to identify them all.

Table 8 lists thirteen words in thirteen language families. Your task, as before, is to classify these families into larger families, if you can discern any connections. I must warn you, before you attempt to classify these thirteen families, that most historical linguists believe there are *no* perceivable connections among them. But why don't we have a look for ourselves.

In Table 8 each family is represented either by a reconstruction or by a modern form of a root that is widespread (or, in a few cases, simply attested in the family). In the table I have waived the requirement for asterisks before reconstructed forms, so as to spare you preconceived notions. Before you examine Table 8 let me give you one final hint. There is one natural class of consonants we have not yet discussed; these are the s-like sounds that linguists call *sibilants*. This class of sounds

TABLE 8 Eurasian Language Families

Language	I/Me/My	You	Who	What	This	That	Bark	Feather	Excrement	Dark	Speak	Take	Day(Light)
A	aku	kaw	t'ai	apa	ini	ian	hu(m)pak	bulu	taki	đađem	ʔutsap	ʔalap	ha(n)daw
B	ni	-k	nor	ser	au	ori	laka	luma	khorots	ifun	esan	eraman	egun
C	-m	te	ken	yo	tä	to	kopa	tulka	sita	pil'mV	kele	kaṗa	yelä
D	ti	sä	dei	tsa-de	he	ha	//gŭ	/go	tsu	kɔ'ui	gui	/kam	
E	ŋä	kʷʌy	näi(ŋ)	su	ʔi	ʔa	q(h)ʷin		kliy	tyaŋ	k(h)a	čŏw	kʷän
F	mini	ti	ken	yä	ku	ta	kặp	tülüg	pargal	balu	kela	kʰapa	nara
G	mi		ka	ya	ku	to	kapa	thʌʌk	si	kur	yalpx	kapu	nal
H	-m	-t	k'e	yaq	ʔənə	ti?	ʔilqə	ičelčx		kel	pʌlm	ɣʌvalʔyn	θχəlwə
I	ja	gu	ana	besʌn	khĭnɛ	ĭnɛ	wʌʈ	pfʊlgo	ɣʊraš	ṭumʈʌŋ	sɛnʌs	yʌʌvʌs	gon
J	-ma	-t	kina		ta			tsulu'k		ðayɛ	kiliyä	kiputi	ʔavə
K	zŏ	yu	nV	sä	ʔi	ʔa	bHats'we	pidwV	kʼurčʼV	HʈʼolV	qʼa	ʔaččwV	ɟinV
L	mẽ	te	kʼi	yo	kŭ	to	ker	petar	sker-d	pol	kel	kap	äier
M	ʔadz	kV	te	ʔan	ʔas	tu	ka	ʔicin	poʔq	tum	qäc	čŏŋ	gəʔn

includes the following members: č, ts, s, š, ǰ, dz, z, ž. Further-more, within this class the first four and the last four constitute well defined subgroups. Try to keep this in mind as you classify the language families in Table 8.

The politically correct answer to Table 8—and the only an-swer that would be acceptable on a Ph.D. oral examination in historical linguistics—is that there is *no* evidence that any of these thirteen families is related to any of the others. Is that what you found? Of course not. For here we have stumbled upon one of the great hoaxes of twentieth-century science. But before we discuss this hoax—its origins, causes, and subsequent development—let us first dispassionately examine the evidence in Table 8.

The first column, which gives the first-person pronoun 'I, me' in thirteen families, immediately suggests one larger group (CFGHJL) in which this pronoun is based on *m*. Families I, K, and M form a second group, with the pronoun based on d^z. The other families (ABDE) have first-person pronouns that resemble neither the pronouns of our first two groups, nor those of each other.

The forms for the second-person pronoun 'you,' given in the second column, show that the group that uses *m* as its first-person pronoun has a second-person pronoun based on *t-* (CFHJL), although information for G here is lacking. A second group, much like IKM, whose first-person pronoun was based on d^z, has a second-person pronoun based on either *g* (IK) or the phonetically similar *k* (ABEM). The form in family D is un-like all the others.

When we examine the words for 'who' in the third column we find that the same first group (CFGHJL) has a form based on *kin* or *ken*, while a second group (now BEIKM) has forms based on *n*. The other two forms, from families A and D, resem-ble each other somewhat (depending on what *t'* stands for), but when we see that these two families nowhere resemble each other in any of the other forms, it is likely that this single re-semblance is merely fortuitous. Thus, after three words, the pic-ture that is emerging, based on the most fundamental and stable vocabulary, is of two large groupings of families, (CFGHJL) and (BEIKM), and two left-over families (A and D) that resemble neither each other nor either of the two larger groupings. We can represent this classification as CFGHJL ‖ BEIKM ‖ A ‖ D, or in the graphic form shown in Figure 7.

I will not take time to discuss each word in Table 8, but I *will* point out some of the most telling evidence supporting the two large groupings we have identified. In addition to the *m-/t-* pronoun system and an interrogative pronoun based on *k-*, the first large grouping reveals words for 'what' (*yo* or *ya*), 'this' (*ku*), 'that' (*to* or *ta*), 'bark (of a tree)' (*kapa*), 'feather' (*tuluk*), 'dark' (*polm*), 'speak' (*kele*), and 'take' (*kapa*). The similarities in most of these forms are obvious enough even to the untrained eye, but a few of the forms are sufficiently deformed as to require explanation. The word for 'feather' in family H, *ičelčlx*, is one such case. I suspect that this form is related to the *tuluk* root. If we begin with a *reduplicated form* of the root as it appears in family J (which just happens to be geographically closest to family H) and add an *i-* prefix to it, we have *i-tsuluk-tsuluk*. From this rather long word one can easily envisage a number of simple phonetic shifts that would result in the attested form: *i-tsuluk-tsuluk* > *i-čuluk-čuluk* > *i-čulux-čulux* > *i-čelux-čelux* > *i-čelx-čelx* > *i-čel-čelx* > *i-čel-člx*, which is the form in family H. Of course, you did not need to suspect a connection of this root with the forms resembling *tuluk* in the other families; family H resembles the other families in the first large grouping in so many obvious ways that this more subtle similarity only confirms the obvious.

The second large grouping is less obvious than the first—both in Table 8 and in the complete literature—and its discovery and elaboration (really rediscovery, since there were impor-

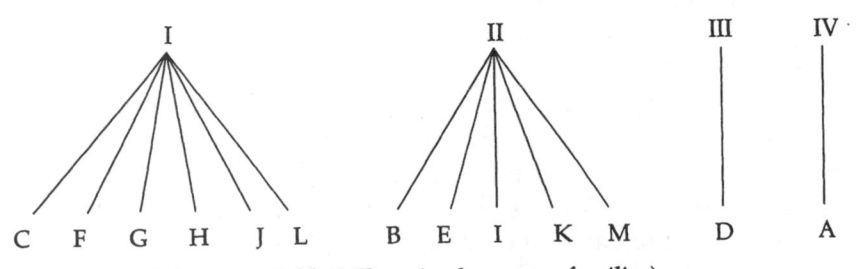

FIGURE 7 Solution to Table 8 (Eurasian language families).

tant precursors) during the past decade represents one of the most important recent advances in historical linguistics. In addition to the *dz-/ku-* pronoun system and an interrogative pronoun based on *na-*, there are words for 'what' (*s–*), 'this' (*ʔi*), 'that' (*ʔa*), 'bark' (*qun*), 'excrement' (*kurots*), 'dark' (*tum*; note that the form in family I appears to be a compound, the first part of which resembles the form in family M, the second part the form in family E), 'speak' (*qa*), 'take' (*čo*), and 'day(light)' (*gun*). These words are not found in every branch, but they are found in at least two or three branches of what consistently constitutes the second large grouping. One possible conclusion might be that the second large grouping is more ancient than the first, and thus has preserved less of its original proto-language. We will examine this possibility further in Chapter 8.

As for the other two families, A and D, they seldom resemble either of the two larger groups, and when there *is* a resemblance it is to no particular family or group of families. Consideration of additional words would corroborate our conclusion that families A and D are quite distinct from both of the large groupings, as well as from each other. There is, however, one similarity between family A and the second large grouping that is hard to overlook. We have noted that the second large grouping (BEIKM) has a characteristic root *tum* 'dark,' which is in fact attested in families I and M. The problem, if we wish to call it that, is that the form for 'dark' in family A looks like a reduplicated form of this same root, namely *ḍəḍəm*, which is one simple phonetic change away from an original *ḍəmḍəm*. This is perhaps an indication that there exist cognates connecting families that we discovered by this second level of comparison, cognates that connect even the large and ancient groupings that we have identified in this chapter. This remarkable prospect will, in fact, be the focus of Chapter 5.

Let us now identify the language families that you have classified in this chapter. Family A is the Austronesian family, which covers most of the Pacific Ocean and includes languages such as Tagalog, Malay, Maori, and Hawaiian. Family B is Basque, a single language spoken on both sides of the Spanish-French border. Family C is Uralic, which covers northern Eurasia and includes such languages as Finnish, Hungarian, and Yukaghir (as we saw in Chapter 2). Family D is the Khoisan family of South Africa, which you distinguished from other African languages in Table 3. Family E is Sino-Tibetan, which you distinguished in Table 5; the best-known of over 200 Sino-Tibetan languages are Chinese, Tibetan, and Burmese. Family F is the Altaic family, consisting of three subfamilies: Turkic, Mongolian, and Tungus; this family stretches across much of Eurasia, from Turkey to northeastern Siberia.

Family G consists of three quite distinct languages, Korean, Japanese, and Ainu, which many linguists consider unrelated either to each other or to any other language. Recent work, however, indicates that they form a group that is likely closest to the Altaic group. (The first-person *mi* in this group comes from Old Japanese; modern Japanese, as well as Korean and Ainu, does not preserve this root.) Family H is the Chukchi-Kamchatkan family, which is found on the peninsulas of the same names in northeastern Siberia, just across the Bering Strait from Alaska. Family I is a single language, Burushaski, spoken in the mountains of northern Pakistan. Family J is Eskimo-Aleut, which (as we saw in the last chapter) extends from the Aleutian Islands in southwestern Alaska across northern Canada to Greenland. Family K is the Caucasian family, located in the Caucasus mountains between the Black Sea and the Caspian Sea; none of its languages is well known—except to linguists, for whom they are renowned for their abundance and variety of consonants. Family L is the Indo-European family, which we met in Chapter 1. Finally, Family M is the Yeniseian family, spoken along the Yenisei River in central Siberia. It consists today of a single language, Ket, but a few other extinct Yeniseian languages are known from historical records.

The first large grouping of families that we discovered (CFGHJL) connects the Indo-European, Uralic, Altaic, Korean-Japanese-Ainu, Chukchi-Kamchatkan, and Eskimo-Aleut families in a more ancient family called Eurasiatic by the American linguist Joseph Greenberg. It also includes the Gilyak (or Nivx) language, spoken on Sakhalin Island and along the facing coast of Asia, a language which space did not permit us to include in Table 8, but which shares many similar words with the other

Eurasiatic families (for example, *ti* 'you,' *ya* 'what,' *xip* 'bark,' *polm* 'make blind,' *qlai* 'converse,' and *kip* 'take,' just to mention those Gilyak forms that appear to be cognate with the Eurasiatic roots exemplified in Table 8).

One of the most impressive pieces of evidence for the validity of the Eurasiatic family is a grammatical pattern whereby plurals of nouns are formed by suffixing -*t* to the noun root (just as -*s* is suffixed to nouns to form English plurals, as for example in 'cat/cat-s'), whereas *duals* of nouns are formed by suffixing -*k*. (A dual may be thought of as a special kind of plural in which the number of objects referred to is *exactly* two, rather than two or more, as with the normal plural suffix.) As early as 1818 this -*k*/-*t* (dual/plural) pattern was noted by Rasmus Rask in two different families that we would today call Uralic and Eskimo-Aleut. It was also Rask who, in addition to being one of the great early Indo-Europeanists, first connected the Aleut language with the Eskimo languages as the Eskimo-Aleut family. In the early days of comparative linguistics, such widespread patterns between families that were obviously not closely related were not automatically dismissed as borrowings or chance resemblances, or buried under any of the other myriad excuses that have become fashionable in recent years to explain away evidence for genetic connections that fall short of the obvious.

In fact, however, the -*k*/-*t* (dual/plural) paradigm is considerably more widespread than Rask realized. In addition to the Uralic and Eskimo-Aleut examples he noted, the same pattern is attested in Altaic, Ainu, Gilyak, and Chukchi-Kamchatkan, all of which are included by Greenberg in Eurasiatic. Outside of Eurasiatic I am not aware of any other language families (or even languages) that exhibit such a paradigm. That this particular grammatical pattern should coincide so well with the *m-*/*t-* pronominal pattern would be a highly unlikely coincidence. Rather, it is precisely such nonrandom distributions of specific words and grammatical affixes that defines valid linguistic families. Why this simple truth is not apparent to a good many supposed experts will be a constant theme of this book.

Greenberg's Eurasiatic family represents his own view of

the nearest relatives of the Indo-European family, a question that has been much discussed since the nineteenth century— often in acrimonious terms. In the late nineteenth century several prominent Indo-Europeanists began to claim that the Indo-European family had not been, and probably could never be, shown to be related to other language families, for a variety of reasons that we will examine here and in Chapter 6. The American historical linguist William Dwight Whitney expressed this pessimistic verdict in 1867, when he wrote that "linguistic science is not now, and cannot ever hope to be, in condition to give an authoritative opinion respecting the unity or variety of our species" (Whitney 1867: 383). The eminent French comparative linguist Antoine Meillet reached the same conclusion in the early twentieth century:

> If we are far from being able to group all the proto-languages, and especially if the comparative grammar of even the best-known groups is imperfect, if the Indo-European family is the only one where such work is truly advanced, if, except for Semitic, Finno-Ugric [part of Uralic], Austronesian, and Bantu, almost all comparative work remains to be done, it goes without saying that the question of the original unity, if not of human language itself, at least of the presently known languages, cannot be approached in any useful fashion. (Meillet 1951 [1924]: 65)

Such pessimistic conclusions persist to the present day, as we see in the following recent statements by an Indo-Europeanist and an Americanist. According to the Indo-Europeanist,

> We can never prove that two given languages are not related. It is always conceivable that they are in fact related, but that the relationship is of such an ancient date that millennia of divergent linguistic changes have completely obscured the original relationship.
>
> Ultimately, this issue is tied up with the question of whether there was a single or a multiple origin of Language (writ large). And this question can be answered only in terms of unverifiable speculations, given the fact that even with the added time depth provided by reconstruction, our knowledge of the history of human languages does not extend beyond ca. 5,000 B.C., a small 'slice' indeed out of the long prehistory of language. (Hock 1986: 566)

According to the Americanist, "the proof of a common origin for the indigenous languages of this hemisphere [the Americas] is not accessible to the comparative method as we know it" (Kaufman 1990: 26).

These statements are thoroughly representative of current received opinion in historical linguistics, according to which the comparative method in linguistics is capable only of discovering such obvious families as Indo-European, Bantu, and Austronesian. More distant relationships are considered beyond the pale of comparative linguistics. But despite this long held and widely shared view, there has always persisted a minority of scholars who protested that the comparative method could indeed go beyond the obvious, and that Indo-European, in particular, is without doubt related to other Eurasian families (as you have discovered in this chapter). Early in this century the Danish linguist Holger Pedersen argued that Indo-European was related to such other families as Semitic, Uralic, Altaic, and Eskimo-Aleut in a family that he named Nostratic. At about the same time the Italian linguist Alfredo Trombetti was exploring long-range linguistic connections around the world, and in the process arrived at the conclusion early in this century that all the world's languages must ultimately be related in a single family, for which he supplied fairly abundant—if sometimes imperfect—evidence. In the United States at this same time, attempts were initiated to consolidate the numerous Native American language families in a smaller number of families. The most influential of these early American taxonomists was Edward Sapir, who made several startling discoveries in the second decade of this century. By 1920, however, Sapir had virtually ceased his taxonomic work, owing at least partially, no doubt, to the heavy criticism he received from his peers.

One of Sapir's students, Morris Swadesh, was also active in the investigation of distant linguistic connections. Swadesh specialized in the Native American languages, but kept an eye on the global picture as well. Like Trombetti, he concluded that all extant languages are very probably related in a single family. He published relatively little evidence for this hypothesis, however, and it must be admitted that some of his etymological conjectures are unconvincing.

Another pioneer in long-range comparison was Greenberg,

but the true nature of his early taxonomic work on African languages in the 1950's was at the time not perceived as a threat to the supposed "standard comparative method," and in fact many comparativists welcomed a little more order on the African continent. But Greenberg's African classification was indeed revolutionary, for it explored linguistic connections that were much more ancient, and much less transparent, than such obvious families as Indo-European and Bantu. His later work on New Guinea languages, Native American languages, and, currently, the Eurasiatic family has followed the same methodology as had his African classification, but, as we shall see, often suffered scathing criticism.

In the early 1960's two Russian scholars, both living in Moscow, began to investigate the further connections of the Indo-European family, building upon Pedersen's Nostratic hypothesis but also cognizant of Trombetti's proposals for distant linguistic connections. Ironically, these two scholars, Aron Dolgopolsky and Vladislav Illich-Svitych, were at first unaware of each other's pursuits, until the coincidence was one day pointed out to them by a mutual friend, Vladimir Dybo. For Illich-Svitych, Nostratic included Afro-Asiatic, Indo-European, Kartvelian, Uralic, Altaic, and Dravidian. The possibility that other families might also be members was not excluded, but Illich-Svitych felt that reliable data for other families was not yet available. Dolgopolsky, on the other hand, included Chukchi-Kamchatkan and Eskimo-Aleut from the beginning, but did not at first include Dravidian. Illich-Svitych was killed in a tragic traffic accident before any of his work had appeared in print, and it was only due to the indefatigable labor of his colleague Dybo that the work Illich-Svitych had in manuscript form at the time of his death was eventually published, with the assistance of Dolgopolsky. Dolgopolsky himself emigrated to Israel in the 1970's and has continued to work on his Nostratic dictionary at the University of Haifa to the present day. A third Russian colleague of Illich-Svitych and Dolgopolsky, Vitaly Shevoroshkin, emigrated to the United States in the 1970's and has been instrumental in popularizing the Nostratic theory as well as in his own work on more distant genetic relationships. We will discuss in Chapter 6 the reasons why Greenberg's Eurasiatic differs from the Russian conception of Nostratic. For the moment, we simply note that both Greenberg and the Nostraticists agree that Indo-European is clearly related to other Eurasian families.

The second large grouping of language families (BEIKM) that you identified in Table 8, known as Dene-Caucasian, connects Basque, Caucasian, Burushaski, Sino-Tibetan, Yeniseian, and the Na-Dene family of the Americas. Na-Dene consists of the Athabaskan family, which we encountered in Table 7, and three other languages spoken on the southeastern coast of Alaska (Eyak, Tlingit, and Haida). Na-Dene was, in fact, one of Sapir's early discoveries, one for which he was severely criticized, though today the family is generally accepted. Sapir also discovered, much to his surprise, that this Na-Dene family appeared to be most closely related to the Sino-Tibetan family of Asia, thus perceiving two of the branches of the Dene-Caucasian family. In light of the harsh criticism his Na-Dene proposal engendered, Sapir never published any of his evidence for a Na-Dene–Sino-Tibetan affinity, and this connection too came to be viewed as spurious by the majority of linguists. In the past decade, however, Sapir's original idea has been resurrected by two Russian linguists, Sergei Starostin and Sergei Nikolaev. Starostin first proposed that the Caucasian, Sino-Tibetan, and Yeniseian families were members of a family he named Sino-Caucasian. Soon thereafter Nikolaev showed that Na-Dene was related to the Caucasian family, and by extension, of course, to Sino-Tibetan and Yeniseian as well. With the addition of Na-Dene, the family was renamed Dene-Caucasian. In the late 1980's the American linguist John Bengtson undertook a comprehensive look at Dene-Caucasian, adding to the family both Basque and Burushaski, ideas that were prefigured in the work of Trombetti and others. Map 6 shows the distribution of both Eurasiatic and Dene-Caucasian. The distribution of Dene-Caucasian is quite striking, its members appearing as isolated islands surrounded for the most part by the vast Eurasiatic family. A possible explanation for this peculiar distribution will be suggested in Chapter 8.

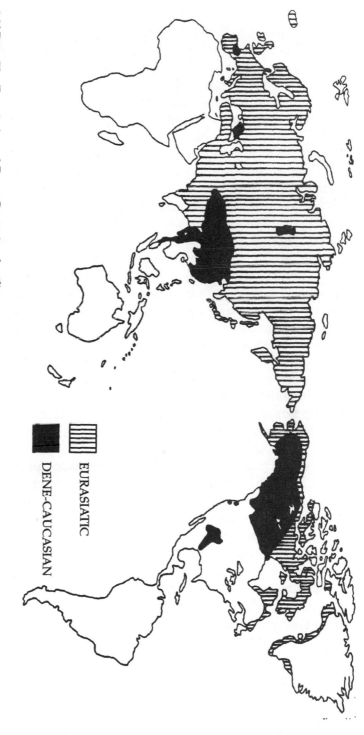

MAP 6 The Eurasiatic and Dene-Caucasian families.

A History of Hysteria

It is time, then, that we begin to address the dilemma reflected throughout this scholarly history. We have compared languages from around the world—Africa, Europe, Asia, and the Americas—and everywhere they could be sorted into obvious families, all of which are accepted as valid. We then applied the same techniques to these obvious families (or proto-languages) and once again arrived at a persuasive classification, this time into two large groupings and two isolated families. Yet the received wisdom among experts is that there is no evidence connecting any of these families. How can this be?

Just how historical linguistics managed to back itself into this quandary embraces a number of subplots, and we will be able to single out only a few of them in the remainder of this chapter. The chapters that then follow will continue the discussion, with regard first to the Native American languages, but also, indeed, with regard to the possibility of a comprehensive classification of the world's languages.

Let us begin with what has probably been the most cited argument for the claim that Indo-European cannot be shown to be related to any other family. According to the experts, linguistic change is so rapid that after around 6,000 years all traces of earlier relationships have been obliterated by constant phonetic and semantic erosion. Conveniently, 6,000 years happens to be the presumed age of the Indo-European family (which means that Proto-Indo-European was spoken around 4,000 B.C.). It follows (or at least it would if these assumptions were true) that even if Proto-Indo-European had once shown an affinity with some other language family, no trace of this earlier relationship could still remain. And if something cannot exist, there is certainly no point in looking for it.

There are several problems with this commonly cited 'explanation." First of all, after 6,000 years everything does not change beyond recognition. Indo-Europeanists have reconstructed the Proto-Indo-European word for 'nephew' as *nēpot-, and this root has passed down into modern Rumanian as *nepot*, a form virtually identical to the word the Indo-Europeans used around their campfires 6,000 years ago. Numerous other examples could be cited—from Indo-European or any other family—to show that this notion that everything changes beyond recognition after 6,000 years is simply false.

Furthermore, you may have already thought to ask, what about the *m-/t-* pronominal pattern that connects Indo-European with several other families? Is this not by itself evidence that Indo-European is related to these other families? The thought certainly occurred to Trombetti early in this century, for he wrote in 1905:

> It is clear that in and of itself the comparison of Finno-Ugric [Uralic] *me* 'I,' *te* 'you' with Indo-European *me-* and *te-* [with the same meaning] is worth just as much as any comparison one might make between the corresponding pronominal forms in the Indo-European languages. The only difference is that the common origin of the Indo-European languages is accepted, while the connection between Indo-European and Finno-Ugric is denied.

In other words, what the experts know is what they have been taught in school.

So what did the Indo-Europeanists make of the embarrassingly wide distribution of the Indo-European pronominal pattern? There were a number of explanations. One was that these pronouns had simply been borrowed from one family to another. Since the first- and second-person pronouns are very rarely borrowed, in any of the world's languages, such an explanation seems most improbable. Another explanation was that these were simply accidental similarities. If, however, the probability of two families having the same first- *and* second-person pronouns is, say, 1 in 20, then the probability that three families would accidentally resemble each other is $(1/20)$ $(1/20)$, or $1/400$. The probability that four families would accidentally resemble each other in their pronouns would be $(1/400)$ $(1/20)$, or $1/8,000$, and the probability of five families showing such an accidental resemblance would be $(1/8,000)$ $(1/20)$, or $1/160,000$. Since we have estimated that there are only about 400 families in the world, our chances of finding an accidental five-way resemblance among their pronouns would be small indeed. And what about the other evidence we saw in Table 8 connecting Indo-European with the other branches of Eurasiatic. Why do all of these "accidental" resemblances fall over and over within the larger Eurasiatic family? The reason, of course, is that these resemblances are not accidental, but rather reflect the language from which Indo-European and the other families derive, Proto-Eurasiatic.

A third explanation for the *m-/t-* pronominal pattern was offered by Meillet, who argued that "pronouns look alike more or less everywhere." Ironically, this same argument has recently been advocated in order to explain the widespread pronominal pattern *n-/m-*, which is found throughout the Americas but rarely, if ever, elsewhere. One is left to wonder why, if indeed pronouns look alike everywhere, the *m-/t-* pattern predominates in Eurasia and is virtually absent in the Americas, whereas the *n-/m-* pattern runs through the Americas and is virtually absent elsewhere. Of course, what this really shows is that Meillet's claim was nonsense. Pronouns do not look alike everywhere and anyone who claims they do just hasn't looked.

We will deal later with other aspects of the Indo-Europeanist mythology, which has effectively stultified historical linguistics in this century. But in closing this chapter let us consider two further questions. Why were the Indo-Europeanists so averse to having Indo-European related to other families by simple linguistic evolution? And how were they able to enforce their views throughout the entire twentieth century, notwithstanding that the fatal flaws therein had already been pointed out, quite clearly, by Trombetti and others at the start of this century?

As regards the first question—the extreme aversion to a simple evolutionary explanation—I can give no definitive answer. It seems to me, however, that a large part of the answer involves the simple ethnocentrism—Eurocentrism in this case—of the scholars involved. The Indo-European family was the crowning achievement of nineteenth-century linguistics, and the European scholars who had studied this family no doubt felt (or at least hoped) that they were as unique as the marvelous family they had discovered. A consequence of their ethnocentric penchant was that when the Indo-Europeanists did dare to seek relatives for their august family, they immediately considered the Semitic family of the Middle East, which included such prestigious languages as Arabic, Hebrew, and Aramaic. The Semitic family, however, is not closely related to Indo-European, being rather a member of the Afro-Asiatic family, so that whatever affinity it may have with Indo-European is remote. The real relatives of Indo-European, unfortunately, were not the relatives the Indo-Europeanists had in mind.

Indeed, if one steps back for a moment—outside this immediate center of discord—one might suspect that this whole line of reasoning underscores the Eurocentric bias. Why are we trying to find relatives for Indo-European? Why is Indo-European given any special attention at all? We started off this book by classifying languages. The *classifications* told us the relationships among the various languages. Now, all of a sudden, we are looking for long-lost relatives of Indo-European, and classification, from which relationships flow, has been largely forgotten. Could the Eurocentric bias be more blatant? To find out what Indo-European is related to, one should simply *classify* all the relevant families, just as we did in Table 8. Whether the results please or displease this or that faction should really not be an issue, so long as we consider ourselves scientists and proceed as scientists.

Though ignorance is not considered an exculpatory plea in a court of law, it seems likely that the early twentieth-century Indo-Europeanists like Meillet really had a very crude understanding of taxonomy. What scholars like Meillet specialized in was reconstructing the vocabulary of Proto-Indo-European and discovering the sound correspondences that connected the various cognates. We will discuss both of these topics in the Epilogue, but they are properly addressed only after one has reached a classification of a set of languages. For the moment we must note that Meillet—for all his acknowledged accomplishments in the field of Indo-European studies—never classified a language in his life; he never discovered a single new relationship; and he really had no idea how one would go about doing such a thing. The blame for Meillet's ignorance, ironically, lies at the doorstep of Sir William Jones, for Jones had described the Indo-European family as a group of five branches from the start. Thus, the Indo-Europeanists never had to *find* a family; it was given to them on a silver platter. And certainly none of the nineteenth-century Indo-Europeanists ever imagined for a minute that their reconstructions or sound correspondences had anything to do with "proving" Indo-European. These quaint ideas, which will be discussed again later, are strictly the baggage of twentieth-century Indo-Europeanists.

But how were the Indo-Europeanists able to perpetuate this mythology throughout the twentieth century? Here I believe they benefited from a shift of focus in this century, from *historical* explanation to *structural* explanation, a sea change that essentially bequeathed historical linguistics to the Indo-Europeanists and let them do with it as they wished. The focus of theoretical linguistics thus shifted to ahistorical explanations, and historical linguistics became equated with Indo-European linguistics. Virtually every introductory textbook deals almost exclusively with Indo-European, devoting perhaps a few pages at the end to "other language families." And none of these textbooks says a word about how one finds language families. Classification, the foundation of historical linguistics, is simply not discussed.

In 1901 the English phonetician Henry Sweet identified many of these prejudices when he wrote:

> In philology, as in all branches of knowledge, it is the specialist who most strenuously opposes any attempt to widen the field of his methods. Hence the advocate of affinity between the Aryan [= Indo-European] and the Finnish [= Finno-Ugric] languages need not be alarmed when he hears that the majority of Aryan philologists reject the hypothesis. In many cases this rejection merely means that our specialist has his hands full already, and shrinks from learning a new set of languages. . . . Even when this passively agnostic attitude develops into aggressive antagonism, it is generally little more than the expression of mere prejudice against dethroning Aryan from its proud isolation and affiliating it to the languages of yellow races; or want of imagination and power of realizing an earlier morphological stage of Aryan; or, lastly, that conservatism and caution which would rather miss a brilliant discovery than run the risk of having mistakes exposed.

Today these same prejudices are still very much alive, but at the same time, as we shall see in the following chapters, they appear these days to be enjoying less and less support. Evidence from outside linguistics—as well as evidence from within comparative linguistics that has been swept under the rug for a century—is leading scholars toward a more complete picture of human prehistory than we have previously dared hope for. Within the perspective of this emerging synthesis, the antiquated ideas of the Indo-Europeanists and their followers persist as no more than a historical curiosity, one that from the point of linguistic taxonomy has led nowhere, and it is unlikely that the Indo-Europeanists will ever again command the field of historical linguistics as their own personal fiefdom.

4

Native Americans

Language in the New World

In the preceding chapter we found that language families like Indo-European can be classified by the same techniques that first uncovered the Indo-European family itself. The comparison of language families across Europe and Asia led us to conclude that Indo-European is just one branch of an even larger (and more ancient) family called Eurasiatic. In this chapter we will apply the same techniques to language families that have been discovered in the Americas, five of which you identified in Table 7.

As you will learn in this chapter, the classification of Native American languages is today one of the most controversial areas of genetic linguistics, the field of linguistics that studies the genealogical relationships of languages and language families. The traditional view throughout this century has been—despite Edward Sapir's attempts at consolidation—that Native American languages belong to a large number of independent families, such as Algonquian, Siouan, or Iroquoian, among which, it is asserted, there are no apparent genetic connections.

By some estimates the number of such independent families in the Americas approaches 200.

In 1987 Joseph Greenberg published *Language in the Americas*, a book in which he drastically reduced the number of independent Native American families. Subsequently, the Greenberg classification was independently discovered by geneticists (Cavalli-Sforza et al. 1988) and corroborated by a study of Native American teeth (Turner 1989). These new discoveries have in turn led to a general scenario for the peopling of the New World, a scenario that tries to integrate the complementary evidence of human language, human genetics, and the archaeological record.

Families Where There Were No Families

But before we discuss these new developments, and the bitter controversy they have engendered, I would like the reader to classify some Native American families without the bias attendant upon knowing the details of this controversy. Table 9 gives thirteen words in thirteen Native American language families. Since few language families in the Americas have been reconstructed, we are forced in most cases to use citations from actual languages rather than reconstructed forms for the families in question. That, of course, is what we were forced to do with such Old World families as Dravidian, the etymological dictionary for which merely lists sets of cognates without reconstructions of any kind. But it is important to stress that even though each word in Table 9 comes from a single language, the root exemplified by that word is in almost all cases attested in other languages of that family, as well. Accordingly, we may be confident that the root existed in the proto-language of that family even though we lack a precise reconstruction for it. In other words, we are comparing not isolated words in isolated languages, but well-attested roots in different language families.

Your task, as before, is to classify these thirteen families into whatever higher-level groupings you can distinguish. I must warn you, however, that the Curator for American Indian

TABLE 9 Native American Language Families

Language	I/Me/My	You	(Give) Hand	Left (Hand)	Knee	Child	Brother/ Son	Sister/ Daughter Aunt	(Sister) Water Bird	(Bat) Throat/ Swallow	(Come) Go
A	-ma	-t	ʔätʸä	siitquq	ʔaye	aŋŋaq	paniy	atsay	imiq qavya	aya	piki-ð
B	ši	nan	lag	s'at'	guhd	gɨt'a	onay(e)	tsik	ʔati čaš	ket	qa
C	ne	ke	maχwa	kes	ketekʷ-ï	t'an'a	ʔtsin	tune	akwä tˢ'ek	məlqʷ	wa
D	na?	ma	makan	kets	ikat	t'anat	t'in	tüne	pinükin č'ik'	mülk'	waŋ
E	na	ma	mane	kasark	pʰuruč'i	t'aŋpam t'inisi	at'on	pane	aqa sik	milqe	wan
F	ne?	ma	maka	kuč'ē	tana	ʔdiino	t'ut'ina	pan	gʷa tsikie	kutu	ma
G	na	ma	man	kuts	ikuet	tuktan	sin	tuntu puna	aka eš'ɛka	murki	wan
H	na	ma	maki	mwenik	tula	tayna	den	thaun epan	yaku tˢïktˢï	malq'a	wen
I	hi	ma	muka	kompe	kat'	maki	ten	äebn	okõa šaga	uamea	w'än
J	no	ma	meʔeŋ	kuču	ikketi	ta?in	tingwa	atunesas penawa	ako čiki	mïrkoi	awani
K	awe	ama	emekun poe		kudo	tane	dēnu	ebuño	tuna sïkïi	eʔmöki	ito
L	no	mi	moken		kaˢege	tavin	ina	tona nene	uaka jïkïdï		wo
M	nu	ma	mako	keč	gete	kra	čina	atonkä	pan ŋo	tˢïpe kot	va

Languages at the Smithsonian Institution, Ives Goddard, maintains that there are no known genetic connections among *any* of the thirteen families listed in Table 9. And most specialists in American Indian languages agree with him. Once again, I'll let you draw your own conclusions.

When one examines the first column of Table 9 one is struck at once by the fact that nine of these thirteen families have a first-person pronoun based on *n-*, and ten of the thirteen have a second-person pronoun based on *m-*. It would appear that—in the Americas at least—pronouns do not "look alike more or less everywhere." There is a distinctive American pattern, *na* 'I,' *ma* 'you,' that has nothing in common with the Eurasiatic pattern, *mi* 'I,' *ti* 'you.' These two American pronouns alone suggest that the thirteen families in Table 9 belong to just three families: A ‖ B ‖ CDEFGHIJKLM. And when we examine the other eleven words, our preliminary conclusions are confirmed over and over and over.

Families A and B resemble the other families almost nowhere. Neither do they resemble each other. On the other hand, families C–M (or a large subset of them) seem to resemble each other at every turn. The family that we first suspected on the basis of the unique pronominal pattern *na/ma* 'I/you,' turns out to have distinctive words for 'hand' (*makan*), 'left (hand)' (*kets*), 'knee' (*kete*), 'child' (*t'ana*), 'son' (*t'ina*), 'daughter' (*t'una*), 'aunt' (*pan*), 'water' (*akwa*), 'bird' (*tˢ'ik*), 'swallow' (*malq'a*), and 'go' (*wan*). One could examine hundreds of additional words and the solution to Table 9 would always be the same, that shown in Figure 8.

The recognition of the distinctive American pronominal

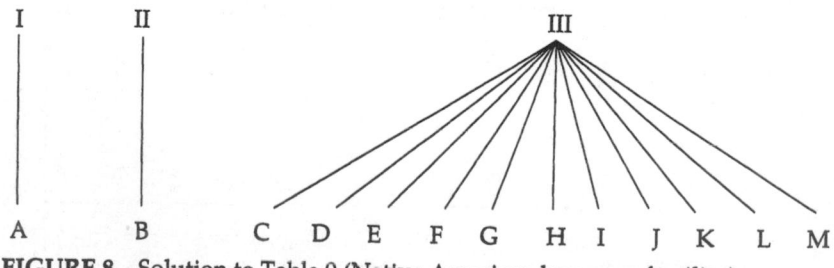

FIGURE 8   Solution to Table 9 (Native American language families).

system, *na/ma* 'I/you,' is in fact almost as old as the recognition of the Eurasiatic system. Already in 1905 Trombetti had devoted an appendix of a book to "The Pronouns 'I' and 'you' in the Principal American Languages." In that appendix he pointed out the broad distribution of the American pattern throughout the indigenous languages of North and South America. A decade later Sapir (apparently unaware of Trombetti's appendix) noted the same pattern and concluded, like Trombetti, that such a broad distribution could only be explained genetically, that is, by assuming that the numerous *n-* 'I' and *m-* 'you' pronouns found over and over in Native American languages must be modern traces of a single ancestral language. In 1918 Sapir wrote, in a personal letter, "Getting down to brass tacks, how in the Hell are you going to explain general American *n-* 'I' except genetically? It's disturbing, I know, but (more) noncommittal conservatism is only dodging, after all, isn't it? Great simplifications are in store for us."

You may well wonder why Sapir found such an idea, a simple evolutionary explanation for linguistic similarities, "disturbing." In fact, Sapir himself considered such evidence exhilarating, as a comment later in the same letter shows: "It seems to me that only now is American linguistics becoming really interesting, at least in its ethnological bearings." But at the same time Sapir knew—from personal experience—that such far-flung families were no more in vogue in American academia than in Europe, where Indo-Europeanists were rejecting all attempts to connect Indo-European with any other family. Sapir himself had sought to show that the Algonquian family, which you identified in Table 7, was most closely related to two languages (Wiyot and Yurok) spoken along the northern California coast, hundreds of miles from the nearest Algonquian language. Sapir's startling discovery was reviewed by the leading Algonquianist of the day, Truman Michelson (the son of the first American Nobel Laureate, Albert Michelson), who derisively dismissed Sapir's putative cognates as "fancied lexicographical similarities." Further, he criticized Sapir for comparing "different morphological elements" and attributed the few remaining similarities to chance resemblances. Michelson concluded his review with a sarcastic dismissal of the whole line of research:

"Enough has been said to show the utter folly of haphazard comparisons unless we have a thorough knowledge of the morphological structure of the languages concerned." Despite this negative verdict, Sapir's proposal connecting Wiyot and Yurok with Algonquian is today universally accepted.

At about this same time Sapir discovered that the Athabaskan family, which you picked out in Table 7, was most closely related to two contiguous languages (Haida and Tlingit) spoken on the southeastern coast of Alaska. This larger family, which Sapir named Na-Dene, was just as harshly criticized by the leading Athabaskanist of the day, Pliny Goddard. Although Sapir had responded in detail to Michelson's attack, he was so disgusted by Goddard's juvenile criticisms that he decided not to respond at all. Apparently, he stopped working on such controversial taxonomic questions altogether at that point, and, as we noted in the preceding chapter, his third major discovery—the connection between Na-Dene and Sino-Tibetan—lay in abeyance for some 60 years before being revived by Russian scholars in the past decade.

Today both of Sapir's earlier proposals are accepted by virtually everyone, and Sapir is regarded as one of the great linguists of the twentieth century, while Michelson and Goddard are little more than footnotes to history. Yet, at the time, their opposition—and that of the influential anthropologist Franz Boas—effectively thwarted any attempt to arrive at more comprehensive linguistic classifications. Scholars like Michelson and Goddard were quite content to have their particular families (Algonquian and Athabaskan, respectively) unrelated to any other family. Not only did that make life easier, it also gave their family the same lustre as that of the proudly isolated Indo-European family. As for the American pronominal pattern, Boas attributed it simply to "obscure psychological causes." Why these "obscure psychological causes" affected only Native Americans was never explained.

For almost half a century, attempts to discover more comprehensive classifications of Native American languages were abandoned, by virtually all scholars. The single major exception was Morris Swadesh, who continued Sapir's work. Swadesh, however, not only was isolated in his work, but was also effectively banished from American academia for supposedly "subversive" political views, and he wound up spending his later years in Mexico, where he died in 1967. Like Trombetti and Sapir before him, Swadesh recognized the significance of the American pronominal pattern (and of other abundant evidence with which he was familiar) and concluded that there was a vast family of languages occupying most of the Americas. He did not, however, attempt a complete marshaling of all the evidence, and his work was thus generally disregarded by the Americanists, who were satisfied with the status quo.

This half-century of quiescence came to an abrupt end in 1987 with the publication of *Language in the Americas*, in which Greenberg offered copious evidence that the Native American languages are to be classified into just three families, not the hundreds that the experts had settled on. These three families are precisely those you discovered in Table 9, whose names I will now identify. Family A is Eskimo-Aleut, which as we saw in the last chapter is the easternmost member of the Eurasiatic family, as revealed in Table 9 by the Eurasiatic pronominal pattern *m-/t-*. Family B is the Athabaskan family, which along with three other languages (Eyak, Tlingit, and Haida) makes up the Na-Dene family that Sapir had identified in 1915.

Families C–M constitute a family that Greenberg named Amerind, a family characterized by the American pronominal system *n-/m-* and a wealth of other cognate words, a few of which you saw in Table 9. Families C–M are, in fact, the eleven branches that Greenberg posited for Amerind, and they are listed in Table 9 in roughly a north to south orientation. Thus, families C–F are found primarily in North America, while families G–M are for the most part restricted to South America. The names that Greenberg gave to these eleven Amerind branches (most of which were built on the work of predecessors like Sapir and Swadesh) are Almosan-Keresiouan (C), Penutian (D), Hokan (E), Central Amerind (F), Chibchan-Paezan (G), Andean (H), Macro-Tucanoan (I), Equatorial (J), Macro-Carib (K), Macro-Panoan (L), and Macro-Ge (M). The distribution of the three Native American families posited by Greenberg is shown in Map 7.

Like Sapir before him, Greenberg knew that his conclusions would be "disturbing" to most Americanists: "I am ... well aware that what is attempted in this work runs against the current trends in Amerindian work and will be received in certain quarters with something akin to outrage." On this point, at least, Greenberg could hardly have been more correct. A year before his book was published, in fact, the Americanist Lyle Campbell–without having even seen the book–urged his colleagues to "shout down" Greenberg's classification, lest it confuse laymen like you. After the book was published, the editor

ESKIMO-ALEUT

NA-DENE

AMERIND

MAP 7 Language families of the Americas.

of *Language*, William Bright, himself an outspoken critic of Greenberg, chose Campbell to review the book—with predictable consequences. The Americanist Terrence Kaufman later warned that Greenberg's "avowed values are subversive and should be explicitly argued against." And the Curator for American Indian languages at the Smithsonian, Ives Goddard, claimed that Greenberg's "technique excludes historical linguistic analysis and, not surprisingly, leads to no reliable conclusions about linguistic history." Small wonder that a noted physical anthropologist, not involved in this debate, recently characterized the reaction to Greenberg's book as "hysterical." Indeed, the kind of verbal abuse that has recently been directed at Greenberg is usually reserved for religious heretics rather than scholars with new ideas.

That Greenberg's book engendered such a violent reaction was due in part to the fact that its conclusions were "disturbing" to the narrow specialists who have dominated Amerindian linguistics in this century. Equally important, however, was the fact that Greenberg was universally recognized—even by his critics—as one of the twentieth century's greatest linguists, having first gained international fame with a revolutionary classification of African languages during the 1950's. When Greenberg began investigating African languages in the late 1940's, there were over a thousand languages on the continent, and the genetic connections among them were largely unknown. Some of the obvious families, such as Bantu, Semitic, and Chadic, had long been recognized, but most of the continent was simply terra incognita. When Greenberg published his classification in 1963 he had reduced this bewildering diversity to just four families: Khoisan, Niger-Kordofanian (including Bantu as a subgroup), Nilo-Saharan (including Nilotic), and Afro-Asiatic (including both Semitic and Chadic as branches). This classification too initially met with criticism (especially from Bantuists, who were disappointed that the Bantu family turned out to be just a twig on the vast Niger-Kordofanian tree), but today this classification is the backbone of African historical linguistics, and Africanists, 30 years later, have come to see that Greenberg made virtually no errors in the entire classification, despite having to deal with hundreds of poorly described languages. Thus, when Greenberg's classification of Native American languages appeared in 1987, it could hardly be overlooked or swept under the rug.

In support of the Amerind family Greenberg presented over 300 sets of cognate words, as well as several dozen grammatical elements such as the by-now famous pronominal pattern *na-/ma-* 'I/you.' Once again the critics were called upon to explain why this pattern—and numerous lexical items—were so widespread in the Americas and virtually absent in the rest of the world. A myriad of explanations were offered. Bright suggested that these pronouns and lexical items were due to "relationships of multilingualism and intense linguistic diffusion" in Asia, before the various Amerind groups migrated to America, and he proposed to call them "Pan-Americanisms." But "Pan-Americanisms" is simply a euphemism contrived to avoid admitting that there are genetic connections among the various Amerind groups, groups that are assumed—contrary to Greenberg's evidence—to be "independent."

In a similar vein—and toward the same end—the English Bantuist Malcolm Guthrie had posited "Bantuisms" to explain the similarities between the Bantu languages and certain West African languages. But whereas "Bantuisms" are today considered little more than a joke, for reasons that we will explore further in Chapter 8, "Pan-Americanisms" are discussed in the Americanist literature even today, as if they represented a serious alternative to common origin. The Americanists' attack on Greenberg has been remarkably like that of the Bantuists four decades earlier. At that time, according to the British historian Colin Flight, "rather than trying to understand what Greenberg had to say, British linguists seem to have done their best to *mis*understand. They acted as if they were determined to miss the point—as if it was their business to spot passages in the text which were loosely worded, ambiguous, or elliptical, and then to place upon these passages the most inept construction that could possibly be devised. In a word, they acted like lawyers" (Flight 1988: 266). Much of the current Americanist criticism of Greenberg has just this flavor.

It is well known in linguistics that pronouns are almost never borrowed, and such promiscuous borrowing, among many different groups, as the Americanists propose is simply unheard of in the linguistic literature. One might also ask how all the people using the pronouns *na-* and *ma-* succeeded in reaching the Americas without leaving a trace of this pattern behind in Asia? Other critics have proposed that the pronouns diffused throughout the Americas after the various peoples had already occupied North and South America. But again, such diffusion of pronouns is simply unknown. Meillet's claim that pronouns look alike everywhere has also been resurrected, though with a new twist. According to these experts, because the consonants *n* and *m* are the most stable consonants over time (which is true), we should *expect* to find an archaic residue of these sounds in the most basic pronouns, around the world. The problem with this explanation is that it is not borne out by the facts. Scholars with a worldwide perspective of the linguistic literature, like Trombetti and Greenberg, noticed the American pattern precisely because they were familiar with what pronominal systems looked like around the world and knew right away the American pattern is unique. It is only the narrow specialist, who knows little of the linguistic literature beyond his small family, who can imagine that the Amerind pronominal pattern is universal.

Yet another explanation for the American pattern has been that these pronouns represent "infant sucking sounds" that have become pronouns in the same way that *mama* is found worldwide with the meaning 'mother.' Once again, the problem is that the American pattern is not widespread outside the Americas, which raises the question why this "infant sucking sound" theory, so popular at the Smithsonian, should apply only to Native Americans. Other, less plausible solutions (even, for example, intervention from extraterrestials) have been mentioned, but the other "explanations" I have laid out are more representative of the current thinking of Amerindian experts.

Ironically, the only explanation *not* mentioned by these scholars is the simple evolutionary one. But in practice, if not in their theoretical pronouncements, these scholars are strictly creationist (like the Indo-Europeanists, whom they so studiously emulate). An evolutionary answer, plausible or not, is simply not acceptable.

An Amerind Root and Its Progeny

Let us consider now, in some detail, just one of the roots that Greenberg posited for the Amerind family, a word for which he gave the semantic gloss 'girl' (he does not give either a phonetic gloss or a Proto-Amerind reconstruction). The putative cognates of this root come from the four North American branches of Amerind (Greenberg cited no forms from South America). Furthermore, the meaning he gave was not uniformly 'girl,' but in some languages was 'son, daughter, child,' or 'small.' Finally, although the two consonants of the root can be clearly identified as initial *t-* and medial *-n-*, the vowel that came between these two consonants could seemingly be any vowel at all. Among the seventeen forms cited by Greenberg, the following at least would seem to be cognate: Proto-Uto-Aztecan **tana* 'son, daughter,' Chumash *taniw* 'small, child,' Yana *t'inī* 'be small,' *t'inī-si* 'child, son, daughter,' Central Sierra Miwok *tūne* 'daughter,' Proto-Central Algonquian **tāna* 'daughter,' Blackfoot *tanna* 'daughter,' and Nootka *t'an'a* 'child.' These comparisons certainly look promising, yet there is a considerable number of loose ends, especially with regard to the varying gender of the forms and the seemingly random medial vowel.

For reasons that need not concern us here, I happened to pick this particular etymology, from among the several hundred Greenberg had proposed, to investigate in greater detail. Ultimately I devoted about six months to an examination of Greenberg's 23 volumes of notebooks on the vocabularies of Native American languages, and I supplemented that with a fairly thorough search of the Americanist literature available to me in the Stanford University library. What I found was that Greenberg's cited forms represented only a fraction of the full range of such forms. Variations on *tana* turned out to be, in fact, as plentiful in South America as in North America. Beyond the seventeen examples that Greenberg had listed for North America, I discovered several hundred additional forms, from both North and South America, that showed the same general pattern that Greenberg had first noticed, *tana* 'child, son, daughter.'

This particular lexical item thus turns out to be a diagnostic trait of the Amerind family comparable in value to the *n-/m*-pronominal pattern. Furthermore, when I studied the several hundred forms I had gathered, it dawned on me one day that there was a strong tendency for the medial vowel of the root to be correlated with the gender of the referent, so that an original Proto-Amerind system such as **tina* 'son, brother,' **tuna* 'sister, daughter,' **tana* 'child, sibling,' could be perceived in this welter of forms, even though many of the forms showed such significant phonetic and/or semantic evolution that this original pattern had come to be obscured.

In Table 9 you met quite a few of these related forms in the columns for 'child,' 'son,' and 'daughter.' The Almosan-Keresiouan examples (in row C) are Nootka *t'ana* 'child,' Mohawk *ʔtsin* 'male, boy,' and Coeur D'Alene *tune* 'niece.' The Penutian examples (in row D) are Totonac *t'anat* 'grandchild,' Molale *t'in* 'elder brother,' and Central Sierra Miwok *tūne* 'daughter.' The Hokan examples (E) are Coahuilteco *t'anpam* 'child,' Yana *t'inīsi* 'child, son, daughter,' and Salinan *at'on* 'younger sister.' In row F, Central Amerind, we find Proto-Uto-Aztecan **tana* 'daughter, son,' Cuicatec *ʔdiino* 'brother,' and Taos *t'ut'ina* 'older sister.'

In the South American branches of Amerind the three grades of the root are equally well attested. In Chibchan-Paezan (G) we have Miskito *tuktan* 'child, boy,' Changuena *sin* 'brother,' and Lenca *tuntu* 'younger sister.' The Andean examples (H) are Aymara *tayna* 'first-born child,' Tehuelche *den* 'brother,' and Tehuelche *thaun* 'sister.' In row I, Macro-Tucanoan, the word for 'child' is not cognate with the forms under discussion (though I might have cited Masaca *tani-mai* 'younger sister' in its place). The masculine and feminine forms, however, come from the same language, Tiquie *ten* 'son' and *ton* 'daughter,' showing that this portion of the original Amerind system I propose has been preserved in a single language down to the present day.

The Equatorial examples in row J are Urubu-Kaapor *taʔin* 'child,' Mocochi *tingwa* 'son, boy,' and Morotoko *atunesas* 'girl.' Macro-Carib (K) examples are Pavishana *tane* 'my son,' Yagua *dēnu* 'male child,' and Nonuya *tona* 'sister,' and examples in Macro-Panoan (L) are Lengua *tawin* 'grandchild,' Vilela *ina* 'son, daughter' (the cognacy of this form is uncertain), and Tacana *tona* 'younger sister.' Finally, in Macro-Ge (M) the word for 'child,' *kra*, is not cognate with these forms. I could have used, for Macro-Ge, Tibagi *togtan* 'girl,' which appears to be a compound whose two parts are the same as the Miskito form cited above, though the gender differs. The other two forms given for Macro-Ge are Guato *čina* 'older brother,' and Piokobyé *atonkä* 'younger sister.'

In light of this hypothesis, it becomes apparent why Greenberg largely overlooked the masculine forms and, indeed, glossed the entire etymology 'girl.' In linguistic evolution, consonants are often affected by vowels that immediately follow them, and different vowels have different effects. Of interest to us, in this case, is the fact that there is a strong tendency for the sequence *ti-* to become *tˢi-*, which in turn often turns into *si-*. The vowels *-u-* and *-a-* tend not to have this effect, which means that many of the masculine forms, deriving from *tina*, would be expected to have evolved into *tˢina* or *sina*, whereas the feminine and neutral forms would have retained their original shapes, *tuna* and *tana*. It is thus easy to see why Greenberg—who, after all, was dealing with hundreds of words across hundreds of languages—should have at first overlooked the often phonetically more deviant masculine forms, connecting only the feminine and neutral forms that preserved both consonants intact. When one examines the hundreds of forms I have collected, one does in fact find many phonetically eroded masculine forms, as well as some with the original *t-* unchanged.

Forms that preserve the initial Amerind consonant more or less intact would include Molale *t'in* 'elder brother,' Yana *t'ini-si* 'child, son, daughter,' Tiquie *ten* 'son,' and Mocochi *tingwa* 'son, boy.' Languages in which the initial *t-* has shifted to *ts-* include Mohawk *ʔtsin* 'male, boy,' Yurok *tˢin* 'young man,' Yuki *tˢina* 'daughter's husband,' Chorti *ih-tˢ'in* 'younger sibling,' Lacandon *i-tsin* 'younger brother,' Southeast Pomo *χa-tˢ'in* 'sister's child,' Yuma *an-tˢen* 'older brother,' Pehuenche *a-tˢena* 'brother,' Amaguaje *tˢin* 'boy,' Siona *tˢijn* 'son,' and Millcayac *tzhœng* 'son.' The final stage, in which *tˢ-* is simplified to *s-*, is seen in such forms as Flathead *sin-tˢeʔ* 'younger brother,' Santa Cruz Costanoan *sinsin* 'nephew,' Tewa *sēŋ* 'man, male,' Proto-Oto-Manguean **si(ʔ)(n)* 'youngster,' and Changuena *sin* 'brother.' The Vilela form, *ina* 'son, daughter,' may represent a final stage where the initial consonant is lost altogether.

There is one further refinement to this analysis that we might make. You have no doubt noticed that quite a few of the initial *t-*'s are followed by apostrophes, e.g. *t'in* 'elder brother' in Molale. This apostrophe signifies that the *t-* is pronounced with a simultaneous closure of the glottis (what you do when you constrict your throat to hold your breath), followed by a release that produces a distinctive popping sound following the *t-*. (Such glottalized consonants are fairly common in the world's languages, but are absent from the well-known European languages.) Inasmuch as some Amerind forms begin with a glottalized *t'-*, while others begin with a plain *t-*, one might ask what the original consonant sounded like in Proto-Amerind. The answer is that it was in all likelihood a glottalized *t'-*, since it is far more likely that original glottalized consonants were simplified to plain consonants in different branches (and different languages) and retained in others, than that plain consonants developed independently in different Amerind branches. Therefore, the original Proto-Amerind system was something like **t'ina* 'son, brother,' **t'una* 'sister, daughter,' **t'ana* 'child, sibling.'

This intricate system of kinship terms, which has left hundreds of slightly modified forms in extant languages, would certainly seem to indicate that the Amerind family is more than a mirage. Yet even this complex lexical item, with three different grades correlated with gender, is but a part of the larger Amerind mosaic, and is often found in conjuction with other Amerind elements. For example, this word is found with the widespread Amerind first-person pronoun in such forms as Proto-Algonquian **ne-tāna* 'my daughter,' Kiowa *nɔ:-tɔ́:* 'my brother,' Paez *ne-tson* 'my brother-in-law,' Manao *no-tany* 'my son,' Baniva *no-tani* 'my son,' and Yavitero *nu-tani-mi* 'my daughter.'

Another prefix that frequently appears with this root is

ʔa-' older . . . ,' as seen in such examples as Proto-Miwok ʔá-ta 'older brother,' Wintun o-tun-če 'older sister,' Shasta ʔá-ču 'older sister,' Washo ʔá-t'u 'older brother,' Coreguaje aʔ-čɨ 'older brother,' aʔ-čo 'older sister,' Guahibo ā-tō 'older brother,' and Paumari ā-dyu 'older brother.'

A number of suffixes are also found with the root under discussion. One of them is a diminutive suffix whose original shape was something like -ihsa or -iʔsa. (A diminutive suffix, for example -ito in Spanish, adds a nuance of smallness or endearment to the noun, and is thus particularly common with words for children.) Examples of this suffix are seen in Proto-Algonquian *ne-tān-ehsa 'my daughter,' Nootka t'an'ē-ʔis 'child,' Mixtec taʔnu iʔša 'younger sister' (where iʔša is a separate word meaning 'child'), Esmeralda tini-usa 'daughter,' and Suhin tino-iče 'young woman.' The suffix occurs with other roots as well, for example Amuesha koy-an-ešaʔ 'girl' and Paez kuen-as 'young woman.'

There is also an in-law suffix, with the general shape -kwa, that is seen in forms such as Proto-Algonquian *ne-tān-kwa 'my sister-in-law,' Columbian ti-kʷa 'father's sister,' Yuki tˢ'i-hwa 'husband's brother,' Iowa ta-gwa 'son-in-law,' Kagaba tu-gwa 'grandchild,' Motilon a-te-gwa 'nephew,' Surinam Carib tī-ʔwo 'brother-in-law,' Tacana u-tse-kwa 'grandchild.' The same suffix also appears on other Amerind words, such as Yurok ne-kwa 'my mother/father-in-law,' Proto-Mixtecan *kuʔn-gwi 'woman's sister,' Cahuapana kaik-kwa 'sister-in-law,' and Krenye pan-çwö 'sister-in-law.'

I have gone into this particular Amerind root in some detail to dispel the notion that Greenberg's comparisons are little more than vague resemblances among a few scattered languages in the Americas. My brief review of the evidence for a single root suggests otherwise, and it seems to me we must conclude that all of these intricate patterns in the roots and affixes of Amerind words can only be reasonably explained as the result of descent with modification from a single earlier language, Proto-Amerind. As Sapir might have remarked, "more non-committal conservatism is only dodging, after all, isn't it?"

The Forest For the Trees

Let us consider one final argument that is often leveled at such ancient and abstract entities as Amerind or Eurasiatic, especially by narrow specialists of the type described by Sweet above. One such specialist, who devotes his life to the study of a single language, laments that whether the Amerind hypothesis is right or wrong really has no impact on his own work, and he would therefore just as soon pay no attention to it. The problem with this line of reasoning, which has been pointed out by both the Nostraticists and Greenberg, is that certain language-specific problems can *only* be solved by considering that language in a larger context. Certain idiosyncratic aspects of a language can never be explained on grounds internal to that language, and the scholar who attempts to do so condemns himself or herself to forever misreading the phenomenon.

The Americanist Howard Berman, for example, in studying the Yurok language of northern California, recently concluded that Yurok "$t^s\bar{a}n$- 'young' is related to t^sin 'young man.' . . . I believe one of these is an old changed form of the other, but I do not know which is which." Without going beyond the Yurok language itself there is no apparent reason why these two words are so similar in sound and meaning. Our specialist believes that one of the two was originally in the language and then gave rise to the other, but he is at a loss to decide which was original or why a new form developed, whichever of the two was there first. But when this unresolved puzzle is considered in light of the evidence of the entire Amerind family, then the presence of these two particular forms in Yurok can be seen as a trivial consequence of the general hypothesis concerning *t'ina/t'una/t'ana* posited above. Yurok preserves two of the three grades of this root, with $t^s\bar{a}n$- 'young' representing the modern reflection, or reflex, of Proto-Amerind *$t'ana$, and t^sin 'young man,' the reflex of Proto-Amerind *$t'ina$. Neither Yurok form, it turns out, developed from the other (at least not within the Yurok language); rather, each developed from a Proto-Amerind kinship system that must have existed at least 12,000 years ago. The solution to the Yurok "problem" turns out to be trivial, but it is available only to those who are willing to consider their language of specialty in a broad genetic context.

Well, where did all these New World peoples come from? Greenberg and colleagues have proposed that the three Native American language families—Amerind, Na-Dene, and Eskimo-Aleut—derive from three separate migrations from Asia. The broad distribution of Amerind languages (seen in Map 7) and its considerable internal diversity both suggest that the first migration brought people speaking Proto-Amerind to the Americas. These people apparently spread very quickly throughout North and South America, which were at the time unoccupied by humans. The second migration, which brought the ancestors of the Na-Dene first to a homeland on the southern coast of Alaska, later saw the Athabaskan expansion into the interior. The final migration brought the ancestors of the Eskimo-Aleut, first to southwestern Alaska, and eventually across the entire northern perimeter of North America as far east as Greenland.

We saw in the preceding chapter that Eskimo-Aleut is the easternmost member of the Eurasiatic family, and that Na-Dene is the easternmost member of the Dene-Caucasian family; hence their immediate Asian relatives are already known. But what about Amerind? Who are its Asian relatives? This question is perhaps more difficult than the other two, but my preliminary conclusion, based on a comparison of all the relevant families of Asia, is that, among all Old World families, Amerind is closest to Eurasiatic. But whereas Eskimo-Aleut is a *branch* of the Eurasiatic family, Amerind is related to Eurasiatic as a whole, and thus has no special ties to Eskimo-Aleut or any other branch of Eurasiatic. At the same time, it must be admitted that Amerind also shares certain roots with Dene-Caucasian, and Sergei Starostin has pointed out numerous similarities between Dene-Caucasian and Eurasiatic. Clearly, the relationship of these three groups to each other (and to other families) is a question that merits further investigation.

5

The Origin of
Language

Are There Global Cognates?

In the preceding chapters we have seen that it is possible to group languages together into families on the basis of similarities in the forms of words used by those languages. In turn, we have found that it is possible to group the more obvious families into even more ancient families, such as Eurasiatic, Nilo-Saharan, and Amerind. Though these more ancient families are less obvious and do not share great quantities of cognates, as the younger, more obvious families sometimes do, they can nonetheless be detected, by the same methods that produced the obvious families. We estimated earlier that there are perhaps 400 obvious families. How many ancient families, or larger groupings, are there? The work of Greenberg and the Russian scholars, and their followers, indicates that there are about a dozen, though a precise number cannot be given because the Russians' Nostratic family, while generally similar to Greenberg's Eurasiatic, includes three families (Afro-Asiatic, Kartvelian, and Dravidian) that Greenberg considers distinct from Eurasiatic. Why the two differ will be dealt with in Chapter 6.

With that framework in mind, our next step is to compare all of the world's families to see whether they share various commonalities, or perhaps to find that we have finally reached the end of the road—where such commonalities as may once have existed have long since been obliterated by linguistic evolution. Such questions have not been seriously investigated for almost a hundred years, primarily because if one accepts the claim of the Indo-Europeanists that the comparative method is limited to the past 6,000 years—and almost everyone does—then the possibility of ever connecting Indo-European (or any of the hundreds of other obvious families) with another family of that antiquity is clearly hopeless. Those precious 6,000 years have allowed the "splendid isolation" of Indo-European to act as a dike against all long-range comparison. And until Greenberg sorted out the higher-level families in Africa, New Guinea, and the Americas, it was not really clear what families might usefully be compared with one another. That situation has now changed fundamentally, and there is no good reason why global comparisons should not be undertaken. It is, after all, an empirical question.

The World's Language Families

Table 10 presents thirteen words in a dozen language families that embrace all of the world's 5,000 extant languages. As in previous tables involving language families, the roots in question have for the most part been posited, not by me, but by specialists in individual families, and have either been reconstructed for that family (or for a large subgroup within it) or shown to exist so widely in modern languages that some such term may be presumed to have existed in the proto-language. A few simple semantic shifts have also been allowed between families, though in most cases the range of meaning is quite specific, as we shall see in the three examples we discuss in more detail. For those who wish to trace down every form cited in Table 10, the Bibliography at the end of this book should prove helpful.

TABLE 10 Language Families Around the World

Language	Who?	What?	Two	Water	One/Finger	Arm$_1$	Arm$_2$	Bend/Knee	Hair	Vaginal/Vulva	Smell/Nose	Squeeze	Seize/Fly (v.)
A	iku	ma	/kam	k''ā	/kɔnu	//kū	≠hā	//gom	/'ū	lkwai	č'ū	xom	d'wa
B	na	de	ball	nki	tok	kani	boko	kutu	sum	buti	čona	kaŋkam	par
C	nani	ni	bala	engi	dike	kono	boko	bongo		butu	kama	pere	
D	k(w)	ma	bwVr	akʷa	tak	ganA		bunge	somm	put	suna	km	pyaRR
E	min	ma	yor	rˢq'a	ert	t'ot'	qe	muql	toma	put'	sun	sxwerp'	p'er
F	yāv	yā	iranʈu	nīru	birelu	kaŋ	kay	menḍa		pūṭa	počču	kamV	parV
G	kʷi	mi	pälä	akʷā	tik	konV	bhāghu(s)	bük(ä)	punče	p'ut'V	snā	kamu	parV
H	kʷi	ma	gnyis	ʔoχʷa	tok	kan	boq	pjut	tˢʰam	put'i	suŋ	k'ēm	phur
I	o-ko-e	m-anu	ʔ(m)bar	namaw	ntoʔ	xeen	baʸa	buku	syām	betik	ijuŋ	ŋgam	apir
J		mina	boula	okho	dik	akan	ben	buku		utu	sɨnna		paru
K	ŋaani	minha	bula	gugu	kuman	mala	paɟiŋ	buŋku		puda	mura	maan	
L	kune	mana	p'āl	akwā	dɨk'i	kano	boko	buka	summe	butie	čuna		taʔ

A final phonetic hint may be of some help. Four of the words in family A have a tilde over a vowel, indicating that the vowel is nasalized. French is well known for its nasal vowels, in words like *bon* [bõ] 'good,' *vin* [væ̃] 'wine,' and *chant* [šã] 'song.' Historically, as the French orthography indicates, nasal vowels almost always derive from earlier sequences combining an oral vowel (for example *o* or *i*) with a nasal consonant (for example *m* or *n*). Thus, it is reasonable to infer that the word for 'nose, smell' in family A, which is *č'ũ*, probably derives from an earlier form *č'um*, *č'un*, or *č'uŋ*. This knowledge should facilitate certain comparisons.

Without further ado, here is your final exam, Table 10. I need hardly remind you that the consensus of most historical linguists is that there are *no* meaningful similarities among such ancient families. Indeed, even the ancient families themselves cannot exist, because of the severe time-depth restrictions on the comparative method in contemporary linguistics. Linguistic evolution, according to the experts, is so swift that the comparative method is only able to discover the obvious; the subtle is simply beyond its temporal grasp. By this time, however, I doubt that such dire warnings from the experts will set you back much.

Well, what did you find? Do these dozen ancient families have anything in common? Or are they all unique and distinct? What you should have found, if you relied on common sense, is that there are many similarities among them, but that it is nonetheless difficult to discern larger subgroupings within what must certainly be a single huge language family. In other words, even this modest little table suggests a single origin for all extant human languages. Since many additional such tables could be produced to corroborate the results of Table 10—or, for that matter, to corroborate the results of earlier tables—the conclusion that all human languages are ultimately related seems inescapable, no matter how unpalatable that idea might be to Indo-Europeanists.

The thirteen words listed in Table 10 represent less than half of the words cited by John Bengtson and me in our attempt to demonstrate a single origin for extant languages (Bengtson and Ruhlen 1994). And the 27 words we chose were just the most widespread; there are numerous additional roots which, while not so widespread, nonetheless provide crucial evidence that all the world's language families, and hence all the world's languages, derive from a common source. Other scholars have in the past decade contributed additional links to this single long chain of evidence. For the most widespread proposals, one may cite, in particular, the work of Václav Blažek, Harold Fleming, Vitaly Shevoroshkin, and Sergei Starostin, though contributions on a smaller scale have been made by many other scholars (some of whom, it must be admitted, have contributed parts to the whole without coming to endorse the whole). Perhaps the problem has been that the chain of evidence is so long, and traverses so many independent kingdoms, that the full import of the evidence has really only been glimpsed, by only a few scholars.

It is hardly necessary to discuss in detail the many similarities that connect all of the families listed in Table 10. Roots that connect them include *ku* 'who,' *ma* 'what,' *pal* 'two,' *akʷa* 'water,' *tik* 'finger,' *kanV* (V indicates a vowel whose precise character is unknown) 'arm,' *boko* 'arm,' *buŋku* 'knee,' *sum* 'hair,' *putV* 'vulva,' *čuna* 'nose, smell,' *kamV* 'squeeze, hold in the hand, seize,' and *parV* 'fly' (v.).

There is also slight evidence that families B and C are closer to each other than to the other families. The words for 'who?' and 'water' can be interpreted in this way. We shall see in Chapter 7 that a close connection between families B and C is strongly supported by the evidence of human genetics, whatever the ultimate fate of these linguistic comparisons. For the time being the linguistic evidence indicates that all the families listed in Table 10 are members of a single large family, but how these different families are related to one another—or, to put it another way, the order in which they split off from one another—is not yet clear. Thus, the proper solution for Table 10 is the solution shown in Figure 9.

The twelve families we compared in Table 10 are Khoisan (A), Nilo-Saharan (B), Niger-Kordofanian (C), Afro-Asiatic (D), Kartvelian (E), Dravidian (F), Eurasiatic (G), Dene-Caucasian (H), Austric (I), Indo-Pacific (J), Australian (K), and Amerind (L). The distribution of these twelve families is shown in Map 8.

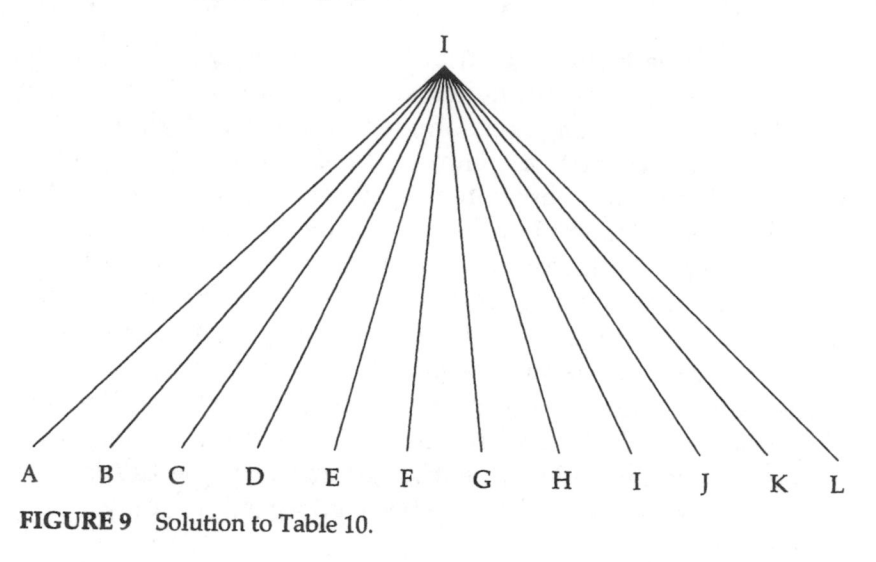

FIGURE 9   Solution to Table 10.

Our critics raise two main criticisms of long-range comparative work, over and over again. One is that the range of semantic variation allowed is so loose that almost any meaning can be connected with any other. The second is that with several hundred languages to choose from in a family like Amerind it is not hard to find one that has a word similar to Latin ak^wa 'water,' for example. In order for you to judge for yourself whether the range of semantic variation is impermissibly large, and whether the roots in Table 10 are truly characteristic of the different families cited in the table, let us consider three of the roots in greater detail, the words for 'water,' 'finger,' and 'two.' All three belong to the basic vocabulary and are thus highly resistant to borrowing. In addition, to the best of my knowledge, no one has ever proposed any sound-symbolic connection between these particular meanings and *any* particular sequence of sounds. So if we find that one meaning is consistently represented by the same phonetic shape in many different language families, the only reasonable explanation is that all these forms have evolved from a common source.

AQ'WA 'water'

Let us begin with the Afro-Asiatic family of North Africa, which seems to have preserved the original form and meaning of this root particularly well. Illich-Svitych reconstructed a root *ʕq(w) 'water,' and more recently the American historian Christopher Ehret has reconstructed two related roots, *akʷ- 'water' and *kʷay 'wet,' to cover the same forms. Before we discuss why these two reconstructions differ, let's take a look at the forms in the modern languages that have retained the root in question. Supporting evidence is found in two of the six branches of Afro-Asiatic, in Omotic (considered by some the most divergent branch of Afro-Asiatic) and in Cushitic. For Omotic we have the following examples: Proto-North Omotic *ak'- 'water, wet,' She k'ai 'wet,' Janjero ak(k)a 'water,' Kaffa ačō 'water,' Mocha āč'o 'water,' Gofa haččā 'water,' Shinasha ač'č'o water,' Badditu watˢ'ē 'water.' Note that in some languages the original consonant k has shifted to č. Modern reflexes of this root in Cushitic languages include Proto-East Cushitic *k'oy- 'wet,' Agaw aqʷ 'water,' Bilin ʕaqʷ 'water,' Xamir aqʷā 'drops of water,' Quara axu 'water,' Avia axū 'water,' Damot agʷo 'water,' Hadiyya woʔo 'water,' Tambaro waha 'water,' Sidamo waho 'water,' and Iraqw ūha 'drink.'

The sound q that appears in some of these forms (and which Illich-Svitych thought was original) is similar to k, except that it is pronounced farther back in the mouth. Since both k and q are found in modern languages—and since either can change into the other—it is not immediately clear which should be taken as original, and thus Illich-Svitych and Ehret differ. Similarly, and for much the same reason, they differ on whether the original consonant, whether k or q, was glottalized, that is, pronounced with a simultaneous constriction of the glottis, which is what the apostrophe in sounds like k' and q' represents. If we are limited to the Afro-Asiatic data there is a certain indeterminacy in the precise nature of the reconstruction (though not on the cognacy of the forms, which seems not in doubt). Consideration of other families where this root is found suggests, as we shall see below, that the original consonant was in fact qʷ, since traces of this consonant are found in different

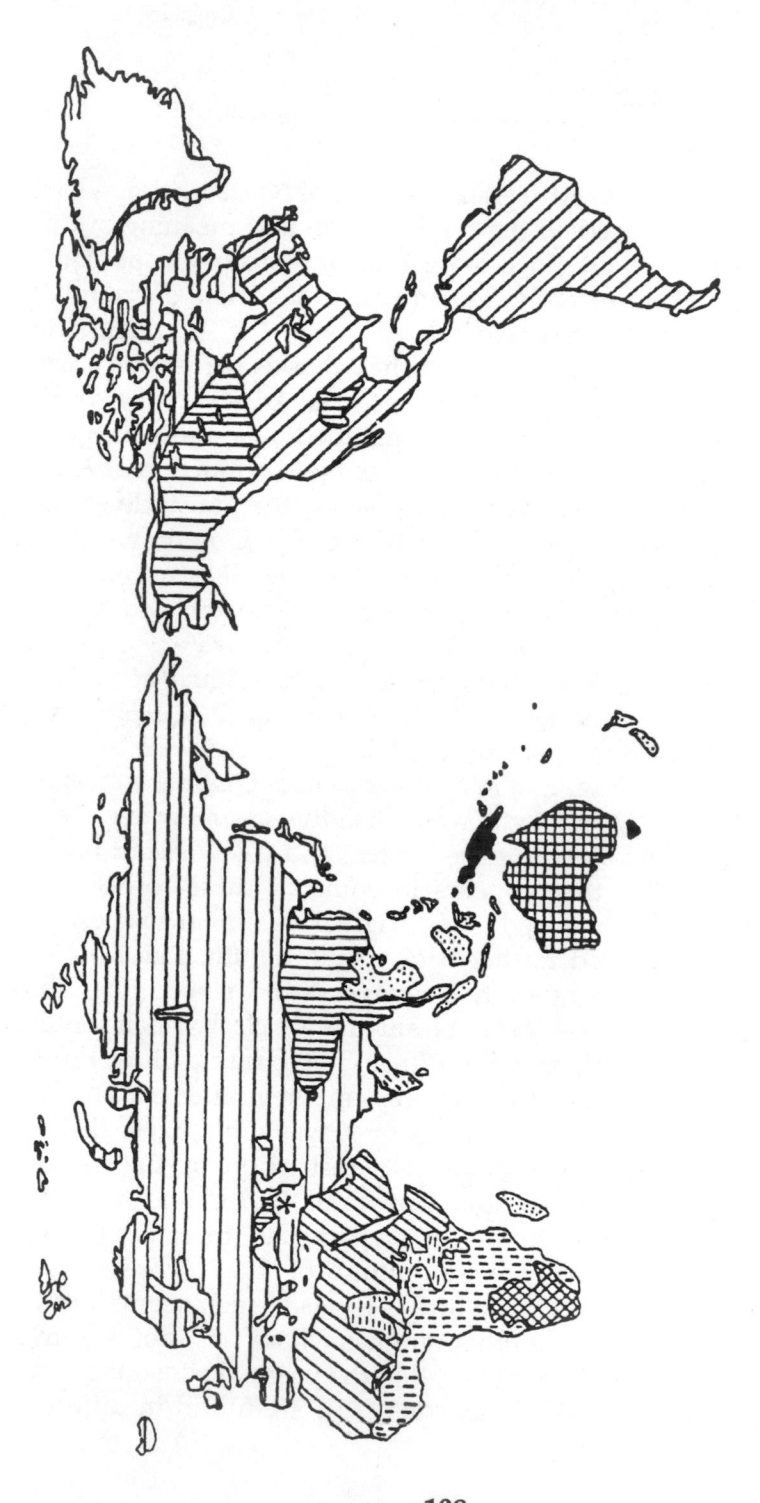

108

MAP 8   Language Families of the World.

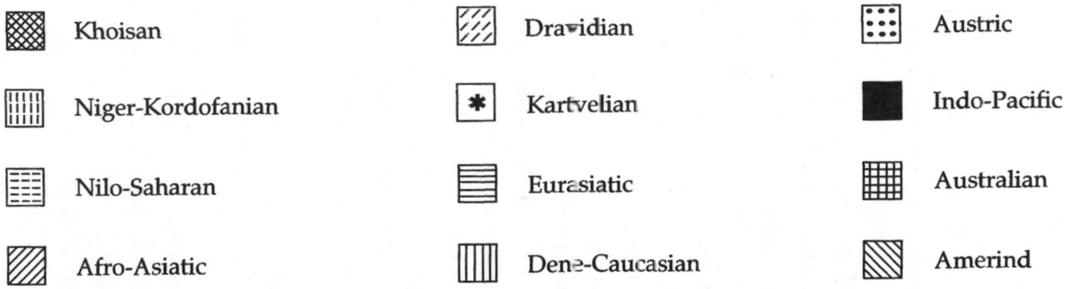

▨ Khoisan   ▧ Dravidian   ⸬ Austric

▥ Niger-Kordofanian   ✳ Kartvelian   ▪ Indo-Pacific

▦ Nilo-Saharan   ▥ Eurasiatic   ▦ Australian

▨ Afro-Asiatic   ▤ Dene-Caucasian   ▨ Amerind

families and it is much more probable (for reasons we can't go into here) that $q^{\prime w}$ was simplified to k^w in most of the families than that original k^w developed into $q^{\prime w}$ independently in different families.

If the original Afro-Asiatic form was indeed $aq^{\prime w}a$, it contained a complex consonant, a labialized glottalized uvular stop $q^{\prime w}$, which may be described as a back k pronounced with simultaneous lip-rounding (this is what the ^{w} signifies) and a simultaneous glottal constriction. You shouldn't be surprised that such complex sounds tend to simplify themselves through normal phonetic processes. For example, $aq^{\prime w}a$ might become aq^wa through the loss of glottalization, or $aq'a$ through the loss of labialization, or aqa through the loss of both. Independent of these simple changes, the uvular consonant q may shift to the simpler velar consonant k, producing forms such as $ak^{\prime w}a$, $ak'a$, ak^wa, or aka. In addition, both labialization and glottalization may break away from the consonant and shift to the beginning of the word, producing forms such as $waq'a$, $wak'a$, $waqa$, $waka$, with a shift of the labial ^{w}, or forms such as $\textipa{P}aq'a$, $\textipa{P}ak^wa$, $\textipa{P}aqa$, or $\textipa{P}aka$, with a shift of the glottalization. A final simple change might weaken the consonant to a fricative (a consonant produced with obstruction but not complete closure of the airstream). Such a change would turn q into χ, and k into x, producing forms like $a\chi^wa$, $a\chi a$, ax^wa, axa, or the like. Thus, if we begin with $aq^{\prime w}a$ there are a number of common phonetic processes that would be expected to produce the variety of phonetic shapes just enumerated. And, as we shall see, it is precisely these kinds of forms that appear around the world, in family after family, from Africa to the Americas, illustrating the evolutionary explanation of descent with modification. Let us turn now to these other families.

In the Khoisan family of southern Africa, similar words are found in all three Khoisan branches. In Northern Khoisan we find !O !Kung *kāū* 'rain' and !Kung *k''ā* 'drink.' In the Central Khoisan branch there is Naron *k''ā* 'drink.' Examples from the Southern branch include |Kam-ka !Ke *k''wā* 'drink,' *kău* 'rain,' ‖Ng !Ke *k''ā* 'drink,' *kāū* 'to rain,' Batwa *k''ā* 'drink,' |Auni *k''āa* 'drink,' Masarwa *k''ā* 'drink,' |Nu ‖En *k''ā* 'drink.'

There are also apparent cognates in the Nilo-Saharan family, though the word I included in Table 10 represents a different root. Nevertheless, the following Nilo-Saharan forms would seem to be related: Fur *kɔi* 'rain,' Nyimang *kwe* 'water,' So *kwɛʔ* 'water,' Ik *čuɛ* 'water,' Mangbetu *éguo* 'water,' Berta *kɔi* 'rain, cloud,' Kwama *uuku* 'water,' Anej *agu-d* 'cloud.'

When we look northward from Afro-Asiatic we immediately encounter the Indo-European family, whose word for 'water' has been reconstructed as $*ak^w\bar{a}$. It is this form that is given under Eurasiatic in Table 10. The resemblance to the Afro-Asiatic forms is more than passing, and was in fact noticed in the early twentieth century by Trombetti. There has, in fact, been some disagreement over the precise reconstruction of this root in Indo-European, and other scholars have posited $*eg^w$- and $*ek^w$-; the latter form is strikingly similar to the Afro-Asiatic form postulated by Ehret. The Indo-European evidence that supports these reconstructions comes from four branches of the family. In the most divergent branch, Anatolian, we find Hittite *eku-* 'water,' Luwian *aku-* 'water,' and Palaic *aḫu-* 'drink.' In the Italic branch we have Latin ak^wa 'water,' whence its Romance derivatives, Italian *akkwa*, Provençal *aiga*, French *o* (orthographically, *eau*), Catalan *aigwa*, Spanish *agwa*, Portuguese *agwa*, Rumanian *apǝ*, and Sardinian *abba*. In the Germanic branch we find Gothic *ahwa* 'river' attested in the earliest Germanic inscriptions, but the root has been lost in most modern Germanic languages. The final branch of Indo-European in which this root is attested is Tocharian, formerly spoken in western China, but for some centuries extinct. Here we find Tocharian A (there were two different dialects attested, A and B) *yok-* 'drink.'

This root appears elsewhere within Eurasiatic, as well. It seems likely that Proto-Uralic **yoka* 'river,' Ainu *wakka* 'water' and *ku* 'drink,' and Japanese *aka* 'bilge water,' all belong with the root here being considered.

A similar root is found in Dene-Caucasian. For the Lezghian branch of the Caucasian family, Starostin has reconstructed Proto-Lezghian $*ʔoχ^wa$ 'drink,' and he considers this form cognate with forms in other branches of the family where the meaning has shifted to 'suck(le),' for example Proto-Nax **-aq-*

'suck(le),' Chechen -*aq*- 'suck,' Proto-Dargi *-*uq*- 'suck(le).' To account for all of these forms Starostin reconstructs a root *$\underline{V}qV$ 'suck' for the Caucasian family, where *V* represents a vowel whose precise quality cannot be determined. Starostin has reconstructed another Caucasian root that he himself notes tends toward confusion with the one just discussed. For Proto-Lezghian he reconstructs *$7o\bar{q}^wa$ 'rain,' while for the Caucasian family as a whole he reconstructs *-$\breve{u}GwV$ 'rain.' It should be noted that both of these roots suggest that the consonant was originally uvular *q* rather than velar *k*.

Elsewhere in Dene-Caucasian, this root may appear as the first part of Burushaski *hʌɣ-um* 'wet' and has been equated by Starostin with Proto-Sino-Tibetan *Ku 'fluid, spill,' as seen in such languages as Newari *kʰwo* 'river,' Khaling *ku* 'water,' and Kachin *kʰu* 'water.'

Only several dozen words have been posited for the Australian family as a whole, but one of these few is Proto-Australian *$gugu$ 'water,' which could very well be a reduplicated form of the root we are investigating. Furthermore, since Proto-Australian did not distinguish *g* from *k*, one could just as well represent the Proto-Australian word as *$kuku$. There has been little serious comparative work on the languages of New Guinea except for an article by Greenberg in which he offered evidence for the Indo-Pacific family. Even basic data on the hundreds of very diverse languages are still scant. There are, nonetheless, several forms that appear similar to the root under discussion (for example Awyu *okho* 'water, river,' Syiagha *okho* 'water,' Yareba *ogo* 'water,' Yonggom *oq* 'water,' Ninggirum *ok* 'water'), and perhaps further research will show this root to be widespread within Indo-Pacific.

Finally, we come to the Americas. The form listed in Table 10 for Amerind, *akwā*, is the Proto-Central Algonquian stem meaning 'from water.' We saw in Chapter 4 that most experts in American Indian languages believe there is *no* evidence connecting Algonquian with other Amerind families of North and South America (except, of course, for the now accepted affinity with the Wiyot and Yurok languages), and therefore this specifically Proto-Central Algonquian form of the word for 'water' should not be found in other, independent, unrelated families.

Let's take a look, running through each of the 11 branches of Amerind that we met in Table 9.

In Almosan-Keresiouan, besides Proto-Central Algonquian *akwā* 'from water,' one finds in Yurok a suffix -*k^w* that is attached to verbs referring to movement in or on water, and in Kutenai a similar suffix, -*q^w*, means 'in water.' Other examples from this branch of Amerind include Quileute *kwāya'* 'water,' Kwakwala *yax* 'thin liquid,' Bella Bella *yug^wa* 'rain,' Snohomish *q^wa?* 'water,' Squamish *q^wu* 'water,' *q^wət^s'* 'wet,' Nisqualli *ko* 'water,' *okokwa* 'drink,' Lkungen *kwa* 'water,' *q^waq^wa?* 'drink,' Twana *qɔ?* 'water,' *yəq^w* 'wash,' Shuswap *kwō* 'water,' Caddo *koko* 'water,' *yoyakka* 'drink,' and Wichita *kik'a* 'drink.'

In the Penutian branch we find Nass *ak̓-s* 'water,' Tsimshian *aks* 'drink,' *yaks* 'wash,' Takelma *ug^w* 'drink,' Siuslaw *in-q'aa* 'river,' Nez Perce *k'u* 'drink,' Molale *?uquns* 'water,' Klamath *joq'* 'wash,' North Sahaptin -*tkwa* 'go in water,' Wintun *wak'ai* 'creek,' *yuqa?* 'wash,' Rumsien *uk* 'drink,' Yokuts *?ukun* 'drink,' Lake Miwok *kiik* 'water,' Saclan *kiko* 'water,' Southern Sierra Miwok *kiky* 'water,' Zuni *k'a* 'water,' *k'i* 'become wet,' Yuki *uk'* 'water,' Chitimacha *?ak-* 'water,' Atakapa *ak* 'water,' Chickasaw *oka?* 'water,' Hitchiti *uki* 'water,' Tetontepec *uu?k* 'drink,' Zoque *?uhk* 'drink,' Yucatec *uk'* 'be thirsty,' *yok-ha* 'river,' and Kekchi *u?ka* 'drink.'

Examples from the Hokan branch are no less numerous: Chimariko *aqa* 'water,' Kashaya *?ahq̓'a* 'water,' *q'o* 'drink,' North Pomo *k̓'a* 'water,' *k'o* 'drink,' Southeast Pomo *χa* 'water,' South Pomo *?ahk̓'a* 'water,' East Pomo *xak^h* 'wet,' Shasta *?at^s^t^s'a* 'water,' Washo *āša?* 'water,' Karok *?ās* 'water,' Esselen *asa(-nax)* 'water,' Chumash *aho* 'water,' Seri *?ax* 'water,' *kiihk* 'wet,' Yuma *axa?* 'water,' Mohave *aha* 'water,' Yavapai *?aha?* 'water,' Diegueño *?axā* 'water,' Quinigua *kwa* 'water,' Tonkawa *?āx* 'water,' Comecrudo *aχ* 'water,' and Tequistlatec *l-axa?* 'water.'

In the Central Amerind branch we have forms such as Proto-Chinantec **g^wa* 'stream, river,' **gū?* 'I drink,' Proto-Central Otomi **?wāi* 'rain' (v.), Otomi *nk'a* 'wet,' Cuicatec *ku?u* 'drink,' and Tewa *p'okwiŋ* 'lake,' *kwaŋ* 'rain.'

All of the Amerind forms cited thus far come from North America. Let's now turn our attention to South America. In the Chibchan-Paezan branch we find Shiriana *koa* 'drink,' Chimila *uk-* 'drink,' Binticua *agan* 'drink,' and Allentiac *aka* 'water.' Examples from the Andean branch of Amerind include Iquito *aqua* 'water,' Quechua *yaku* 'water,' *hoq'o* 'get wet,' Aymara *oqo* 'swallow,' Mapudungu *ko* 'water,' Genneken *iagup* 'water,' and Yamana *aka* 'lake.' From the Macro-Tucanoan branch one may cite Cubeo *oko* 'water,' Bahukiwa *oko* 'water,' *uku-mi* 'he is drinking,' *okobo* 'rain,' Tucano *axko* 'water,' Erulia *oxko* 'water, rain,' Barasano *oko* 'water,' Wanana *ko* 'water,' Yahuna *okoa* 'rain,' and Auake *okõa* 'water, river.'

The root is also well attested in the Equatorial branch: Esmeralda *kebi-axa* 'let's drink,' Ayore *oxiʔ* 'drink,' Guaranoco *axi* 'drink,' Proto-Tupi *ɨʔu* 'drink,' *akɨm* 'wet,' Kabishana *äku* 'water,' Amniape *äkü* 'water,' Wayoro *ügü* 'water,' Mekens *ɨkɨ* 'water,' Guaraní *akɨ̄* 'wet,' *ɨʔu* 'drink,' Kamayura *ʔakɨm* 'wet,' *ɨʔu* 'drink,' Quitemo *ako* 'water,' Uaraicu *uaka* 'wash,' Terena *oko* 'rain,' Chipaya *axʷ* 'wash,' Guana *uko* 'rain,' Apurina *ĩāka* 'wet,' and Amarakaeri *ĩyãko* 'lake.'

Macro-Carib examples include Witoto *hoko* 'wash,' Yagua *xa* 'water,' Taulipang *aiʔku* 'wet,' Macusi *u-wuku* 'my drink,' *aiku* 'wet,' and Waiwai *woku* 'drink.' In Macro-Panoan we have Lule *uk* 'drink,' Guachi *euak* 'water,' Caduveo *yakip(a)* 'drink,' Suhin *i-yoke* 'drink,' Mayoruna *uaka* 'water,' *oakanu* 'drink,' Culino *yaku* 'water,' *waka* 'river,' Amahuaca *wakum* 'water,' *aiyaki* 'drink,' Nocoman *wakoja* 'river,' Huarayo *hakua* 'wash,' and Cavineña *igi* 'drink.'

Finally, in the Macro-Ge branch, we find such examples as Bororo *ku* 'drink' (n.), Koraveka *ako* 'drink!' (v.), Fulnio *waka* 'lake,' Caraja *axu* 'lake,' Kamakan *kwa* 'drink,' Palmas *goi* 'water,' Apucarana *(n)goyo* 'water,' Delbergia *ŋgɔyo* 'water,' Proto-Ge *ŋo* 'water,' *hiko* 'wet,' *-kõ* 'drink,' Apinage *inko* 'water, river,' Crengez *ko* 'water,' Cayapo *ŋgo* 'water,' *ikon* 'drink,' Chavante *kõ* 'water,' Cherente *kö* 'water,' Chicriaba *ku* 'water,' Aponegicran *waiko* 'drink,' and Suya *ikone* 'drink.'

The Amerind forms just cited are only a selection of what seem to me the most obvious cognates. Yet even this brief survey suggests strongly that the Proto-Central Algonquian form *akwā* 'from water' is cognate with numerous other forms found in every branch of the Amerind family. The evidence is overwhelming that the Proto-Amerind language possessed a word for 'water' that was very similar to the forms we found in the Old World. Furthermore, the Amerind evidence indicates that the original consonant was $q^{\prime w}$, since the uvular consonant (q), glottalization ($'$), and labialization (^{w}) are all attested in various languages. An original form very similar to that reconstructed for Proto-Afro-Asiatic, *$aq^{\prime w}a$, could, through the simple phonetic processes mentioned above, have given rise to the dozens of slightly different shapes we have just examined. I believe it did.

TIK 'finger, one'

Another striking resemblance among the world's language families is a word whose original meaning was probably 'finger' (though it has evolved to 'one' and 'hand' [= 'fingers'] in many languages), and whose original form was something like *tik*. I first became aware of the widespread nature of this root at a public lecture that Greenberg gave at Stanford in 1977, in which he mentioned three roots that were widely distributed around the world: *tik* 'finger,' *pal* 'two' (which we will look at in the following section), and *par* 'to fly.' As you no doubt noticed in your examination of Table 10, no less than eight of the twelve families show traces of *tik* 'finger, one,' namely, Nilo-Saharan (B), Niger-Kordofanian (C), Afro-Asiatic (D), Eurasiatic (G), Dene-Caucasian (H), Austric (I), Indo-Pacific (J), and Amerind (L). Let us take a look at the precise evidence that each of these families offers for the *tik* root.

One of the roots that Greenberg originally proposed for the Nilo-Saharan family (which he discovered) was a word for 'one' of the general shape *t–k*, exemplified in such forms as Fur *tɔk* 'one,' Maba *tək* 'one,' Nera *dɔkk-u* 'one,' Dinka *tok* 'one,' Berta *dúkóni* 'one,' Mangbetu *t'ɛ* 'one,' Kwama *seek-o* 'one,' Bari *to* 'one,' Jur *tok* 'one,' Twampa *dèʔ* 'one,' and Komo *dé* 'one.' In 1972 the American linguist Edgar Gregersen presented substantial evidence connecting two of Greenberg's four African families, Nilo-Saharan and Niger-Kordofanian. One of the pieces of evidence he offered was Niger-Kordofanian forms that appeared cognate with the Nilo-Saharan forms just cited. Examples from the Niger-Kordofanian family include Fulup *sik ~ sex* 'finger' (the symbol ~ separates variant pronunciations of certain words; English 'harass,' for example, is pronounced by different people with the stress on the first or second syllable), Nalu *te* 'finger,' Gur *dike* 'one,' Gwa *dogbo* 'one,' Fon *dòkpá* 'one,' Ewe *dèká* 'one,' Tonga *tiho* 'finger,' Chopi *tˢiho* 'finger,' Ki-Bira *zika* 'finger,' and Ba-Kiokwa *zigu* 'finger.'

What appears to be the same root has been reconstructed by Russian scholars for the Afro-Asiatic family of North Africa, Proto-Afro-Asiatic **tak* 'one.' This reconstructed form accounts for such modern reflexes as Oromo *toko* 'one,' Peripheral West Gurage *təgu (əmmat)* 'only one,' Yaaku *tegei* 'hand,' Saho *ti* 'one,' Bilin *tu* 'one,' Tsamai *dōkko* 'one,' Nefusa *tukod̦* 'finger,' Hausa *(d̦aya) tak* 'only one,' Gisiga *tēkoy* 'one,' Gidder *te-teka* 'one,' and Logone *tku* 'first.'

What can only be interpreted as the same root is abundantly attested in the Eurasiatic family, from Europe through Asia into North America. Indo-Europeanists have reconstructed a root **deik-* 'to point,' but it would appear that this verbal use is a secondary development within Indo-European since Indo-European also preserves the nominal use we have seen in the other families in forms such as Latin *dig-itus* 'finger' and *in-dek-s* 'forefinger.' It is simpler to assume that the verbal use is an innovation of Indo-European, since in the other families—and even partially in Indo-European—the word is normally a noun. The development of a verbal action from the name of the body part involved is a quite common semantic development, which should cause no concern. Even in English one may say that he "fingered" the guilty party. It is considered likely that English 'toe' developed from this same root via earlier stages of Proto-Germanic **taihwō* 'toe' and Old English *tahe* 'toe.' It also seems likely that another Proto-Indo-European root, **dekm̩* '10,' is related to the other forms; it is common, for obvious reasons, for the numbers 1, 5, and 10 to be derived from words for 'finger(s).'

Traces of this root are also found in most of the other branches of Eurasiatic. In Uralic it appears to have been preserved in only two languages, Votyak *odik* 'one' and Zyrian *ōtik* 'one.' In the Turkic branch of Altaic we find such forms as Chuvash *tek* 'only, just,' Uighur *tek* 'only, merely,' Chagatai *tek* 'only, single,' and Turkish *tek* 'only,' *teken* 'one by one.' In Korean there is *(t)tayki* 'one, thing' and *teki* 'one, guy, thing,' while Old Korean showed *tēk* '10.' Ainu exhibits two reflexes of the *tik* root, *tek* 'hand' and *atiki* 'five'; Japanese *te* 'hand' has lost the final consonant, but is otherwise virtually identical with the corresponding Ainu word. The Kamchadal language of the Chukchi-Kamchatkan family has a word *itygin* 'paw, foot' that is probably cognate with the other forms.

The *tik* root is clearly attested in both branches of the Eskimo-Aleut family and Proto-Eskimo-Aleut **q(ɨ)tɨk* 'middle finger' has been reconstructed by a Russian scholar, Oleg Mudrak. In the Central Yupik dialect of Eskimo we find Kuskokwim *tik(-iq)* 'index finger,' and the Inupiaq language of Greenland has *tik(-iq)* 'index finger' and *tikkuagpaa* 'he points to it.' In the Attu dialect of Aleut we find *tik(-laq)* 'middle finger,' *atgu* 'finger,' *taɣataq* 'one,' and the Atka dialect has *atakan* 'one.'

We come next to the Dene-Caucasian family, in which the root is attested in at least three of the branches. Proto-Sino-Tibetan appears to have had two competing forms, **tyak* and **tyik* 'one.' The first variant gave rise to Chinese **t'įek* 'one, single' in one branch of Sino-Tibetan. The second variant is represented in the other branch of the family, where Proto-Tibeto-Burman **tyik* 'one' accounts for forms such as Rai *tik(-pu)* 'one,' Nung *thi* 'one,' and Tibetan *(g-)tśig* 'one.' In the Yeniseian family we have Ket *tәk* 'finger,' Pumpokol *tok* 'finger,' and Kott *tog-an* 'finger.' In Na-Dene the initial *t-* has apparently developed into *t'-* in forms such as Haida *(s-)t'a* 'with the fingers,' Tlingit *t'eeq* 'finger,' *t'ek* 'one,' Eyak *tikhi* 'one,' Sarsi *tlik'-(aza)* 'one,' Kutchin *(ī-)łag* 'one,' Hupa *ła?* 'one,' and Navajo *łá?* 'one.'

At least three branches of Austric—Austroasiatic, Daic, and Miao-Yao—have preserved traces of this root. In the first family we have Proto-Austroasiatic **(k-)tig* 'hand, arm,' from which developed such modern forms as Kharia *ti?* 'hand,' Riang *ti?* 'hand,' Wa *tai?* 'hand,' Khmer *ṭai* 'hand,' Vietnamese *tay* 'hand,' and Proto-Aslian **tik ~ *tiŋ* 'hand.' In Daic we find

Li **dliaŋ* 'finger,' Northern Li *tleaŋ ~ theŋ* 'finger,' and Loi *thɛŋ ~ ćiaŋ* 'finger.' The Proto-Aslian form **tiŋ* 'hand' and Daic forms such as Northern Li *theŋ* 'finger' suggest that perhaps Proto-Austronesian **(tu-)diŋ* 'point with the finger' is also cognate with the Austroasiatic and Daic forms. In any event, Proto-Miao-Yao **ntoʔ* 'finger' would clearly seem to be cognate (and is in fact very similar to the Yeniseian forms cited above). In the two branches of this family we have Proto-Yao **doʔ* 'finger' and Proto-Miao **ntai* 'point with the finger.'

The Indo-Pacific family, centered on New Guinea, is one of the least studied families in the world, yet it is one with great diversity. From the scant information we have on this family one may point to the following forms as perhaps being related to the root under discusssion: Southern Tasmanian *motook* 'forefinger,' Southeastern Tasmanian *togue* 'hand,' Proto-Karonan **dik* 'one,' Boven Mbian *tek* 'fingernail,' and Digul *tuk* 'fingernail.'

Finally, the *tik* root is well attested in Amerind languages of both North and South America, though frequently the initial *t-* has evolved to *tˢ-* (or *č-*) under the influence of the following *-i-*, just as we saw in Chapter 4 with Amerind *t'ina* 'son, brother.' From the North American branches one might cite such examples as Nootka *takʷa* 'only,' Mohawk *tsiʔer* 'finger,' Southern Sierra Miwok *tˢik'aʔ* 'index finger,' Wintun *tiq-eles* 'ten,' Nisenan *tok-* 'hand,' Mixe *toʔk ~ tuk'* 'one,' Sayula *tuʔk* 'one,' Tzeltal *tukal* 'alone,' Quiche *tik'ex* 'carry in the hand,' Proto-Hokan **dik'i* 'finger,' Karok *tīk* 'finger, hand,' Achumawi *(wa-)túči* 'finger,' Washo *tsek* 'finger,' Yana *-tˢ'gi-* 'alone,' East Pomo *bī'ya-tsūkai* 'finger,' Arraarra *teeh'k* 'hand,' Pehtsik *tiki-vash* 'hand,' Akwa'ala *ašit-dek* 'one,'; Nahua *tˢïïkiaʔa* 'one,' Pima Bajo *čīč* 'one,' Tarahumara *sika* 'hand,' Mazatec *čikaʔã* 'alone,' and Mangue *tike* 'one.'

Examples from the South American branches of Amerind are no less abundant: Chibcha *ytiquyn* 'finger,' *ačik* 'by ones,' Borunca *e'tsik* 'one,' Guatuso *dooki* 'one,' Shiriana *īthak* 'hand,' Ulua *tinka-mak* 'finger,' Paez *tɛɛč* 'one,' Cahuapana *itekla* 'finger, hand,' Jebero *itökla* 'finger, hand,' Qawashqar *tākso* 'one,' Siona *tekua* 'one,' Siona *teg-li* 'five,' Canichana *eu-tixle* 'finger,' Yupua *di(x)ka* 'arm,' Uasöna *dikaga* 'arm,' Upano *tˢikitik* 'one,' Aguaruna *tikiǰ* 'one,' Murato *ťiči* 'hand,' Uru *ťĭ* 'one,' Chipaya *zek* 'one,' Itene *taka* 'one,' Guamo *dixi* 'finger,' Katembri *tika* 'toe,' Yuracare *teče* 'thumb,' Kukura *tikua* 'finger,' Accawai *tigina* 'one,' Yagua *teki* 'one,' Imihita *meux-tsekoa* 'finger,' Trio *tinki* 'one,' Ocaina *dikabu* 'arm,' Mataco *otejji* 'one,' Tagnani *etegueno* 'finger,' Sensi *(nawiš)-tikoe* 'one (finger)' Cavineña *eme-toko* 'hand,' Botocudo *(po-)čik* 'one (finger),' *ǰik* 'alone,' and Proto-Ge **(pɨ-)ťi* 'one.'

PAL 'two'

The final word from Table 10 that we will consider in depth is a word for 'two' with the general shape *pal*. In Dolgopolsky's attempt to discover which meanings are most stable over time in human language, the number 'two' ranked second in stability. (His complete list, in order of stability, was I/me, two, you (singular), who/what, tongue, name, eye, heart, tooth, no/not, fingernail/toenail, louse/nit, tear(drop), water, dead, hand, night, blood, horn (of an animal), full, sun, ear, and salt.)

In his pioneering classification of African languages, Greenberg noted a root of the general shape *pal* 'two' in both Nilo-Saharan and Niger-Kordofanian, and Gregersen later suggested this parallel as one of the traits connecting these two families in a larger Congo-Saharan family. For Nilo-Saharan we find examples such as Nubian *bar(-si)* 'twin,' Merarit *wírre* 'two,' Kunama *báarè* 'two,' *ibā* 'twin,' Maba *mbar* 'two,' Mesalit *mbarrá* 'two,' Tama *warri* 'two,' Baka *brūe* 'two,' and Ilit *ball-ame* 'two.' In most of these forms *-l-* has changed to *-r-*, a very common sound change. Niger-Kordofanian examples include Temne *(kə)bari* 'twin,' Nalu *bele* 'two,' Mende *fele* 'two,' Mano *pere* 'two,' Sya *pla* 'two,' Nimbari *bala* 'two,' Daka *bara* 'two,' Messo *bala* 'two,' Proto-Bantu **bàdí ~ *bìdí* 'two,' **bádì* 'side.'

In North Africa, traces of this root have been preserved in three branches of the Afro-Asiatic family. In the Cushitic branch we have Saho *baray* 'second' and Oromo *bíra* 'second.' In the Omotic branch the meaning has shifted from 'second' to 'other': Kafa *barā* 'other,' Mocha *baro* 'other,' and Dime *bal* 'other.' Examples from the Chadic branch include Proto-Central Chadic *(kV-)bwVr 'two,' Ngamo *bolo* 'two,' Karekare *belu* 'two,' Maxa *bolo* 'two,' Kirfi *mbalu* 'two,' Bele *bolo* 'two,' Galambu *mbaal* 'two,' and Gera *mbalu* 'two.'

In the Eurasiatic family only Indo-European and Uralic have preserved this root, and in both families the meaning has shifted from 'two' to 'half' or 'side.' Proto-Indo-European *pol 'half, side' is seen in Sanskrit *(ka-)palam* 'half,' Albanian *palë* 'side, part, pair,' Old Church Slavic *polŭ* 'side, half,' and Russian *pol-* 'half.' Proto-Uralic *pälä 'half, side' has given rise to a host of modern reflexes, including Yurak Samoyed *peele* 'half,' Selkup *pεle* 'half,' Kamassian *pjeel* 'half, side,' Hungarian *fele* 'half, (one) side (of two),' Vogul *pääl* 'side, half,' Saami *bæle* 'side, half, one of a pair,' Mordvin *pel'* 'side,' *pele* 'half,' and Votyak *pal* 'side, half.'

The Dravidian family also appears to have preserved this root, but the meaning has apparently evolved from 'half, side' to 'part, share,' a not implausible shift. Proto-Dravidian *pāl 'part, portion' is reflected in such modern forms as Tamil *pāl* 'part, portion, share,' Malayalam *pāl* 'part,' Kannada *pāl* 'division, part,' Tulu *pālu̥* 'share, portion, part,' Telugu *pālu* 'share, portion,' and Parji *pēla* 'portion.'

Bengtson and I found no trace of this root in the Dene-Caucasian family, but Austric examples occur in at least Austroasiatic and Austronesian. Proto-Austroasiatic *ʔ(m)bar 'two' has been reconstructed to account for such modern forms as Santali *bar* 'two,' Kharia *(u-)bar* 'two,' *(am-)bar* 'you two,' Juang *ambar* 'two,' Remo *ʔmbār* 'two,' Khmu' *bār* 'two,' Bahnar *ʔbar* 'two,' Jeh *bal* 'two,' Old Mon *ʔbar* 'two,' Old Khmer *ber* two,' Sakai *hmbar* 'two,' Palaung *ār* 'two,' *par* 'you two,' Proto-Aslian *ʔmbār* 'two,' and Temiar *bər(-nar)* 'two.' In the Austronesian family the root under discussion appears in the Proto-Austronesian word for 'twin,' *kə(m)bal ~ *kə(m)bar 'twin,' a modern reflex of which is Javanese *kĕmbar* 'twin,' *kĕbar* 'doubled.'

As noted previously, our knowledge of the Indo-Pacific family is scant. Nevertheless, there are forms in at least three of its branches that appear cognate with the forms cited above. In the Andaman Islands we find Biada *(ik-)pāūr(-da)* 'two,' Kede *(ír-)pōl* 'two,' Chariar *(nér-)pól* 'two,' and Juwoi *(ró-)pāūr* 'two'; in Tasmania we have Southeastern Tasmanian *boula ~ bura* 'two' and Southern Tasmanian *pooalih* 'two'; and on the island of New Guinea there are examples such as Ndani *bere* 'two' and Sauweri *pere* 'two.'

The root in question is abundantly attested in the Australian family, and in fact the Proto-Australian word for 'two' has been reconstructed as **pula* or **bula* 'two.' In Australian languages *p* and *b* are not perceived as different sounds: in some languages, particularly in the west, *p* predominates; in other languages, *b* predominates. Thus, whether one posits **p* or **b* for Proto-Australian is a matter more of convention than of substance, but there have been heated debates over which symbol is more appropriate. The larger context that we are considering here, however, indicates to me that *p* is the original sound, which has evolved into *b* in some languages. Such a scenario is also supported by what we know about language change. At the beginning of a word it is common for the sounds *p, t, k* to change into *b, d, g,* respectively. On the other hand, a change of initial *b, d, g* into *p, t, k,* respectively, is rare. Not only is this root the normal word for 'two' in Proto-Australian, but it has also evolved into a dual affix for pronouns in the Pama-Nyungan branch, for which two dual pronouns have been reconstructed, **(nyuN)palV* '(you) two,' **pula* 'they two.'

The final family that exhibits this root is Amerind. North American examples seem to be restricted to Penutian, where we find forms such as Wintun *palo(-l)* 'two,' Wappo *p'ala* 'twins,' Atakapa *happalst* 'two,' and Huave *apool* 'snap in two.' Examples from the South American branches of Amerind are more plentiful: Chiripo *bor* 'two,' Xinca *bial ~ piar* 'two,' Bribri *bul ~ bur* 'two,' Cacaopera *burru* 'two,' Sanuma *-palo* (a repetitive suffix added to a verb to indicate that something is done over and over), *polakapi* 'two,' Cayapo *pal'u* 'two,' Colorado *palu* 'two,' Quechua *pula* 'both,' Aymara *paya* 'two,' Yamana *sa-pai* 'you-two' (*sa-* = 'thou'), Yahgan *(i-)pai* '(we) two,' Tuyuka *pealo* 'two,' Wanana *pilia* 'two,' Desana *peru* 'two,' Yupua *apara* 'two,' Proto-Nambikwara **p'āl(-in)* 'two,' Catuquina *upaua* 'two,' Hubde *mbeere* 'two,' Ticuna *peia* 'two,' and Caraho *pa-* 'we-two-inclusive' (that is, 'you and me').

I believe that the three roots that we have just examined in some detail indicate three things. First, the semantic connections among the forms are not farfetched; indeed, they are as tightly controlled (or more so) than the semantic connections *within* established families. Second, we are not dealing with a few isolated forms scattered across several continents, but with roots that are abundantly attested in family after family and which have often been posited by scholars who are totally opposed to long-range comparison. Third, all of the world's extant languages, and all historically attested languages, have evolved from a single earlier language.

MAMA, PAPA, and KAKA

I mentioned in the Prologue that most linguists consider kin terms like 'mama' and 'papa' to be sound symbolic. Such terms have long been known to occur in languages from every corner of the earth. The presence of these particular kin terms in numerous language families that were supposed to be "independent" posed a problem: how could all of these unrelated families share the same words for 'mother' and 'father' without the terms being due to descent from a common source? In the 1950's the great Russian linguist Roman Jakobson (who spent the later decades of his life in the United States) proposed a solution to this problem. He suggested that words such as 'mama' and 'papa' occurred so widely around the world because the consonants *m* and *p*, and the vowel *a*, are among the first sounds learned by young children. In general, children learn the sounds of a language—any language—in roughly the same order, with easy sounds like *p*, *m* and *a* appearing first, and difficult sounds like *r* and *θ* appearing last (all of us have probably known older children who still substitute *w* for *r*). Of course different languages have different sounds, and the developmental trends are hardly ironclad, allowing for a good deal of individual variation. Nonetheless, no one doubts that the acquisition of a child's sound system tends to proceed along these lines. Since forms like *mama* and *papa* would be among the first to appear in all languages, it is only natural, Jakobson argued, that these most basic forms would become attached to the most basic semantic concepts, 'mother' and 'father.' Their broad distribution is thus a special case of convergence, and such terms do not endanger the independence of the innumerable families that have them.

But is Jakobson's explanation for the broad distribution of 'mama' and 'papa' really correct? Part of its appeal, besides its admitted ingenuity, was that it resolved the problem of common words shared by independent families. But we have seen in this chapter—and in this book—that these hundreds of independent families are not really independent at all. There are many grammatical and lexical elements that go far beyond the narrow confines of such obvious groupings as Indo-European, Bantu, or Algonquian. But if this is true, how can we be sure that 'mama' and 'papa' themselves are not due more to simple common origin than to Jakobson's ingenious explanation? What indicates to me that Jakobson's solution is basically deficient is the existence of other kin terms, besides 'mama' and 'papa,' that are almost as widespread as these two, but for which Jakobson's child-language explanation seems inapplicable. Specifically, there is a very widely attested form *kaka* that is associated with the meaning 'older brother' (or closely related concepts like 'uncle, brother, older sibling') in many supposedly unrelated families. Examples of this root in the Old World would include forms such as Yukaghir *aka* 'older brother,' Proto-Uralic **ekä* 'older male relative, uncle,' Proto-Altaic **āka* 'older brother,' Ryukyuan (a language closely related to Japanese) *aka* 'older brother,' Gilyak *ikin* 'older brother,' Proto-Tibeto-Burman **ik* 'older brother,' Proto-Yao **kɔ* 'older brother,' and Proto-Austronesian **kaka* 'older brother.'

In the Americas the root is abundantly attested in Amerind languages of both North and South America. North American examples include Nisqualli *kukh* 'older brother,' Bodega Miwok *kaaka* 'uncle,' Southern Sierra Miwok *kaka* 'uncle,' Yuki *kík-an* 'maternal uncle,' Zuni *kaka* 'maternal uncle,' Natchez *kāka* 'older brother,' Totonac *kuku* 'uncle,' Achomawi *kex* 'uncle,' East Pomo *kēq* 'uncle,' North Pomo *-ki-* 'older brother,' Kashaya *-ki-* 'older brother,' Salinan *kaai* 'older brother,' Jicaque *kokam* 'uncle,'

Varohio *kukuri* 'paternal uncle,' Tirub *kega* 'uncle,' Matagalpa *kuku-ke* 'uncle,' and Paya *uku* 'uncle.' In South America we find examples such as Yeba *kako* 'uncle,' Masaca *kokomai* 'uncle,' Waraicu *ghuk* 'uncle,' Manao *ghooko* 'maternal uncle,' Sanamaika *koko* 'uncle,' Mashco *kokoa* 'uncle,' Kushichineri *koko* 'uncle,' Cuniba *kuku* 'uncle,' Canamari *ghughu* 'uncle,' Piro *koko* 'uncle,' Apiaca *koko* 'uncle,' Bakairi *kxuɣu* 'uncle,' Pimenteira *kuckú* 'uncle,' Cavineña *ekoko* 'uncle,' Panobo *kuka* 'uncle,' Pacawara *kuko* 'uncle,' Palmas *kĕke-* 'older sibling,' Apucarana *kanki* 'older brother,' and Oti *koaka* 'brother.'

Why are these forms a problem for Jakobson's explanation? Could his analysis of *mama* and *papa* not be extended to cover *kaka* 'older brother'? I think not. First of all, velar consonants like *k* and *g*, unlike *m* and *p*, are not learned particularly early in child language acquisition. Is it then plausible that older brothers should appear in the child's world at just the moment when velar consonants are developing? Of course the older brothers will have been there all along, so why do children around the world wait to acquire their velar consonants before they get around to naming their older siblings? The organization of human societies is not likely such that the arbitrary association of velar consonants and older brothers could come about independently in family after family. These forms must be the result of common origin, not of convergence. But if *kaka* has a genetic explanation, why should we assume that there is no genetic component in the multitude of *mama* and *papa* forms around the world? I believe there is, and that Jakobson's explanation was exaggerated, if not completely mistaken.

6

A Window on the World

What Has Been Resolved

In the preceding chapters I have tried to summarize the line of reasoning that leads to the conclusion that all of the world's languages share a common origin. The essence of the proof is that similarities among languages, and among language families, can only reasonably be explained by assuming that they reflect a prior unity. I have been at some pains, however, to admit that these proposals do not enjoy wide acceptance within the linguistic establishment, where, in fact, they are almost universally condemned as "futile," "subversive," or worse. How then can we reconcile the apparent abundance of evidence for a single origin with the resolute rejection by historical linguists—not simply of global cognates—but of *any* connection between Indo-European and another family?

There is no single answer to this complex question, but it is certainly possible to identify some of the underlying causes, and indeed some of these have been discussed, sporadically, in previous chapters. The eclipse of historical studies by synchronic research in the twentieth century; the consequent identification of historical linguistics with Indo-European linguistics;

the reluctance of Indo-Europeanists to broaden their horizons; a Eurocentric bias inherited from the nineteenth century; a misunderstanding of the role of classification in historical linguistics; the drift toward ever more narrow specialization, in scholarship generally; the consequent failure of textbooks and curricula to deal with the broader issues; the peculiar drift toward comparing only minuscule numbers of languages— all of these factors have conspired to produce the current controversies.

Sanctity at All Costs

When proposals for connecting Indo-European with other families were first seriously advanced in the early twentieth century, by scholars such as Pedersen, they were immediately opposed. But it is difficult to determine to what extent the ensuing opposition was based on a desire to keep Indo-European "independent" at all costs, and to what extent it was based on the Indo-Europeanists' not understanding the true basis of linguistic classification, and thus of linguistic affinity itself. A whole variety of demands had to be met before Indo-European's kinship to another family would be conceded, demands so constraining that they effectively blocked that possibility altogether. But they were demands that had in fact played no role at all in the discovery of Indo-European, or of the many other obvious families that had already been fully accepted by the beginning of the twentieth century. In recent years some experts have claimed that ancient families demand more evidence than do shallow, obvious families—though the rationale behind this claim is far from obvious, and no such distinction had been enforced when Indo-European itself was assembled from Germanic, Romance, Celtic and the others.

Whatever their reasons may have been, the Indo-Europeanists of the early twentieth century were determined that no connection of Indo-European with another family was to be countenanced. They could, after all, have accepted the evidence that Indo-European was one member of a larger, and more ancient, Eurasiatic family, but they chose not to. Instead, they initiated a century-long chronicle of unlikely explanations for linguistic similarities. Some of these have already been discussed. The French Indo-Europeanist Antoine Meillet, for example, claimed that "pronouns look alike everywhere without this fact implying a common origin" in order to explain the presence of the Indo-European pattern *m-/t-* 'I, you' in other Eurasian families, but he failed to explain why this pattern is not found in other parts of the world. A psychologist, Wilhelm Wundt, proposed that the sound *m* is psychologically associated with the meaning 'near,' whereas the sound *t* was psychologically associated with the meaning 'far,' thus furnishing the linguists with a natural explanation for why the first-person pronoun should be based on *m* and the second-person pronoun on *t*. Had Wundt investigated pronoun systems from around the world he would have found that the *m-/t-* pattern is not widespread except in Eurasiatic. Consequently, either the Eurasiatic peoples are "psychologically different" (whatever that might mean) from other human beings, or we need to seek a different explanation for the presence of this particular pattern in Eurasian languages.

The predominance of a *different* pronoun system, *n-/m-* 'I, you,' in the Americas has also been explained by this hypothesis (here, too, disregarding the evidence of the world's languages). It has also been explained by mass borrowing; as "infant sucking sounds"; as an archaic residue of stable sounds; as a consequence of "obscure psychological causes"; as the result of sociolinguistic mixture in Asia before the ancestors entered the Americas; and by a host of other, equally exotic or implausible phenomena. Almost the only explanation that has not been entertained is the simple evolutionary one, whereby these similarities are interpreted as modern witnesses of an earlier historical unity.

Whatever the intellectual dynamics of the early twentieth century, it is clear that today most historical linguists have no appreciation of the fundamental difference between classification and reconstruction, often using the two terms as if they were synonymous. According to one of Greenberg's Americanist critics, "a temporal ceiling of 7,000 to 8,000 years is inherent in the methods of comparative linguistic reconstruction. We can recover genetic relationships that are that old, but probably no earlier than that" (Kaufman 1990: 23). In the first of his two sentences Kaufman is talking about reconstruction, yet in the second he jumps to the topic of genetic relationship, as if the two were one and the same. But as you have seen throughout this book, genetic relationships come to light from the classifying of languages; they are not the product of reconstruction. You have discovered quite a few genetic relationships in the course of analyzing the various tables in this book, but have you reconstructed anything along the way? One attempts to reconstruct a family only after it has been identified, that is, only when its genetic affinity is well established. In the Epilogue we will return to the question of reconstruction, as well as other concerns of traditional historical linguists, but the abiding concern of this book is classification—the identification of language families at all levels—which must be considered the initial step in comparative linguistics. Once this initial step has been completed, one can then turn to such traditional topics as reconstruction and sound correspondences.

It is only in the twentieth century that historical linguists began to cite reconstruction and sound correspondences as the "proof" of genetic relationships, an association that would not have occurred to nineteenth-century Indo-Europeanists. By the time August Schleicher first attempted to reconstruct Proto-Indo-European in the 1850's the validity of Indo-European had been taken for granted for almost 40 years. Nor was the discovery of regular sound correspondences among the branches of Indo-European in the 1870's considered to play any role in proving Indo-European. It is only later that we find statements to the effect that "the ultimate proof of genetic relationship, and to many linguists' minds the only real proof, lies in a successful reconstruction of the ancestral forms from which the systematically corresponding cognates can be derived. . . . It is through the procedure of comparative reconstruction, then, that we can establish *language families*, such as those of Indo-European, Uralic, Dravidian, Altaic, Sino-Tibetan, Malayo-Polynesian, Bantu, Semitic, or Uto-Aztecan" (Hock 1986: 567).

Greenberg on the Griddle

With regard to Greenberg's method of multilateral comparison, the English historical linguist Theodora Bynon remarks that "it is clear that, as far as the historical linguist is concerned, it [multilateral comparison] can in no way serve as a substitute for reconstruction, for to him the mere fact of relationship is of little interest in itself" (Bynon 1977: 272). This is a peculiar statement inasmuch as Greenberg has never claimed that multilateral comparison is a substitute for reconstruction; rather, it is multilateral comparison that provides the historical linguist with the *wherewithal* for reconstruction, *a set of related languages.*

Explicit discussions of how one discovers language families are rare in the writings of nineteenth-century Indo-Europeanists, precisely because Indo-European was taken for granted. The German Indo-Europeanist Bertold Delbrück described the discovery of Indo-European as follows:

> My starting point is that specific result of comparative linguistics that is not in doubt and cannot be in doubt. It was proved by [Franz] Bopp and others that the so-called Indo-European languages were related. The proof was produced by juxtaposing words and forms of similar meaning. When one considers that in these languages the formation of the inflectional forms of the verb, noun, and pronoun agrees in essentials and likewise that an extraordinary number of inflected words agree in their lexical parts, the assumption of chance agreement must appear absurd. (Delbrück 1880: 121–22)

We have arrived here at the heart of the controversy between Greenberg and his critics. The usual perception is of Greenberg on one side, with his personal techniques of "multilateral comparison," and the traditional historical linguists on the other side, defending the "standard comparative method" against Greenberg's supposedly intuitive approach. In reality, there is no opposition between the two sides, which are rather complementary. Greenberg's work is simply taxonomy, the classification of different languages into families (and subfamilies) and in its theoretical basis his method differs little from biological taxonomy, or indeed taxonomy in any field. The evolutionary biologist Ernst Mayr has described the initial step in the comparative method as follows: "From the earliest days, organisms were grouped into classes by their outward appearance, into grasses, birds, butterflies, snails, and others. Such grouping 'by inspection' is the expressly stated or unspoken starting point of virtually all systems of classification" (Mayr 1988: 268). For most modern historical linguists, unfortunately, this principle not only has been unspoken, but even unrecognized.

The "standard comparative method," as usually defined (incorrectly, in my view), begins where Greenberg leaves off. Once you *have* families, discovered by classification, what do you *do* with them? What historical linguists have done throughout the twentieth century has been to attempt to reconstruct proto-languages and to discover the sound correspondences that connect and explain the various cognates in a family. Somehow what is really the *second* stage of historical linguistics, reconstruction, has become confused with the *first*, classification. That the two sides in this controversy were engaged in fundamentally different work should have been obvious to everyone from the start, inasmuch as Greenberg has never reconstructed anything in his taxonomic work (though he has in fact written papers on reconstruction), whereas Greenberg's critics—virtually all of the Indo-Europeanists and all of the Americanists—have never classified a single language; in other words, they have never discovered a single new genetic relationship. There has been no change in our understanding of the classification of the Indo-European languages since Hittite was discovered early in this century, and, as we have seen, any connection between Indo-European and any other language family has been resolutely denied. As for New World taxonomy, it had actually been regressing toward an ever-increasing number of "independent families" prior to Greenberg's revolutionary classification.

According to Watkins (1990: 292–93),

A genetic linguistic relationship is first assumed, or hypothesized, by inspection or whatever. At that point must begin the careful and above all systematic comparison, which will lead, if the hypothesis or supposition of genetic relationship is correct, to the reconstruction of the linguistic history of the languages concerned, including the discovery of the attendant sound laws, which are a part of that history.

In other words, systematic comparison requires the postulation, reconstruction, or restoration of a common original, and of a set of rules by which that original is transformed into the later attested languages. That is what we mean by linguistic history. It is the history which is, de facto, the proof of the genetic relation. The implication is clearly that if the careful comparison of such languages does not yield a reconstruction of linguistic history as we know it, the presumption that the languages are related is at best uninteresting, and at worst, in grave jeopardy.

In other words, unless you reconstruct the proto-families with regular sound correspondences and then explain precisely how each proto-form evolved into all of its modern reflexes, this linguist (ironically, an Indo-Europeanist) won't buy your classification. Watkins (1990: 295) continues:

If I believe in Indo-European, Algonquian, or Austronesian, it is because scholars have done the necessary systematic explanation and produced the requisite historical results. If I do not believe in an Amerind, Eurasiatic, or Nostratic, it is because scholars have so far neither done the one nor produced the other. To spell it out: because scholars have neither done the necessary systematic explanation [regular sound correspondences: MR], nor produced the requisite historical results [reconstructions: MR]. And there is no other way.

In fact, however, Indo-European, Algonquian, and Austronesian were all recognized—and accepted—as valid families long before linguists began to reconstruct their proto-languages or concern themselves with regular sound correspondences. Furthermore, as the quotation from Delbrück shows, the nineteenth-century Indo-Europeanists who first reconstructed Indo-European and worked out the sound laws connecting the various branches of the family never for a moment imagined that this work had anything to do with "proving" Indo-European. The validity of Indo-European was simply not in doubt. Obvious families like Indo-European and Algonquian were discovered in precisely the way you discovered them in Tables 2 and 7, by recognizing obvious similarities in basic vocabulary that set these families off from the others.

There is a final, disastrous consequence of the requirement of reconstruction with regular sound correspondences, in order to establish genetic affinity. In order to reconstruct proto-languages with regular sound correspondences, one must have a rather large corpus of evidence; otherwise, there will simply not be enough examples of sound correspondences to detect them (even should they exist). According to Kaufman (1990: 18), one must have at least 500 words of basic vocabulary and 100 points of grammar before one can begin to do "serious comparative work." Nice work if you can get it, but such a priori demands cannot be taken seriously. Indo-Europeanists have accepted the (long-extinct) Lydian language as being an Indo-European language, of the extinct Anatolian branch, *on the basis of a handful of words*. Other extinct and poorly documented languages, such as Venetic and Messapic, are also accepted as Indo-European languages, on the basis of equally meager evidence. In the Americas, we have the case of Shebayo, the original language of Trinidad. As one of the first Native American groups to encounter the European invasion, the Shebayo found that theirs was also one of the first languages to be extinguished by that invasion. When the language vanished at the end of the seventeenth century, the sum total of our knowledge was a vocabulary list of fifteen words. Despite this paucity of information, the Shebayo language has been classified as a member of the Arawakan group of the Equatorial branch of Amerind, and the Arawakan affiliation, at least, is uncontroversial.

That one can in fact classify languages correctly on the basis of a dozen or so words should come as no surprise to you, since you have done precisely that throughout this book. Each family is defined by a set of diagnostic cognates. If, then, several diagnostic cognates from one specific family appear in a small amount of data from some obscure or extinct language, then it is a fairly safe bet that this language is a member of that family. In cases where additional data later become available, the initial classification of the language is almost always confirmed, in spades. It is all well and good for Kaufman, Watkins, and others to demand this or that, but in the real world the scholars who do the classifying have often made do with much less than the ideal quantities of data.

Notice further that Watkins and Kaufman dwell on theoretical desiderata, and avoid addressing empirical questions such as why the *m-/t-* pronoun pattern is found throughout northern Eurasia, why the *n-/m-* pronoun pattern and *t'ina/t'ana/*

t'una 'son, child, daughter' are found throughout the Americas, and why lexical items like *aqʷa* 'water,' *tik* 'finger, one,' and *pal* 'two' are distributed around the world. In his avoidance of the substance of Greenberg's work and the Nostraticists' work, it would seem that Watkins is more interested in *preventing* Indo-European from being connected to any other family than in finding out what Indo-European's true relatives might be. Were a biologist to demand a complete reconstruction of Proto-Mammal, together with a complete explanation of how this creature evolved into every living mammal, before he would accept the fact that human beings are related to cats and bats, he would not be taken seriously. Yet it is just this kind of linguistic nonsense that has been taught in universities by Indo-Europeanists for so long that most linguists are unaware of its mythical nature.

Finally, Watkins (1990: 295) claims that

> a comparison of the language groups in Greenberg's 'Eurasiatic' family . . . with those in Illič-Svityč and others' 'Nostratic' family shows, if nothing else, the perceptual variability—and consequent fragility—of such inspections. Thus, 'Eurasiatic' includes not only Korean and Japanese, but also Ainu, Gilyak, Chukotian, and Eskimo-Aleut; 'Nostratic' excludes some of these, but includes Khartvelian, Dravidian, and at least the 'Semito-Hamitic' component of Afro-Asiatic, which for Greenberg (and for me) are separate families. Are these just trivial differences, and am I being nit-picky to point them out?

First of all, there is no " 'Semito-Hamitic' component" in Afro-Asiatic (nor is there any "Hamitic" component, for that matter, as Greenberg showed), and indeed the whole idea of "racial components" in language is today considered without merit. "Semito-Hamitic" is merely an older term for Afro-Asiatic that has fallen into disrepute because of its racist connotations. As for the differences between Eurasiatic and Nostratic, these are due not to "perceptual variability," but to differences in the methodologies used by Greenberg and the Nostraticists—and it is difficult to believe that Watkins is unaware of these differences.

So why do the two differ? Nostratic has traditionally been defined as those families that are related to Indo-European. Furthermore, the Nostraticists only compare families that have been reconstructed, and the Chukchi-Kamchatkan and Eskimo-Aleut families, for example, have often been left out of their comparisons simply because no one had yet reconstructed them to their satisfaction. In their emphasis on reconstruction and regular sound correspondences, the Nostraticists appear closer to the traditional approach of comparative linguistics, and in fact one not infrequently finds Indo-Europeanists endorsing the methodology of the Nostraticists, if not their actual results, while at the same time condemning Greenberg's multilateral approach. Yet notwithstanding this supposed theoretical affinity between the traditionalists and the Nostraticists, it is apparent that the Nostraticists and Greenberg are allies in seeking to exceed the artificial limits that have been arbitrarily imposed by the Indo-Europeanists.

In contrast to the Nostratic methodology, Greenberg's approach does not require the prior reconstruction of families before they can be compared with others (nor was this ever required of Indo-European, or its branches). Moreover, Greenberg's methodology accords Indo-European no special importance; it is just one family among many to be classified. Who, then, is right? There are really two independent questions. On the question whether Indo-European *is related to* other families, Greenberg and the Nostraticists are in complete agreement, and indeed the cognates each has suggested (for Eurasiatic and Nostratic, respectively) overlap to a great extent and (in cases such as the *-k/-t* dual/plural affix) continue genetic links that had already been recognized in the nineteenth century.

On the other hand, if we ask which is the better *family*, here Eurasiatic must be considered to have the edge. Recall that a family, or taxon, is defined as a set of languages (or language families) all of which are more closely related to each other than any of them is to any languages (or language families) outside that set. By failing to consider families just because there were no reconstructions available, Nostraticists have lost the necessary taxonomic basis for a valid family. Historically valid families cannot depend on which families have, or have not, had the good fortune to have been reconstructed by Western scholars. Rather, families must be defined by a set of exclusively shared lexical and grammatical items. And on this basis it is quite clear that Chukchi-Kamchatkan and Eskimo-Aleut, even lacking reconstructions, are both closer to Indo-European than Afro-Asiatic or Dravidian is. It should be noted that several Nostraticists have come to the same conclusion in recent years, and Starostin, for one, now considers Afro-Asiatic and Dravidian to be related to Nostratic *at greater remove*, rather than a *part* of it. His views are thus virtually identical with those of Greenberg. The strength of Nostratic studies has been the discovery of a substantial number of cognate roots shared by Indo-European and other families. Its chief defect, deriving from the lack of a proper classificatory basis, has been in giving Indo-European undue importance. It is simply not permissible to define a family as those families that are related to a particular family—Indo-European, in the case of Nostratic.

Another alleged requirement of genetic relationship that has been demanded by some comparative linguists is the presence of an "exclusively shared aberration" in two languages, or language families. Thus, for example, the fact that English uses a different root to form the comparative and superlative of the adjective 'good,' namely, 'better' and 'best,' while German shows exactly the same irregularity in *gut/besser/best*, is sometimes cited as the kind of "magic bullet" that provides absolute proof of genetic affinity. It is argued that languages could never share such an irregularity without being genetically related. However, although the presence of such an irregular pattern in two different languages might be conceded to be *sufficient* proof of genetic affinity, one may seriously question whether it is *necessary*. In fact, when we do find such exclusively shared aberrations they are almost always shared by languages that are so closely related, as are English and German, that the question of genetic affinity is not even at issue, having already been determined by great numbers of similarities in basic vocabulary.

The true basis of genetic affinity among languages is not the rigamarole that Indo-Europeanists and their followers have come to demand. It is, rather, the presence of widespread similarities in the basic vocabulary of different languages (or language families) that determine their classifications, and hence their affinities. Darwin recognized this simple basis of biological taxonomy quite clearly in 1871:

> We can understand why a classification founded on any single charac-
> ter or organ—even an organ so wonderfully complex and important
> as the brain—or on the high development of mental faculties, is al-
> most sure to prove unsatisfactory. . . . For this object numerous points
> of resemblance are of much more importance than the amount of sim-
> ilarity or dissimilarity in a few points. If two languages were found to
> resemble each other in a multitude of words and points of construc-
> tion, they would be universally recognised as having sprung from a
> common source, notwithstanding that they differed greatly in some
> few words or points of construction. . . . Hence we can see how it is
> that resemblances in several unimportant structures, in useless and ru-
> dimentary organs, or not now functionally active, or in an embryolog-
> ical condition, are by far the most serviceable for classification; for
> they can hardly be due to adaptations within a late period; and thus
> they reveal the old lines of descent or of true affinity. (Darwin
> 1871[1936]: 513–14)

Unfortunately, it is a lesson that has been largely forgotten by
historical linguists during the twentieth century.

Since early in the twentieth century, Indo-Europeanists
have directed their attention to what constitutes "proof" of linguistic affinity. How will we *know*, they asked, when Indo-
European has been shown to be related to some other family?
But this demand for "proof" by the Indo-Europeanists is really
beside the point, for "proof" is a mathematical concept not applicable to empirical sciences like linguistics, biology, or even
physics. In these areas we do not so much "prove" something
as provide what seems like the *most likely* explanation of a nonrandom set of data. Thus, if one is asked whether this book—
or even the entire linguistic literature—"proves" that all the
world's languages are related, I would answer that this is a
proposition that cannot be proved in a mathematical sense, but
that the modicum of data presented in this book nonetheless
strongly suggests that a common origin for all extant languages
is the simplest, and most likely, explanation of the linguistic
similarities observed in the various tables. If all of the relevant
literature pertaining to these matters had been produced here,
the evidence for a common origin of all languages would
have been inescapable, if not technically proved. Very few readers, however, would have been willing to wade through the
thousands of pages that a complete rendering of that evidence
would have required. I have tried to lay out the essence of the

evidence; those who wish to pursue the various different lines should consult the Bibliography at the end of this book for a general orientation to the literature.

A final charge that is often leveled at Greenberg's work is that since there is no way of *disproving* his results, they remain one man's speculation, which can be neither confirmed nor disconfirmed by the scientific method. In fact, however, Greenberg's results *can* be disconfirmed, either by presenting a better classification or by showing that certain languages have been misclassified, neither of which has been done by his critics.

Let us consider specifically how one might go about disconfirming Amerind. Greenberg and I have discovered a lexical item, *t'ina/t'ana/t'una* 'son, child, daughter,' that is abundantly attested in the Amerind languages of North and South America. Critics often dismiss such evidence with the argument that with hundreds of Amerind languages to choose from, one can find just about anything one wants. As Campbell put it, "given the large number of target [that is, Amerind] languages, Greenberg could hardly miss finding what he was looking for." Other scholars compare the ease with which superficially similar forms can be found to "shooting fish in a barrel." Now if we consider that the Amerind family contains roughly 500 of the world's 5,000 languages, this means that we have produced our case for *t'ina/t'ana/t'una* using approximately 10 percent of the world's languages. If finding such forms is really as easy as shooting fish in a barrel, then finding such forms in non-Amerind languages should be nine times easier. Let our critics—all the king's horses (the Indo-Europeanists) and all the king's men (the Americanists)—put together a case for *t'ina/ t'ana/t'una*, in non-Amerind languages, that involves the gender-induced ablaut and the specific Amerind prefixes and suffixes we discussed in Chapter 4. This would be an easy way to disprove Greenberg's speculations. Critics often allege that a graduate student over a weekend could do as much. So far, however, no grad students—nor indeed any tenured professors—have done it. The reason is they can't, because the forms do not exist in non-Amerind languages. Greenberg's results cannot be disproven, not because they have no empirical basis, but because they are correct.

One of the consequences of the current confusion in historical linguistics—over how exactly one proves that two languages (or language families) are related—is that even the experts have a hard time distinguishing what is known from what is not known. In fact, most historical linguists probably have little more firsthand knowledge of the evidence for genetic affinity among the world's languages than you do. Very few Indo-Europeanists, I would venture to say, have ever even glanced at the evidence for Bantu, Nilo-Saharan, Austroasiatic, Australian, or Amerind. So even your brief acquaintance with some of these families in the course of this book constitutes a deeper investigation of these families than most experts ever attempt. The problem with modern historical linguistics, as it is currently practiced, is that a specialist is expected to know *everything* concerning his or her family of specialization but need not know *anything* about other families. This compartmentalized view of knowledge has led, as we have seen in the case of Amerind *t'ina/t'ana/t'una* 'son, child, daughter,' to a situation in which specialists fail to perceive even the most abundantly attested patterns, simply because no one has a knowledge of what exists outside his narrow niche. One might call this collective myopia.

What would happen if we were to bring to the debate an experienced taxonomist from Mars, and ask her to render an opinion on the classification of the earth's languages? Let us assume that we would present this taxonomist with all the relevant data and then ask her for her conclusions. What would she say? Most of today's experts would be shocked, I suspect, by how little her assessment would coincide with conventional wisdom. When she found—in the first five minutes—that Greenberg's Amerind family is better supported by the evidence than is any of his four African families, the experts would be at a loss to explain why these four families are accepted by almost everyone—and appear in every encyclopaedia—while the more robust Amerind family is currently denigrated and ridiculed by most Americanists. When she then arrived at the conclusion that all the world's languages are obviously related, today's experts would be even more aghast. How could she possibly leap to such far-fetched conclusions without first having reconstructed all the intermediate families? She would have done so the same way that Sir William Jones arrived at the Indo-European family—without first reconstructing Proto-Celtic, Proto-Germanic, or proto-anything-else. Sir William saw simply that these languages shared certain similarities that set them off from other languages. And our taxonomist from Mars would see the same kinds of resemblances among the world's language families that Jones saw among the languages of Europe and Southwest Asia. Her conclusion would thus be no different than his, except in time depth and geographical breadth.

The Global Configuration

In concluding this chapter I would like to sketch what I expect would be the full configuration that our hypothetical taxonomist from Mars would identify. The immediate conclusion that all the world's languages are related in a single family is apparent from the outset, and is one of her *first* conclusions. The contention that all the intermediate nodes must first be worked out before more ancient families can even be approached is so blatantly contradicted by the examples of Indo-European, Algonquian, and Austronesian, not to mention taxonomic practice in zoology and botany, that it is difficult to understand how anyone could give it any credence at all—much less make it a requirement for genetic affinity. It is the subgrouping of this single human family that represents the most challenging problem for linguistic taxonomy, a challenge that is now only in its infancy. Nevertheless, certain reasonable conclusions within the larger problem can be reached, on the basis of the evidence now available.

It is ironic that Africa, which has perhaps the greatest linguistic diversity on the face of the earth, is today not a focus of controversy, ironic that the classification that Greenberg proposed in 1963 is now so widely accepted that its general validity is nowhere in doubt. One tends to forget that Greenberg's African classification initially met with the same kind of hostile criticism, especially from the British Bantuists, that his American classification is currently receiving from Americanists. The English historian Colin Flight (1988: 265–66) describes the British reaction to Greenberg's African classification in the following terms:

> In British circles even Westermann [a German linguist who had worked on West African languages] was believed to have been 'overoptimistic' in his attempts at classification. His claim to have demonstrated the existence of genetic relationships among the 'West Sudanic' languages was regarded by British linguists as highly suspect; and by taking this conclusion for granted and extending it still further, Greenberg seemed to them to be indulging in irresponsible speculation. . . . It was not easy to classify African languages, as Greenberg seemed to think; it was very difficult, perhaps insuperably so. Moreover, this pessimistic attitude towards the linguistic data was reinforced by the conception of African history as an everlasting orgy of random violence—a vicious circle which had been broken thanks to European intervention. If African history was chaos, and if African languages were the product of that history, then order was not to be looked for.

Order, however, was what Greenberg found. After over a decade of research that began in the late 1940's, Greenberg proposed that all native African languages belonged to one of just four families: Khoisan, Niger-Kordofanian, Nilo-Saharan, and Afro-Asiatic. In order to appreciate the magnitude of the simplification that Greenberg had brought to our understanding of the classification of African languages, I need mention only that in 1950 there were over 1,000 African languages, a few well-known families like Bantu, and next to no understanding of the relationships of most African languages to the handful of recognized families. Greenberg's classification not only revolutionized African linguistics, it later was found to be a fruitful explanation for the patterning of both human genes and the archaeological record in Africa, as we will explore in some depth in Chapter 8.

Yet another irony of Greenberg's African work, which is only now coming to be grasped by the linguistic community, is that his classification went far, far beyond the arbitrary ceiling of 6,000 years that had been imposed by the Indo-Europeanists. No one who examines the evidence can fail to perceive that Nilo-Saharan is vastly more heterogeneous than Indo-European, and hence no doubt far more ancient, but this obvious fact was overlooked by most historical linguists at the time, who were content—and even grateful—to have a little order on the African continent. It took Greenberg almost a decade to arrive at the Nilo-Saharan hypothesis, yet it took him less than a year—in the mid-1950's—to arrive at the Amerind hypothesis. It is again ironic that the hypothesis that consumed a decade of work is today uncontroversial, while the hypothesis that imposed itself in a matter of months—Amerind—is today rejected by Americanist experts across the board.

Most Khoisan languages are today found in southern Africa, often in such inhospitable regions as the Kalahari Desert, but there are indications that the Khoisan family was once much more widespread, and that it has only recently been confined to a smaller territory by the precipitate expansion of the Bantu peoples from West Africa, which we will examine in greater detail in Chapter 8. Two isolated languages found in East Africa not far from Lake Victoria—Sandawe and Hadza—use clicks like those in the other Khoisan languages, and have been linked by Greenberg to the rest of the Khoisan family, though they are clearly the most divergent (that is, most distinctive) members of the family. Surprisingly, since they are located quite close to each other, they show little similarity to one another.

Because a high percentage of Khoisan words begin with clicks, this family poses a special problem for those attempting to connect it with other language families that do not use clicks. Since the origin of these clicks is not known (hypotheses range from their being early sounds in the development of human language that survive only in Khoisan, to a more recent origin within the family by normal phonetic evolution), it is not immediately clear with which sounds in other families the clicks should be compared. Yet despite this rather substantial handicap, we *have* identified a number of roots connecting Khoisan with the world's other families, and if the origin of the Khoisan clicks can ever be resolved, it is likely that the number of apparent cognates with other families will increase significantly.

The Niger-Kordofanian family covers more of sub-Saharan Africa than does any other family, but most of that territory has seen speakers of Niger-Kordofanian languages only within the past two millennia, as a result of the Bantu expansion. The family as a whole consists of two separate and very unequal parts.

The Kordofanian branch is a small group of languages spoken in the southern Sudan that appears to be only distantly related to the other branch of the family, Niger-Congo. In light of the civil war that has ravaged the southern Sudan for almost a decade, the fate of these Kordofanian peoples is unknown. Most of the branches of the Niger-Congo group are found in West Africa, from Senegal eastward to northern Zaire, and it is in this region that the original homeland of the family is to be sought. The recent Bantu expansion from eastern Nigeria only confirms this conclusion.

Nilo-Saharan is a very diverse family that consists of perhaps ten subgroups located for the most part in north Central Africa and East Africa. The American linguist Edgar Gregersen (1972) has proposed that Nilo-Saharan and Niger-Kordofanian should be joined in a higher-level family that he calls Congo-Saharan. This proposal, which would join the two African families whose speakers are predominantly Negroid, has so far not won wide acceptance within the linguistic community, but, as we shall see in Chapter 8, such a grouping is supported by the distribution of genes in Africa and may well be correct.

The Afro-Asiatic family consists of a half-dozen branches, two of which—Semitic and Chadic—you discovered in Tables 2 and 3. The other branches are Berber, once widely spoken across North Africa, but now largely engulfed by the Arabic expansion; Ancient Egyptian, now extinct; and the Cushitic and Omotic branches of northeast Africa. The family is considerably older than Indo-European, but nonetheless fairly uncontroversial. The main point of contention has been the inclusion of the Chadic branch, but the opposition here seems to have been based on nonlinguistic factors rather than the actual linguistic evidence. Chadic speakers are Negroid, while the rest of the family tends to be Caucasoid, and some scholars have apparently hesitated to include a black branch in an otherwise white family. The linguistic evidence connecting Chadic with the rest of Afro-Asiatic is, however, straightforward.

In Eurasia there is the Eurasiatic family, as defined by Greenberg, with the position of the Kartvelian family of Georgia as yet unclear. Kartvelian may very well turn out to belong to Eurasiatic, as the Nostraticists claim, or it may be more removed from Eurasiatic, as Greenberg contends, perhaps having a special relationship with Afro-Asiatic. It does seem, however, that Afro-Asiatic is distinct from Eurasiatic, and probably Dravidian is, too. Neither Greenberg nor the Nostraticists denies that all three are related, but at what remove from one another is the question to be answered.

The other ancient family found in Eurasia, Dene-Caucasian, comprises a heterogeneous group of geographically isolated languages and subfamilies: Basque, Caucasian, Burushaski, Yeniseian, Sino-Tibetan, and, in North America, Na-Dene. This family appears to be more archaic than Eurasiatic, and a possible explanation for this fact will be offered in Chapter 8. Bengtson has suggested that Basque, Caucasian, and Burushaski form a subgroup within Dene-Caucasian, and he has offered evidence to support this conclusion. Bengtson also includes the extinct Sumerian language in Dene-Caucasian, but this affiliation seems less secure.

The Austric family of Southeast Asia consists of four subfamilies: Austroasiatic, Miao-Yao, Daic, and Austronesian, the last two of which appear to be closest to each other. The Austroasiatic subfamily consists of two branches, Munda and Mon-Khmer. The small Munda branch is restricted to northern India, while the Mon-Khmer branch, more numerous in both languages and speakers, is spread across much of Southeast Asia, often interspersed with languages of other families. Vietnamese and Khmer (or Cambodian) are the two best-known Mon-Khmer languages, and the only two that have attained the status of national languages. The Miao-Yao family is made up of just two branches, Miao and Yao, each of which may be considered a single language with very divergent dialects. The various Miao and Yao dialects are spread across much of Southeast Asia, from Southern China to Northern Thailand, in numerous villages isolated from one another by other language families.

The Daic languages, of which Thai and Laotian are the two best known and the only ones to achieve the status of national languages, are found in Southern China, northern Vietnam, Laos, and Thailand. Austronesian languages are found on Taiwan, which is probably the original homeland of the family, but also on islands throughout the Pacific Ocean, and even on Madagascar, in the Indian Ocean close to Africa. The present Chinese domination of Taiwan is a consequence of a recent migration from the mainland that began only in 1626. Over six millennia earlier a previous migration from the mainland, of people closely related to the Daic family, had led to the original Austronesian occupation of the island, which turned out to be the first small step in what was one of the longest—and most hazardous—migrations in human history. We will take a more careful look at this migration in Chapter 8. Though there are approximately 1,000 Austronesian languages, the age of the family is thought to be comparable to that of Indo-European, and there is virtually no controversy over which languages do or do not belong to the family. The internal structure of the family, however, is poorly understood.

There is no general consensus on the nearest relatives of the Austric family. In fact, even the idea of an Austric family has received little scholarly attention in recent years, though the family was first proposed early in the twentieth century. The possibility that Austric and Dene-Caucasian are especially close is, in my view, worthy of further study.

In Oceania we have three families: Austronesian (a subfamily of Austric), Indo-Pacific (distributed largely in New Guinea), and Australian. As we have just seen, the Austronesian family reflects a migration from Southeast Asia that began only some six millennia ago. Though it is by far the most broadly distributed of the three Oceanic families, the more circumscribed Indo-Pacific and Australian families are clearly much more ancient. Archaeological evidence indicates that both New Guinea and Australia were inhabited by modern humans at least 40,000 years ago, and perhaps 10,000 to 15,000 years earlier than that.

The island of New Guinea has long been renowned for its extraordinary linguistic diversity, even though the interior valleys of the highlands were unknown to Westerners until the 1930's. It is only in the last few decades that a complete mapping of the languages of New Guinea has been completed, and the final count shows over 700 indigenous languages, in addition to a sprinkling of Austronesian languages scattered along the coast. In 1971 Greenberg presented evidence that the non-

Austronesian languages of New Guinea—as well as certain languages on islands to the east and west of New Guinea—belong to an extremely diverse and ancient family that he named Indo-Pacific. The Australian linguist Stephen Wurm, who directed much of the linguistic mapping in New Guinea, has proposed a somewhat less inclusive family than Greenberg had, which he calls the Trans-New Guinea phylum. Wurm's proposed family includes about 70 percent of the languages Greenberg included in Indo-Pacific.

At the present time the evidence connecting Indo-Pacific to the world's other language families is sparse, comparable perhaps to the relatively weak links between Khoisan and other families. Part of the problem is our general lack of knowledge of these languages and the almost complete lack of meaningful historical studies. But an equal part of the problem is that there is truly great linguistic diversity in New Guinea, far greater than that found in the Americas, for example. Despite these impediments, there do appear to be some threads connecting Indo-Pacific with the world's other language families, threads that further research can be expected to strengthen.

Despite its great antiquity, often estimated at 40,000 years, the Australian family is surprisingly uncontroversial, and it is now generally accepted that all native Australian languages belong to a single Australian family. Within this family there is great diversity on the northern coast (Arnhem Land), but a fairly homogenous subgroup, Pama-Nyungan, covers most of the Australian continent. Relatively few roots have been posited as diagnostic of the entire Australian family, but some of these, such as *pula* 'two' and *-pal* (dual in pronouns), appear to have clear cognates in other families outside Australia, as we saw in Chapter 5.

In the Americas our taxonomist from Mars would quickly detect the same three families that Greenberg proposed in 1987: Eskimo-Aleut, Na-Dene, and Amerind. Furthermore, she would be at a loss to understand the current controversies over what is really a simple, straightforward, and well-supported classification. In order to understand the origin of this controversy our Martian taxonomist would have to know the history of linguistics here, rather than historical linguistics. And without such knowledge she would find the present debate merely perplexing.

What we currently lack is an overall tree of human phylogeny based on language. One can see that all the world's families are related, and it is possible to recognize certain ancient families, such as Nilo-Saharan, Eurasiatic, and Amerind. But unfortunately there is as yet no understanding of the order in which these various groups branched off from the original linguistic trunk. Though one may hope that linguistic evidence may one day shed light on this difficult, but crucial, question, for the moment we must rely on evidence from other fields. Toward that end, we will turn now to the work of human geneticists, who have been attacking this same problem.

7

Genes

Biology and Language

If the conclusions we have reached in the first six chapters are correct, and all the world's languages can be shown to share a common origin, how might one explain that fact? In the final two chapters, I will try to place these linguistic conclusions and questions within the larger context of human evolution.

The perceived relationship between language and race—or, to give it its proper term, *ethnicity*—has a long and complex history. In broadest outline, however, it is clear that the views of nineteenth-century scholars were often diametrically opposed to those current today. During the nineteenth century, many European scholars believed that the Indo-European family represented the most advanced form of human language, and languages in other parts of the world were thought to represent more primitive stages in the development of language. It was even suggested that the Khoisan languages of South Africa, with their chatter of clicks, might represent a level of language intermediate between the rudimentary linguistic abilities of chimpanzees, monkeys, and apes, on the one hand, and the fully developed European languages, on the other.

During the twentieth century a totally different outlook developed. A careful study of languages around the world has led linguists to conclude that there are, in fact, no primitive languages anywhere on earth. All extant human languages are today considered of equal "complexity" by virtually all linguists, despite the fact that there is no recognized way of measuring complexity in language. Across the same decades, biologists were coming to understand that there are no primitive *peoples* on earth either. All humans exhibit very similar cognitive and linguistic abilities, across the entire species; differences between languages do not represent differences in brain structure, and it is well known that any human child is capable of learning any human language to which he or she is exposed.

In our technologically advanced society we tend to assume that people with less technology, such as the highlanders of Papua New Guinea, also have less advanced languages and perhaps less advanced mental capacities. But biology and linguistics concur that such is not the case. Furthermore, just as we are a single species today, despite the abundance of cultural, linguistic, and genetic differences that distinguish various populations, so too have we been a single species for perhaps the past 100,000 years—that is, since our species first evolved. Stephen Jay Gould eloquently expressed this idea as follows:

> At some point, modern *Homo sapiens* split off from an ancestral group and founded our own species. They were us from the beginning, are us now, and shall be us until we blow ourselves up or genetically engineer ourselves out of current existence. *Homo sapiens* ... is an entity, not a tendency. Once we arose as a species—and 100,000 to 250,000 years ago in Africa is our best current assessment of time and place—we were probably pretty much ourselves in terms of mental organization. ... I would reverse our usual perspective. ... We are stunned by what our Ice Age ancestors could do. I think that we should look the other way, onward from the origin of our species. Is it not remarkable that all of what we call civilization, all of agriculture, of the arts and sciences, of technology, of life in complex cities, could be built by the unchanged power resident in the mind of a creature who evolved a large brain for reasons obviously unrelated to this future potential?

Correlations on a Grand Scale

Despite the fact that there is no *intrinsic* connection between language and ethnicity, and the fact that different languages and different ethnic groups do not represent different stages of our evolution, during the past decade several teams of human geneticists, from a number of countries, have discovered a significant correlation between linguistic and biological classifications in many areas of the world, including, among others, Africa, Sardinia, Europe, and the Americas. In the most comprehensive worldwide study of nuclear genetic material (for example, blood groups, proteins, enzymes), Luca Cavalli-Sforza and his colleagues reported significant similarity between the population clusters they had identified on the basis of gene frequencies and the language families that had been posited by linguists such as Greenberg. A brief summary of their results was published in 1988 and the full monograph appeared in 1994. Cavalli-Sforza's comparison of the genetic clusters and language families is shown in Figure 10.

These results were not warmly received by either Indo-Europeanists or Americanists. What they found disconcerting was not just that there was a correlation between genes and languages (though even this result could hardly have been anticipated by linguists), but rather that some of the larger groupings coincided with vast linguistic families like Eurasiatic/Nostratic, Amerind, Austric, and Indo-Pacific that traditional historical linguists had been burying under scorn and disparagement. Cavalli-Sforza's finding that on the basis of their genes Native Americans fell into the same three families that Greenberg had postulated the year before on the basis of language was greeted with astonishment and dismay at the Smithsonian Institution. Astonishment because the Curator for American Indian languages, Ives Goddard, had already proclaimed that Greenberg's work "led to no reliable conclusions about linguistic history," and dismay because Greenberg's results had been independently corroborated by research in another field of study.

In the face of these disturbing results, the Smithsonian put

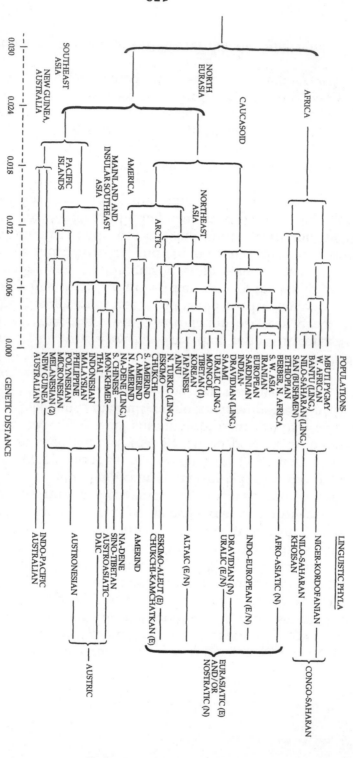

FIGURE 10 A Comparison of biological and linguistic classifications, after Cavalli-Sforza et al., 1988.

In this tree, (ling.) indicates populations pooled on the basis of linguistic classification. (1) Tibetans are associated genetically with the Northeast Asian cluster, but linguistically with the Sino-Tibetan phylum. (2) Melanesians speak, in part, Indo-Pacific languages. Genetic data are not currently available for Kartvelian or (North) Caucasian populations.

up a united front. In a lengthy article, Goddard and six staff biologists argued that Cavalli-Sforza's results were "undermined by analysis of an inadequate database by inappropriate methods and by several conceptual flaws in subsequent interpretations" (Bateman et al. 1990: 2). Their article is full of pretentious jargon (human beings are referred to as "extant hominids"), and they include a delightful figure showing that "languages evolved after the ability to speak," but the substantive criticism, if one can call it that, is either erroneous or uninformed.

In their response to this article, Cavalli-Sforza and colleagues pointed out that their database rests on three standard reference books, known to all specialists in the field, and almost 3,000 articles. It is the largest database ever assembled on such genetic traits as blood groups, proteins, and enzymes. As for the inappropriate methods, Cavalli-Sforza has for three decades been among the leaders in the field of human genetics both in developing analytical techiniques for the study of gene distributions and in applying them to the investigation of human phylogeny. The Smithsonian group had shown such naiveté that Cavalli-Sforza and colleagues concluded that they must be "unfamiliar with the data, methods, and models of human population genetics." In a later response the Smithsonian group acknowledged that that was so. What had begun as an assault on the genetic findings wound up as yet another defeat for the anti-Greenberg forces.

Having spent the past century denying that Indo-European had any recognizable linguistic relatives, the Indo-Europeanists were equally disenchanted with the genetic results. The genetic support for a Eurasiatic, or even Nostratic, family confirmed a grouping that Indo-Europeanists had chosen not to accept—and had exiled beyond the temporal limits of the comparative method. One irate Indo-Europeanist, Paul Hopper, angrily denounced the "linguistic hustlers" [Greenberg and the Nostraticists] for duping "responsible human biologists" like Cavalli-Sforza into "invoking the results of comparative linguistics to support arguments about the distribution of human genes" (Hopper 1989: 818). Hopper also condemned the fact that

> We see . . . mitochondrial DNA and other gene distributional studies being calibrated against 'the' genetic classification of such internally diverse 'families' as Niger-Kordofanian, Afro-Asiatic, Nilo-Saharan, Austro-Asiatic, and so on . . . , apparently as if these were factually established genetic categories of languages rather than broad-based guesses about distant linguistic and other relatationships whose ultimate nature is in fact very uncertain. (Hopper 1989: 818)

Notwithstanding this tirade, both Afro-Asiatic and Austroasiatic are universally accepted as valid linguistic families, apparently with the sole exception of a few hardliners like Hopper, for whom anything beyond Indo-European, Algonquian, or Bantu is suspect. The charge that Greenberg and the Nostraticists had somehow influenced Cavalli-Sforza is unsubstantiated by Hopper and is, in any case, unfounded as well. Greenberg and Cavalli-Sforza arrived at their conclusions independently, on the basis of different data and different methods, a fundamental truth that no amount of gainsaying can obscure.

Let us turn now to the meaning of the genetic results illustrated in Figure 10. Does this figure imply that there are genes that predispose a person to speak a particular language? Not at all. It has long been known—and is today universally accepted—that any human child will learn whatever language is spoken in the surrounding culture. A person of Chinese ancestry who is raised in France will speak French as well as any Frenchman, and a person of French ancestry raised in Beijing will speak Chinese with no trace of a foreign accent. There certainly are genes that predispose the human child to learn to talk (and to walk and see), but the language that a child learns depends entirely on the surrounding environment.

If, then, there is no *direct* connection between a person's genes and the language he speaks, how are we to explain the high degree of correlation between language families (as postulated by linguists) and human populations (as defined by gene frequencies)? The answer is that language families and biologically distinct human populations are, jointly, the consequence of certain historical (or more often prehistorical) events. For example, when Australia was first occupied by humans over 40,000 years ago, this initial population brought with them both a specific language (Proto-Australian) and a specific gene pool. Since that time Proto-Australian has differentiated into several hundred distinct languages, and the gene pools of the various populations that speak these languages have also diverged in various ways. And because of, or despite, this parallel but independent development, all Australian languages are more similar to one another (as seen for example in a characteristic pronominal pattern) than any of them is to any language (or family) outside Australia, and all Australian aboriginal populations are genetically closer to one another than any is to human populations elsewhere in the world. The correlation of Australian languages and genes is simply the reflection of a specific historical event—the settlement of Australia.

In a similar manner, the correlation of language and genes in the Americas has been interpreted by Greenberg and colleagues as reflecting three separate waves of migration from Asia. The initial migration brought a population speaking Proto-Amerind, from which all modern Amerind languages derive. Significantly, not only is Amerind the most diverse of the three linguistically, but the speakers of the Amerind languages are also the most diverse genetically. Later migrations brought the ancestors of the Na-Dene and Eskimo-Aleut families, both of which are considerably more homogeneous in their languages and genes than is Amerind.

It is, of course, obvious that language and genes do not always coincide. Black Americans speak English though their genes largely reflect their African origin—a fact that occasions no mystery. Nor is this the only historically documented case of a population switching languages; it has happened for a whole variety of reasons, the slave trade being just one. Would not such language switching so seriously scramble the correlation between language and genes that ultimately there would be no consistent pattern at all? Apparently not, or at least that is the conclusion of Cavalli-Sforza and colleagues (1990: 18):

> The central question is *why there should be any congruence between genetic and linguistic evolution.* The main reason is that the two evolutions follow in principle the same history, namely, sequence of fissions. Two populations that have separated begin a process of differentiation of both genes and languages. These processes need not have exactly constant evolutionary rates, but rough proportionality with time is a rea-

sonable expectation for both. They should therefore be qualitatively congruent, except for later events such as gene flow or language replacement. These may blur the genetic and the linguistic picture, but our conclusion is that they do not obscure it entirely.

We found in Chapter 5 that comparative linguistics can delineate about a dozen language families (see Map 8), all of which are related to one another in a single large, and no doubt very ancient, family. How these dozen families are related to each other—that is, the order in which the different branches split off—currently is unknown. But precisely such a subgrouping is offered by the genetic data, and it is tempting to suspect that, if the linguistic and genetic classifications correspond so closely in the lower-level branchings like Eurasiatic/Nostratic, Austric, and Amerind, then they will likely correspond in the more ancient groupings as well. It is clear in any event that the genetic studies supply at least a hypothesis about the differentiation of our species, something that linguistic studies have not yet attained. Using linguistic labels for the different populations, we might express the genetic structure of the human population, as worked out by Cavalli-Sforza and colleagues, in terms of the diagram shown in Figure 11.

Certain aspects of this (somewhat simplified) family tree require comment. First, we should note that African Pygmies speak languages belonging to either the Nilo-Saharan or Niger-Kordofanian families. It is assumed that Pygmies once spoke their own language(s), but that, through living in symbiosis with other Africans, in prehistorical times, they adopted languages belonging to these two families.

There is a population called "Ethiopian" in Figure 10 that I have omitted in Figure 11. These are a people who associate genetically with sub-Saharan Africans while speaking languages belonging to the Afro-Asiatic family. Cavalli-Sforza attributes this anomaly to a recent admixture between a majority of Africans and a minority of Caucasoids. The Khoisan family also appears to represent an admixture of a majority of Africans and a minority of Caucasoids, but at a considerably earlier date.

Another discrepancy in the linguistic evidence is that neither Eurasiatic nor Nostratic appears as a distinct unit in the genetic tree. Instead, the American languages (both Na-Dene

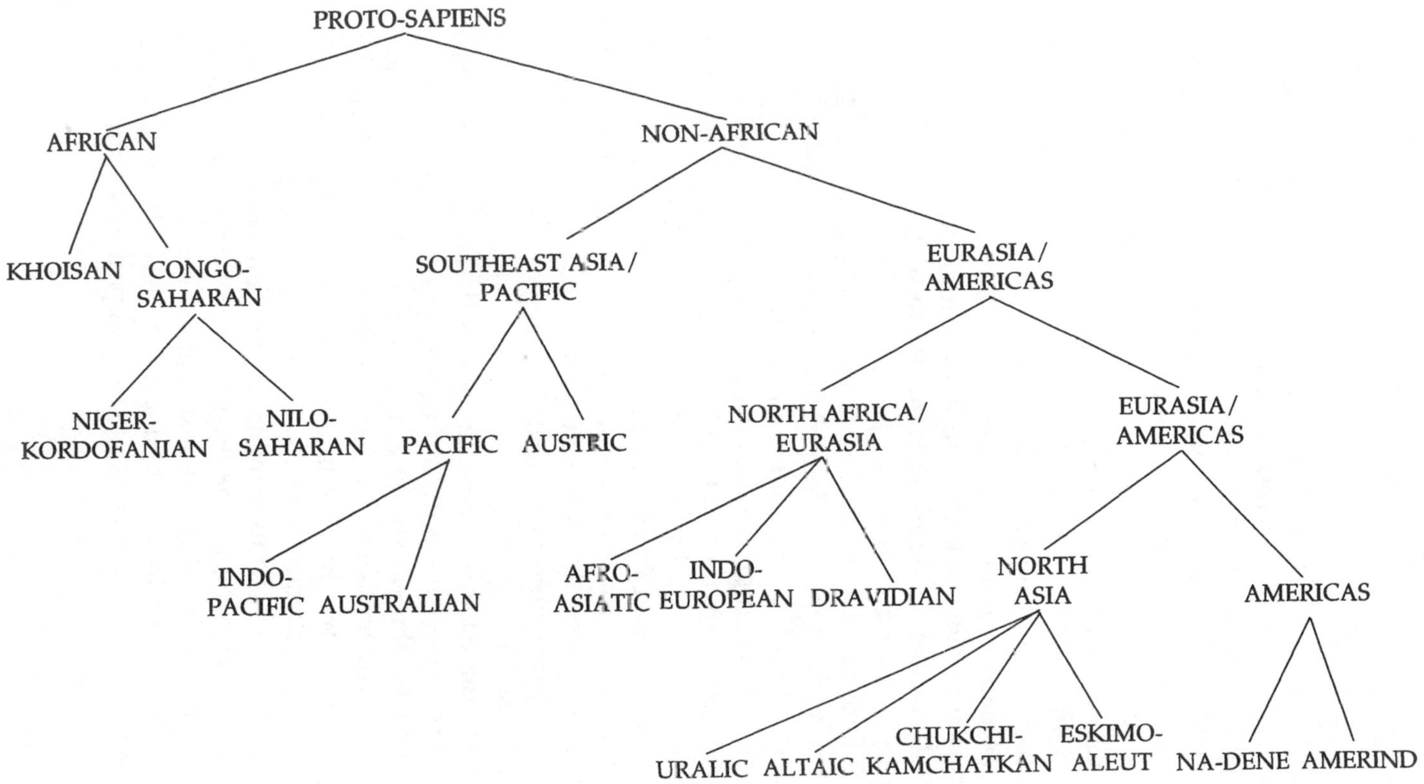

FIGURE 11   The genetic structure of the human population after Cavalli-Sforza et al. (1988).

and Amerind) appear closer genetically to the Asian branches of Eurasiatic than either is to the European branch (Indo-European). Nor are they close to either of Nostratic's two posited extensions to Eurasiatic (Dravidian and Afro-Asiatic); but because Indo-European-speaking peoples have been in continuous contact with both Afro-Asiatic- and Dravidian-speaking peoples, one might suspect that the association of Indo-European with these two families reflects gene flow over a long period of time. Linguistically, Indo-European seems closer to the members of the North Asia node in Figure 11 (Uralic, Altaic, Chukchi-Kamchatkan, and Eskimo-Aleut).

The most striking discrepancy between the linguistic evidence, as we have worked it out in the earlier chapters, and the genetic tree given in Figure 11 is that the Dene-Caucasian family is not to be found in the tree. Its absence is a consequence of several factors. First, genetic data were lacking for the Caucasian family, the Yeniseian family, and Burushaski; for that reason these families do not figure in the tree.

The Basque language is of course completely distinct from other European languages, and Cavalli-Sforza et al. (1994) show that Basque genes do in fact exhibit certain striking dissimilarities, such as a high frequency of Rh-negative genes, from the other European populations. But from a global perspective the Basque genes associate so closely with the other European populations that surround them that the Basques do not appear in Figures 10 and 11.

Of the three Dene-Caucasian groups that do appear in Figure 10, each associates with a different genetic cluster. Tibetan associates with the Northeast Asia cluster; south Chinese, with the Austric cluster; and Na-Dene, with the Amerind cluster. Though not shown in this figure, the north Chinese appear closer to the Northeast Asia cluster. A possible explanation of why the Dene-Caucasian families do not associate genetically with one another, despite the linguistic similarities we noted in Table 8, will be offered in the next chapter. For the moment we will simply observe that there appears to have been considerable genetic admixture between these groups and the surrounding populations.

The evidence we have been discussing up to this point is based on classical genetic markers such as blood groups and proteins. Recently, a team of geneticists led by the late Allan Wilson has been investigating human phylogeny on the basis of mitochondrial DNA, which is inherited strictly along the female line and is therefore easier to trace genealogically than nuclear genes. They found, as did the Cavalli-Sforza team using nuclear material, that the most basic cleavage in the human population separates sub-Saharan African populations from the rest of the world. This finding has recently been challenged as not the only—or perhaps even the best—solution to the problem, but it has not been shown to be incorrect. Inasmuch as the Cavalli-Sforza group arrived at the same results by different means, this basic division seems likely to be correct, though we have noted that linguistic evidence supporting this basic split is currently lacking.

The mitochondrial DNA of Native Americans has been studied by a number of molecular biologists, especially Douglas Wallace and his colleagues. Wallace has found that Native Americans who speak Amerind languages carry one of four maternal lineages of mitochondrial DNA that are found in Asian populations but not in European or African groups. Furthermore, the Na-Dene appear to have only a single lineage, which would imply that the Na-Dene and the Amerinds derive from different Asian populations and came to the Americas by separate migrations at what were no doubt quite different times. Other molecular biologists dispute Wallace's interpretation of his data, however, arguing that the four lineages could have come to the Americas in separate waves rather than within a single group. We should note that, although mitochondrial DNA is potentially an immensely powerful tool for the reconstruction of human prehistory, its use is only in its infancy, and further data and analysis will be required before any final conclusions can be reached. Nonetheless, the general congruence of Wallace's results with Greenberg's findings would seem to be significant—complementing, as it does, the similar conclusions derived from nuclear genetic material and human dentition.

Correlations on a Local Scale

Although Cavalli-Sforza's global results have garnered the most attention in the popular press, he has also found considerable parallelism between genes and languages in geographically more delimited areas (Cavalli-Sforza et al. 1994). Moreover, several other genetic laboratories around the world have also reported a strong correlation between genes and languages in various regions (for example Europe, Africa, Sardinia), or even in the dialects of individual languages (for example Yanomama).

In the United States the laboratory of Robert Sokal has published a series of papers focusing on the relationship between the distribution of genes and the distribution of languages in Europe. In one study they utilized a technique called "wombling" to identify biological boundaries at which gene frequencies change rapidly. They found

> ... 33 boundaries marking rapid genetic change. ... Of these, 31 represent modern boundaries between language families, languages within language families, or marked dialects. The two remaining boundaries are modern relics of ancient ethnic differences not affecting current speech. Once more, there is a close association between genetic and linguistic variation. (Sokal 1991: 132–33)

As regards the origin of these boundaries, Sokal and colleagues concluded that

> The demonstration of a linguistic component in addition to geographic differentiation ... and the near ubiquity of linguistic boundaries along the zones of rapid genetic change in Europe ... suggest historical as well as geographic components reponsible for the genetic differentiation of the European language families. Some of the observed genetic differences can clearly be associated with historical migration patterns of populations representing speakers of various languages, these speakers differing aboriginally in gene frequencies. (Sokal et al. 1990: 170)

Sokal and his colleagues Neal Oden and Guido Barbujani have applied the technique of wombling to a single Amerind tribe of South America, the Yanomama Indians. This tribe is thought to have expanded in both population size and territory over just the past hundred years, and today the Yanomama occupy some two dozen villages along the Brazil-Venezuela border. These villages belong to one of four dialect clusters (Yanomami, Yanomamö, Sanuma, and Ninam), and indeed the four recognized dialects are sufficiently dissimilar from one another that they might legitimately be considered separate languages. Sokal and colleagues concluded that "at the level of variation among dialect groups as well as within such groups the regions of rapid genetic change agree with observable linguistic differences. These findings support conclusions from other studies on the relation of genetics and language" (Barbujani, Oden, and Sokal 1989: 386).

In Switzerland, the genetics laboratory of André Langaney has found a high degree of correlation between the genes and languages of African populations:

> A rather clear distinction may . . . be made between Bantu and West Africans. As a matter of fact, they seem to form two overlapping but different clusters. . . . Concerning East Africans, the genetic data support quite clearly the main ethnic groupings defined by the linguistic approach. . . . Genetic results also completely concur with two other specific ethnic distinctions inside Africa, commonly known as Pygmies and Khoisan. . . . [I]t seems that a quite clear distinction may be made between East Africans, West Africans, Pygmies, Bantu, and Khoisan. These genetic differentiations agree mostly with linguistic rather than with purely geographical divisions. . . . East African Cushites and Ethiosemites, which both belong to the Afroasiatic linguistic family, appear to constitute a rather homogeneous and well-differentiated genetic group. . . . Genetic data, without any doubt, always separate Khoisan from other African populations. . . . It appears that most of the genetic peculiarities concerning present populations can be explained, when confronted with historical and linguistic sources, rather than being considered as examples of founder effects, random genetic drift, or frequency convergence. . . . Most of the time, genetic specificities correspond to linguistic differentiations. (Excoffier et al. 1987: 166–67; 181–82; 185)

These and other studies of the relationship between human genetics and comparative linguistics seem to be leading toward a better understanding of the origin and spread of modern humans around the earth. Beyond these two fields, archaeology, clearly, has a vital role to play in unraveling this intricate and complex history, and the integration of these three fields will be the subject of my concluding chapter. In closing here, however, it is fitting that we pay homage to Darwin, who, in *The Origin of Species* (1859), foresaw that biological and linguistic evolution would have to proceed along parallel lines:

> If we possessed a perfect pedigree of mankind, a genealogical arrangement of the races of man would afford the best classification of the various languages now spoken throughout the world; and if all extinct languages, and all intermediate and slowly changing dialects, were to be included, such an arrangement would be the only possible one.

8

The Emerging Synthesis

On the Origin of Modern Humans

There is today one species of animal that is found in virtually every nook and cranny of this planet, and it is not the cockroach. In scientific terminology the species (actually subspecies) is named *Homo sapiens sapiens*; in popular books like this one, these animals are often referred to as modern humans; in everyday parlance, they are usually just called people. But their past contrasts dramatically with their current ubiquity: if we go back just 100,000 years, a mere moment in biological time, the species appears to have been restricted to Africa; and if we go back only another 100,000 years or so the species does not exist at all. Where this animal originated, and how its various populations spread throughout the world, is the subject of this concluding chapter.

Our earlier inquiries have been concerned primarily with the question how can one use language to investigate human prehistory. We have also seen that geneticists—independently pursuing their own techniques of analysis and their own data—have arrived at conclusions very similar to those we reached on the basis of language. A third field in which human prehistory is a prime concern—indeed the *central* concern—is archaeology. For most of the twentieth century these three fields have gone their own separate ways, each developing its own goals, methods, and results. Yet all three have had as one goal a better understanding of human prehistory. During the past decade there has been a growing effort by a number of scholars to integrate the knowledge from these three diverse disciplines into a more general, but more precise, picture of the origin and spread of modern humans. The British archaeologist Colin Renfrew has coined the term the "Emerging Synthesis" to describe this increasingly cooperative effort. Needless to say, all the details of this vast and complex story are not yet known, but greater progress seems to have been made in the past decade than in the entire preceding century. In what follows we shall examine a few of the more important recent developments. For a comprehensive overview of the Emerging Synthesis, which discusses human genetics, linguistic families, and the archaeological record for the entire world, the reader should consult Cavalli-Sforza et al. (1994), but the following should serve as a useful overview.

An African Homeland?

There have been in recent years two general theories regarding where and when modern humans originated. According to the "Out of Africa" model, which is supported by most geneticists and many paleoanthropologists, modern humans migrated out of Africa sometime within the past 100,000 years, and in so doing replaced other hominids, such as Neanderthal Man in Europe and Solo Man in Asia, who were already occupying Eurasia. According to this view there was very little genetic admixture between the immigrants and the previous occupants of Eurasia. The second model of human origins, called "Multiregional Evolution," contends that there was no *recent* migration out of Africa, but rather that modern humans evolved from populations of *Homo erectus* that had been in Eurasia for the past million years. According to this theory, which is supported by some paleoanthropologists, modern humans developed independently in different regions at different times.

In recent years it would appear that the "Out of Africa" model has gained the upper hand. The genetic studies of Cavalli-Sforza and colleagues place the basic split in the human tree between sub-Saharan Africans and everyone else, and they date this split at some time after 100,000 B.P. Studies of mitochondrial DNA have posited the same basic split, though it has been claimed that other interpretations of these data are equally good. Beyond the structure of the genetic tree, whose primary division in Africa favors the theory of an African homeland for modern humans, the fact that sub-Saharan Africans show greater genetic diversity—both mitochondrial and nuclear—than do populations elsewhere in the world would also favor an African homeland, since one expects the greatest diversity in those areas that have been inhabited the longest, and in which, accordingly, variant forms will have had the longest time to emerge and accumulate. Furthermore, the oldest fossils of modern humans, as well as the oldest artifacts associated with modern humans, appear in the African archaeological record long before they appear elsewhere in the world. All of these considerations would appear to point toward an African homeland.

At present, linguistics is not particularly informative on these questions. As noted earlier, no one has yet devised a general linguistic subgrouping of the entire human family that might indicate the linguistic homeland of us all, and linguistics is all but useless at suggesting dates, at least at this time depth. Nevertheless, the linguistic evidence does support a recent, as opposed to a very ancient, date for the origin of modern languages, for otherwise the global linguistic similarities we have seen would not exist. On these grounds, at least, the linguistic evidence seems to favor the "Out of Africa" model over the "Multiregional Evolution" model. Furthermore, as with the genetic data, the greatest linguistic diversity appears to be in Africa. If you look again at Map 8 you will see that Africa contains four distinct (and very diverse) families in a relatively restricted geographical area, whereas directly north of Africa, in Europe, we encounter the Eurasiatic family, a single, coherent unit that literally circumnavigates the globe, extending across Eurasia into the Americas as far as Greenland. In the Americas a single family, Amerind, occupies most of North and South America. Yet despite the enormous geographical distribution of both Eurasiatic and Amerind, each is characterized by a single pronominal pattern. In Africa the pronominal patterns are more divergent than this even within each of the three sub-Saharan families. In sum, the linguistic evidence would seem to be at least consistent with the "Out of Africa" theory, if not demonstrably supportive of it.

Although the linguistic evidence cannot at the present time answer all the questions one might like to ask about human evolution, in certain areas, at least, it can provide us with compelling theories concerning the origin and spread of language families, and therefore of the speakers of their component languages. In the remainder of this chapter I will discuss several different episodes, large and small, in the Emerging Synthesis where the linguistic evidence, sometimes in conjunction with the genetic and archaeological evidence, seems to offer us a satisfying—or at least plausible—hypothesis for the distribution of a particular language family. Let us begin with the Dene-Caucasian family, whose peculiar geographical distribution we first noted in Map 6.

The Remnant Dene-Caucasians

In Table 8 we discovered a language family called Dene-Caucasian—a family conceived and elaborated by linguists only in the last decade—that comprises Basque, Caucasian, Burushaski, Sino-Tibetan, Yeniseian, and Na-Dene. Not only are its member families isolated from one another, separated by languages belonging to the Eurasiatic family, but the family as a whole fails to appear as a cohesive unit in the genetic tree of the world's populations shown in Figure 10—partly, of course, because genetic data were lacking for Caucasian, Yeniseian, and Burushaski. We also found that the four Dene-Caucasian populations on which information is available—Basque, Tibetan, south Chinese, and Na-Dene—each affiliated with a different genetic cluster. How are we to explain these contrary facts?

It seems to me that the discontiguous locations of the Dene-Caucasian families shown in Map 6—surrounded on all sides, so to speak, by Eurasiatic languages—suggest that we are dealing with two separate migrations. The map indicates that a first wave of expansion by Dene-Caucasian peoples was later overwhelmed by the Eurasiatic expansion, which left the formerly widespread Dene-Caucasian family restricted to isolated pockets in the least accessible—and most defensible—areas of its former occupation. The Basques in the Pyrenees mountains of northern Spain, the Caucasian peoples in the Caucasus mountains, and the Burushaski in the Hindu Kush mountains of northern Pakistan would appear to represent such remnant populations. The reasons for the survival of the other Dene-Caucasian families—Yeniseian, Sino-Tibetan, and Na-Dene—are less clear.

From a linguistic point of view, Eurasiatic seems to be a more obvious family than Dene-Caucasian, supported by more abundant and more transparent cognates, and this too would indicate that the Dene-Caucasian migration preceded the Eurasiatic expansion.

Why then did the Dene-Caucasian genes not appear as a unique cluster in Figure 10? Here, I believe, Basque gives us the answer. Recall from the last chapter that from a worldwide perspective the Basque genes are so similar to other European populations that Cavalli-Sforza lumped them in a single European cluster. But in a more detailed study focusing on Europe it *is* possible to find some genetic traits that characterize the Basques, such as the highest frequency of the Rh-negative gene of any population in the world. Despite their completely distinct language, which bears virtually no similarities to any other European languages, there has certainly been significant gene flow between the Basques and a later migration of people who moved into Europe within the past 10,000 years, replacing all of the languages previously spoken in Europe—except for Basque—with Indo-European languages.

It remains to be seen what the Caucasian, Burushaski, and Yeniseian genes will reveal, but it seems not unlikely that we will find considerable admixture with surrounding peoples there as well. As for Tibetan, it is believed that these people were once pastoral nomads on the steppes north of China who apparently adopted a Sino-Tibetan language. If this is so, their genes would still reflect this northern origin and their association with the Northeast Asia genetic cluster. I suspect that the association of Na-Dene with Amerind in Figure 10 is also the result of gene flow between these two contiguous populations over the past six or seven millennia.

In addition to whatever genetic differences there may have already been between the various Dene-Caucasian branches, in each case the populations speaking these languages have undergone genetic admixture with different populations in different parts of the world, to the point, at least for the Basques, that they are now genetically more similar to their neighbors than they are to their ancestral cousins elsewhere in the world. Notice that in cases of long-term gene flow between different peoples, the languages, rather than the genes, often preserve a clearer picture of the earliest state. The Basque language is totally distinct from its neighbors; the Basque genes are not. Why don't languages mix the way people do? I think the answer is obvious. Languages don't have sex.

The Peopling of the Americas

One of the areas where the Emerging Synthesis has had remarkable success in the past decade has been in understanding the original peopling of the New World, that is, the origins of the peoples who were living in the Americas prior to the arrival of Columbus in 1492. In Table 7 you found that Native American languages fall into three basic families, Eskimo-Aleut, Na-Dene, and Amerind, as postulated by Greenberg in 1987. This same classification was independently discovered by Cavalli-Sforza and colleagues (1988) on the basis of genes, and by Christy Turner (1989) on the basis of teeth. When three independent lines of evidence converge on a single solution, there is a strong presumption that that solution is correct.

The archaeological record in the New World provides a means of dating at least the first wave of immigration from Asia, the wave that brought the Amerind people to the Americas. What is clear in the archaeological record of the New World is that after about 11,500 B.P. there is abundant evidence of human occupation throughout North America (represented by the so-called Clovis culture that was first identified in Clovis, New Mexico), and only a thousand years later we find evidence of human occupation at the southern tip of South America. Before 11,500 B.P. there is almost no evidence of human occupation anywhere in the Americas, and the few purported sites of earlier occupation (one at the Meadowcroft Rock Shelter, Pennsylvania, dated to 16,000 B.P., one at Monte Verde, Chile dated to 13,000 B.P., and one at Pedra Furada, Brazil, reported to be over 40,000 years old) seem more likely to be the result of misanalysis than of genuine early occupation. Nevertheless, it must be acknowledged that the Pennsylvanian and Chilean sites have been excavated by respected archaeologists, and their conclusions have not been demonstrated to be incorrect, though they have certainly been shown to be discordant with most of the other evidence that now exists. A report on the Brazilian site has not yet been published, but because of the very early date and the apparently meager and controversial nature of the evidence, it seems unlikely that this one site will by itself forge a new scenario for the peopling of the Americas.

Perhaps future archaeological work in the New World will alter our current understandings, but for now the weight of the evidence very heavily favors the arrival of modern humans in the New World (there were never any earlier varieties of hominids in the Americas) around 11,500 B.P., followed by a rapid expansion throughout both North and South America and into the West Indies, perhaps in as short a time as one millennium.

For a single population to increase sufficiently in numbers to be able to expand through two continents in a thousand years, covering an expanse of close to 8,000 miles at an average of 8 miles a year, would seem to be a rather astounding accomplishment. Yet this is what the archaeological record indicates did happen, and biological models simulating this problem suggest that such a rapid expansion through unoccupied territory is indeed feasible. Furthermore, since these first Americans were entering a part of the world that had never seen humans before, there was an abundance of game that could be—and was—hunted. In fact, during the millennium in which the Amerind peoples spread through the Americas, countless species of large mammals became extinct, and we are led inescapably to the conclusion that they were hunted to extinction (though climatic change, attending the retreat of the ice sheet, has also been advanced as a principal cause of these extinctions).

Is there any linguistic evidence for such a rapid expansion? I believe there is. Recall that one of the lines of evidence supporting the Amerind family is a set of kinship terms in which the quality of the first vowel is determined by the gender of the person being referred to. On the basis of the evidence found in the modern Amerind languages, we can postulate that Proto-Amerind must have had three morphologically related words: *t'ina 'son, brother,' *t'ana 'child, sibling,' *t'una 'daughter, sister.' This complex system would be expected to break down—that is, to simplify itself—in largely predictable ways, and, as we have noted, no modern Amerind language preserves all three grades of this root. A few have two; many preserve one; and many others have none. What is important about this example is that all three grades of the root are equally well attested in both North and South America, as can be seen in Table 9. What this implies is that not only did these terms exist in the Proto-Amerind language that entered North America with the first immigrants, but they must also have still existed in the language of the first immigrants to South America, since all three grades are well attested in modern languages there as well. A rapid expansion through North and South America, which is supported by the archaeological record, would have played a crucial role in preserving this distinctive Amerind pattern on two continents.

One could of course hypothesize that the three different forms were brought to South America by different migrations from North America. However, the presence of two grades in a single South American language, such as Tiquie *ten* 'son,' *ton* 'daughter,' guarantees that at least this portion of the pattern was brought into South America as a system inherited from

Proto-Amerind (unless one hews to the unlikely possibility that *ten* 'son' and *ton* 'daughter' came into South America by separate migrations and were then reassembled in Tiquie in precisely the Proto-Amerind pattern). Furthermore, there is some evidence that South America was settled by what was essentially a single migration from North America. Once the narrow Isthmus of Panama was populated by the first migration from the north, there would have been a human barrier at this narrow juncture that would have impeded the easy passage of other Amerind groups from farther north. There are in fact indications that all of the South American Amerind languages constitute a single branch of the Amerind family (Ruhlen 1991b).

The Amerind population as a whole appears to be closer—both genetically and linguistically—to populations found in northern Asia than to populations anywhere else in the world. In the genetic tree shown in Figure 10, Amerind is closest to the Eurasiatic-speaking families of North Asia, as part of a vast genetic cluster that stretches from northern Africa through Eurasia and throughout the New World. In linguistic terms this huge cluster, which was considered one of the best supported nodes in the tree, consists essentially of Afro-Asiatic, Eurasiatic, and Amerind (the relationship of Dene-Caucasian to this cluster is unclear, for the reasons discussed above). It is striking that it was in just these families that we found the specific form aq'^wa 'water': Proto-Afro-Asiatic *aq'^wa 'water,' Proto-Indo-European *$ak^w\bar{a}$ 'water,' and Proto-Amerind *aq'^wa 'water.' The other families that appear to have retained this root show a more phonetically eroded form in which the consonant (q^w) has generally been simplified to k, as for example in Proto-Australian *$kuku$ 'water.'

The other two Native American families, Na-Dene and Eskimo-Aleut, represent two later waves of migration from Asia to North America. Na-Dene, whose homeland in the New World can be traced to the southern coast of Alaska, represents the easternmost extension of the Dene-Caucasian family. The homeland of the Eskimo-Aleut family, which spreads across North America to Greenland, was probably in southwestern Alaska, at the juncture of the Aleut and Eskimo languages. This family, as we have seen, represents the easternmost extension of the Eurasiatic family. But it is more difficult to attach dates to the second and third migrations because we are no longer dealing with a clean archaeological slate. It seems likely, however, that the Na-Dene family entered the Americas sometime between 10,000 and 5,000 B.P., and that the Eskimo-Aleut entered somewhat later.

The Bantu Expansion

I turn now to three episodes in the Emerging Synthesis in which the growth of agriculture seems to have played a major role in human migrations. Bear in mind that until around 10,000 years ago all human groups, in all areas of the world, subsisted by hunting and gathering. Farming and the domestication of animals were unknown. At about this time the retreat of the last great glaciers produced a warmer climate in the tropical and temperate zones, and the warming led in turn to the development of farming in several different regions of the world, no doubt independently: southwest Asia (the Fertile Crescent), China, the New Guinea highlands, southern Mexico, and western South America. The initial development of agriculture—with its accompanying tools—is known as the Neolithic Revolution. Its development appears to have proceeded at varying speeds, most quickly in southwest Asia and China, less rapidly elsewhere. In all of these cases, however, there appear to have been subsequent dispersals of the populations that had initiated the development of agriculture. The three episodes we shall examine are the spread of the Bantu across southern Africa, beginning about 2,300 years ago; the Austronesian expansion, which originated in southern China about 8,000 years ago and spread south to Indonesia and east across most of the Pacific islands; and Colin Renfrew's recent attempt to trace the origins of the Indo-European languages to an agricultural expansion from a base in Anatolia (modern Turkey), beginning about 8,000 years ago. In contrast to the Bantu and Austronesian examples, Renfrew's proposals for Indo-European remain highly controversial.

The Bantu migration is today a classic example of how linguistic, archaeological, and genetic data can be brought to bear on the same problem. Thanks to the complementary evidence of these three fields, the Bantu expansion is today fairly well understood, though (as we shall see) only a few short years ago it was the subject of a bitter controversy, not unlike that currently swirling around Amerind.

By the close of the eighteenth century, several scholars had noticed that the languages in the southern third of Africa exhibited an astonishing degree of similarity. Languages spoken over 2,000 miles apart seemed to be little more than dialects of a single language, as you discovered in Table 3. In 1858 the German scholar Wilhelm Bleek named this vast, but homogeneous, family Bantu. One of the salient characteristics of Bantu languages is that nouns are divided into a number of classes, much as Latin, German, and Russian nouns are divided into masculine, feminine, and neuter classes. In Bantu languages, however, there can be up to a dozen or more such classes, and although some classes have a well-defined semantic basis (for example personal, animate, paired objects, liquids, plants), other classes lack any obvious semantic basis and must be considered arbitrary sets. Depending on the noun class to which it belongs, each Bantu noun is preceded by a prefix that is different in the singular and plural forms. For example, the Bantu root -*ntu* 'man' belongs to the personal class in which the singular prefix is *mu*- and the plural prefix is *ba*-. Thus we have *muntu* 'man,' *bantu* 'men,' and it is this second term that Bleek adopted as the name of the family.

Because the Bantu languages are so similar, these early scholars concluded that their current vast distribution must be of relatively recent date, and the several hundred Bantu languages must be the modern descendants of a single Proto-Bantu language spoken sometime in the past. But where and when Proto-Bantu was spoken—and how and why this original population spread so rapidly throughout southern Africa—was not satisfactorily resolved until the second half of this century.

During the 1950's a controversy erupted over the homeland and subsequent spread of the various Bantu peoples. On one side was a young American linguist, Joseph Greenberg, who had produced a complete classification of African languages, a classification ten years in the making that went far beyond all previous attempts at synthesis. On the other side was the leading Bantuist of the era, Malcolm Guthrie, the head of the School of Oriental and African Studies at the University of London, at the time one of the leading centers of African language research in the world. Each proposed a scenario to account for the origin and spread of the Bantu peoples—and their scenarios were diametrically opposed. Greenberg located the Bantu homeland in the area of the Nigeria-Cameroon border, specifically in the central Benue valley of eastern Nigeria. Guthrie placed the Bantu homeland over a thousand miles to the southeast, in what is today Zaire (and then was the Belgian Congo).

The line of reasoning that led Greenberg to his conclusions was roughly as follows. If one first considers just the Bantu languages, one finds that the area of their greatest diversity—and hence the area where they have been diverging the longest—is in the extreme northwest of the Bantu-speaking area. There were hints of this even in Table 3, where, of the four Bantu languages listed, Duala (B), spoken in this extreme northwestern zone, seemed more divergent than do the other three Bantu languages (Mbundu [G], Swahili [J], Zulu [D]), the latter three often sharing almost identical forms. Had I chosen to give you a table just of Bantu languages, you would have seen immediately that the languages of the northwest region differ in significant ways from the rest of Bantu. The principle that the area with the greatest divergence is likely to be the region inhabited for the longest period of time is known in linguistics as the Age-Area hypothesis, and it is one of the techniques used to identify the original homeland of a family of languages.

The second step in Greenberg's argument rested on finding the Bantu family's closest relatives. If a language is widely dispersed, but its closest relative occupies only a small region, the usual historical explanation is that the broadly dispersed language was originally spoken in a much more circumscribed area, side by side with its closest relative, and spread to its present distribution only later. This is sometimes referred to as the *principle of least moves*. To see how this principle works, consider the Vietnamese language, which is spoken along the coast of Southeast Asia from China to the southern tip of Vietnam. It is reasonable to assume that this language spread along the coast in one direction or the other, but which, and from where? It so happens that Vietnamese is most closely related to a relatively obscure language known as Muong, spoken by just over 700,000 people in the northern regions of Vietnam, and this fact suggests that Vietnamese originally spread from this northern region southward to its present distribution. The fact that Vietnamese dialects in the north are more divergent than those in the south—which invokes the Age-Area hypothesis—confirms the hypothesis of a northern origin.

Who Bantu's closest relatives were was no mystery, as Greenberg was well aware, for there had long been identified in West Africa, in the area of Nigeria, a group of languages that were commonly referred to as "Semi-Bantu." These languages were generally considered a subgroup of an even larger family called West Sudanic. Not only do the Bantu, "Semi-Bantu," and West Sudanic languages show similar words, but there are traces of the Bantu noun-class system throughout the West Sudanic family. Greenberg noted that still other languages show these class markers and accordingly renamed this enlarged West Sudanic family Niger-Congo. He also objected that there was no more reason to call Bantu's closest relatives "Semi-Bantu" than there would be to call Dutch, German, and Swedish "Semi-English," and therefore abandoned the term, selecting Benue-Cross as the name of the subgroup of Niger-Congo to which the entire Bantu family belonged. He noted that had Bantu been a single language, spoken alongside the other Benue-Cross languages, it would have been accepted as a member of that group without dissent because of the obvious similarities. It was thus such nonlinguistic factors as its broad distribution and great numbers of speakers that had led to the false dichotomy between Bantu and West Sudanic. Taxonomically, Bantu could hardly be considered anything other than one member of one subgroup of West Sudanic, or even of the larger group Greenberg called Niger-Congo. In short, Greenberg presented evidence for a vast Niger-Congo family, the half-dozen or so subgroups of which are all located in West Africa. One member (Bantu) of one subgroup (Benue-Cross) had, within relatively recent times, expanded from this original homeland throughout southern Africa, in the process giving rise to the Bantu family.

Guthrie saw things quite differently. First of all, he made no attempt to conceal his disdain—perhaps even contempt—for Greenberg's methods and results. "Clearly the serious investigation of the prehistory of Africa demands something more than speculative hypotheses, and for this reason it is essential that any conclusions drawn from linguistic information shall be based on a firm basis of codified data," he declared (Guthrie 1962). Guthrie proposed a new approach: "In order to meet the fundamental condition that hypotheses should be built only on facts that are demonstrably true, I began some fifteen years ago to adopt a quite different method of comparative study. The aim of the investigation was to produce results in prehistory that would be based on verifiable observations" (Guthrie 1962).

Without going into the details of Guthrie's new approach, his conclusions on Bantu origins ran roughly as follows. The Proto-Bantu were located in southeastern Zaire, from whence, at a certain time, they began to expand in all directions, leading to the present Bantu distribution. Guthrie put the homeland in Zaire because it was in this area that Bantu roots seemed to be best preserved; as one progressed in any direction from this nucleus, as Guthrie called it, the Bantu traits gradually dissipated. In the northwest region of the Bantu territory, in particular, the aberrant traits became particularly distinctive, and farther on, in West Africa, there were merely traces of Bantu-like features.

Guthrie was not really interested in why features in scattered languages across West Africa were uncannily similar to Bantu, and would have preferred to ignore them, had this problem—and others—not been raised by his own colleagues. There were several problems with Guthrie's proposals, in particular the Bantu-like features in the West African languages and the deviant Bantu forms in the northwestern region, both of which had to be explained somehow. But for historians like Roland

Oliver at Guthrie's own school, the central issue was not just mapping the current distribution of Bantu languages, but in *explaining* what historical processes might have led to the present distribution. What advantage, or advantages, could have allowed one small population to overrun the southern third of Africa? It had already been suggested that iron-making, which had arisen in Nigeria some time prior to the Bantu expansion, might have given the Proto-Bantu the impetus to expand throughout southern Africa—at the expense of hunter-gatherers, who lacked any form of metallurgy. Oliver suspected, rather, that it was agriculture—or a combination of agriculture and iron-working—that had enabled the Bantu to expand so explosively. When pressed to explain these recalcitrant data, Guthrie refined his theory.

Perhaps, he speculated, before the Proto-Bantu expansion from Zaire ensued, there had been a Pre-Bantu stage, at which time the Bantu ancestors lived far to the north, around Lake Chad. One group from this area made its way to Zaire and became the Proto-Bantu; another group migrated westward, and it was through contact with this group that various West African languages absorbed Bantu features, for which Guthrie proposed the name "Bantuisms." But except for the absorbed Bantuisms in the West African languages, there is no trace of this Pre-Bantu group, nor is there any trace of Pre-Bantu peoples, or their descendants, around Lake Chad. And as for the deviant northwest Bantu forms, Guthrie chided Greenberg for "ignoring such things as terrain and vegetation" and proposed that the poor preservation of these languages was "probably due to a greater rate of decay under forest conditions." The fact that climate is not known to have *any* affect on linguistic evolution was ignored, overlooked, or forgotten.

When pressed by Oliver on the question how the Proto-Bantu in Zaire came to possess the knowledge of metal-working that ignited the Bantu expansion, Guthrie speculated that perhaps a band of Nigerians, "refugees from the slave raids of iron-using chiefs," had brought metallurgy to the Proto-Bantu. According to the British historian Colin Flight, who has studied the historical aspects of the Bantu controversy in a series of penetrating articles:

Oliver's reaction [to Guthrie's proposals] was muted. He was not averse to speculation as such, yet there had to be some limit to what was permissible. . . . Even if Guthrie was right [in locating the Bantu homeland in Zaire], the imaginary Nigerians were not to be taken seriously. Isolated migrations by small groups of people—refugees, warriors, blacksmiths, hunters—might or might not have occurred; but the Bantu expansion was not to be explained by reference to petty events of this kind. (Flight 1988: 823)

Oliver struggled on for some time in a vain attempt to reconcile Guthrie's views with Greenberg's. Gradually, however, as the archaeological record in sub-Saharan Africa came to better known (Phillipson 1977), and as Greenberg's linguistic arguments came to be more appreciated, there emerged a consensus that Greenberg had been correct in virtually every aspect of the controversy. According to Flight, Guthrie's historical work "was a disaster. The evidence could hardly have been more completely misconstrued. . . . It ought to have been obvious to everyone, perhaps not from the beginning, but at least by 1962, that his reconstruction [of Bantu prehistory] was wrong—not just wrong in certain details, but grossly and gratuitously wrong" (Flight 1980: 108).

The present view of Bantu origins places the homeland near the Nigeria-Cameroon border, exactly where Greenberg put it four decades ago, and dates the beginning of the Bantu expansion to around 300 B.C. This area, situated just north of the equatorial rain forest, had long posed a problem for those seeking to explain the Bantu migration southward. How had the Proto-Bantu traversed this dense jungle, which was inimicable to all forms of agriculture, and gone on to populate southern Africa? One possibility was that they had somehow moved directly south, perhaps following the coastline of West Africa. Or perhaps they had bypassed the rain forest entirely, moving first eastward along its northern fringe until they arrived in the Great Lakes region of East Africa, where the rain forest ends and a movement to the south would have been feasible. Archaeological evidence indicates that both of these routes were taken.

These two different paths gave rise to a Western group and an Eastern group of Bantu languages, but the distinction was soon blurred by a westward movement of members of the Eastern group, who eventually merged with the Western group. Early in the first millennium A.D. the Eastern group began to expand southward and eastward to the coast. Meanwhile, the western stream was expanding eastward, and by the fifth century A.D. had established a center in Zaire, from which further expansion, beginning in the eleventh century A.D., carried Western Bantu languages over much of East Africa, replacing the Eastern Bantu dialects formerly spoken there.

As for the prime impetus for the Bantu migration, current opinion sees agriculture as having been chiefly responsible. Iron-working was adopted by some Bantu groups, and no doubt played a significant role in certain regions, but it does not appear to have been part of the original Proto-Bantu tool kit. Rather, it was the cultivation of yams in West Africa, and later various cereals from East Africa, that set in motion the Bantu expansion a little over two millennia ago. In the words of the British archaeologist David Phillipson, who has studied the Bantu migration extensively, "we can therefore see what a marked degree of similarity there is between the archaeological sequence of the Iron Age in subequatorial Africa and the linguistic evidence for the spread and development of the Bantu languages and their speakers" (Phillipson 1977: 114).

Recently, as we noted in the preceding chapter, human geneticists have found that Bantu is a meaningful entity in their field as well. According to Cavalli-Sforza (1991: 109), "Bantu—originally a linguistic category—can now be extended to designate a group of populations having both a linguistic and a genetic basis."

The Austronesian Expansion

The Bantu expansion was by no means the first large-scale dispersal of modern humans that was instigated by the development of agriculture; in fact, it was one of the later episodes. Much earlier, an expansion that began in southern China ultimately led to the peopling of almost every island in the Pacific

Ocean, as well as Madagascar, far to the west, off the east coast of Africa.

At the time of the inception of agriculture in China, most of the Pacific islands were uninhabited. Australia and New Guinea—as well as the islands that connected them with Southeast Asia—had been occupied since at least 40,000 B.P., and perhaps even as early as 50,000 years ago. A few of the islands to the east of New Guinea were also inhabited, but beyond the Solomon Islands all the rest of the Pacific islands remained unoccupied.

The archaeological record of Southeast Asia indicates that the Neolithic revolution in this part of the world began in China around 8,000 years ago. Evidence of the cultivation of millet, in the Yellow River basin, and of rice, to the south, in the Yangzi basin, dates to about that time. By 5,000 B.P. farming had spread from this agricultural center southward to Vietnam and Thailand and eastward to the coast of China. From this time period archaeologists have uncovered villages with their accompanying pottery, stone and bone tools, boats and paddles, rice, and the bones of such domesticated animals as dogs, pigs, chicken, and cattle.

About 6,000 years ago one or more of these agricultural groups crossed the Strait of Formosa (now the Taiwan Strait) and became the first inhabitants of Taiwan. And from Taiwan these shipbuilding agriculturists spread first southward to the Philippines, and then eastward and westward throughout most of Oceania. The archaeological record indicates that the northern Philippines were reached by 5,000 B.P., and 500 years later these migrants had spread as far south as Java and Timor, as far west as Malaysia, and eastward to the southern coast of New Guinea. By around 3,200 B.P. the expansion had reached Madagascar, far to the west, and had spread as far east as Samoa, in the central Pacific, and the Mariana Islands and Guam, in Micronesia. During the next millennium the expansion spread to encompass the remainder of Micronesia. The final step in this vast human dispersal was the occupation of the Polynesian islands: by 400 A.D. the Hawaiian Islands and Easter Island—the most northern and eastern islands of Polynesia—had been occupied; while New Zealand—the most southern island group in Polynesia—was not reached until around 800 A.D.

This bare-bones account is based entirely on the archaeological record, as worked out by the English archaeologist Peter Bellwood (1991) and others, and of necessity presents little more than a relative chronology of one of the broadest dispersals in human prehistory. Unmentioned are the extraordinary navigational skills these peoples developed, and the remarkable boats they constructed to facilitate trans-oceanic voyages across hundreds, even thousands, of miles of open water. Overlooked too are such details as the fact that the crops that initially propelled the expansion, rice and millet, were in the course of the expansion replaced by other crops more suited to new lands and new soils, such as tropical fruits and tubers. The original culture changed in other ways, too, for example establishing regional variations in pottery design. No doubt there were local developments in languages and genes as well, the former diverging owing to separation and long isolation, the latter mixed along the way with the genes of various aboriginal populations—in those regions where there *were* aboriginal populations.

But who were the people who carried this culture throughout the Pacific and left these artifacts? And what languages did they speak? Here, as in the Bantu case, the artifacts themselves reveal nothing of the language of the people who used them. Yet in both cases it is clear who these people were, and it seems certain that the people who carried this particular Southeast Asian culture throughout the Pacific were the ancestors of those who today speak Austronesian languages. The dispersal is accordingly known as the Austronesian expansion.

It is striking how well the internal subgrouping of the Austronesian language family, which is based solely on linguistic evidence, corroborates the archaeological evidence just surveyed. According to the American linguist Robert Blust, the primary division in the family is between those languages spoken on Taiwan and those spoken elsewhere. (The Chinese occupation of Taiwan did not begin until 1626, over five millennia after the initial Austronesian occupation of the island.) It is even possible that the aboriginal Taiwanese languages constitute three distinct primary branches and that all of the extra-Taiwanese languages collectively constitute a fourth. The other divisions in the huge family posited by Blust—again, on strictly linguistic evidence—accord well with the archaeological record, and the vast, but homogeneous, Polynesian family constitutes simply the final branching in the family tree.

If the people who became the Austronesian family came to Taiwan from the mainland, one might legitimately ask what populations found today in Southeast Asia are closest to Austronesian. The American linguist Paul Benedict answered this question a half-century ago. Benedict showed that Austronesian was related to a group of fairly obscure languages spoken in southern China, which he named Tai-Kadai. Thai and Laotian (which are really dialects of one language, despite their separate names) are the only well-known members in this group. The implication is thus that one group from the Tai-Kadai cluster managed to navigate the Strait of Formosa and populate a previously uninhabited island, and in so doing became the Proto-Austronesians.

What is known of human genetics in this part of the world also fits rather well with the picture of the Austronesian dispersal worked out on archaeological and linguistic grounds, as seen in Figure 10. In the genetic tree the six Austronesian populations are closest to three Southeast Asian populations, one of which is Thai. In fact, three of the Austronesian groups (Indonesian, Malaysian, Phillipine) are closer genetically to the three Southeast Asian groups than they are to the other three Austronesian groups (Melanesian, Micronesian, and Polynesian). No doubt admixture with local populations during the Austronesian dispersal is at least partly responsible for this discrepancy.

Discrepancies aside, the archaeological record, the linguistic evidence, and the distribution of human genes all allow us— once again—to assemble a satisfying panorama of one of the greatest migrations in human prehistory.

The Indo-European Expansion

The Indo-European family has more speakers, and is spoken more widely around the globe, than is any other comparable language family. Its enormous distribution is due to two important expansions. The more recent, set in motion by Christopher Columbus five centuries ago, carried Indo-European languages like English, Spanish, Portuguese, French, and Dutch to the farthest corners of the earth. The more ancient, which is the one that concerns us here, was responsible for the original distribution of Indo-European languages as attested prior to 1492, which (as we saw in Map 1) extended from Iceland to India.

Inasmuch as the Indo-European family was first discovered over two centuries ago, and since that time has been the subject of more historical work than have all the other language families in the world combined, you might well expect that the Proto-Indo-European homeland and its subsequent path of dispersion would be one of the best understood of all human migrations. Such, however, is not the case. In fact, just about every aspect of the Indo-European dispersal—its place of origin, its timing, its path, and the former cultures it overran—remains even today a major center of controversy among linguists, archaeologists, and geneticists, and it is fair to say that no consensus has yet emerged on these questions. Indeed, even the question of who should resolve the issue of Indo-European origins—the linguists or the archaeologists—elicits sharply opposing views. The American archaeologist Marija Gimbutas has claimed that "it is quite obvious that the solution of Indo-European origins—on a spatial and temporal basis—is in the hands of the archaeologists" (quoted in Dolgopolsky 1988: 7). Dolgopolsky, however, maintains that "linguists are ultimately responsible for determining the geographical and cultural parameters of the Proto-Indo-European community, and . . . any attempt on the part of the archaeologists to reach a conclusion without due consideration of all the relevant linguistic data is liable to lead them into serious error" (Dolgopolsky 1988: 7).

Let us, then, begin our search for Indo-European origins with what is known and agreed upon, and from this firm foundation enter the shadowy territories of interpretation and dispute. The archaeological record of Europe and the Near East shows quite clearly that agriculture developed for the first time (anywhere in the world) around 10,000 years ago, in a Fertile Crescent that extended from Anatolia (modern Turkey) to Mesopotamia (modern Iraq). Agriculture, involving wheat and barley, was well established in Anatolia by 7,000 B.C., and from here its spread may be traced in the archaeological record first to Greece, between 6,000 and 5,000 B.C., then to the nearby Balkans, and on to central and north-central Europe. It took no more than one millennium for farming to spread from Greece as far as Germany and Poland. A separate, and probably later, development carried agriculture to southern Italy, and then into France, Spain, and the British Isles. By 3,000 B.C. agriculture had reached England, and by 2,000 B.C. it is found on the Atlantic coast of Portugal.

How and why, then, did agriculture spread from the Near East to Europe? These are questions that the silent artifacts of the archaeological record cannot answer. Two possibilities immediately suggest themselves. The first is that farming was continuously borrowed by neighboring groups who perceived the agricultural life to be superior to their own hunting-and-gathering lifestyle. If this were the case, then there would have been no movement of people, simply the gradual spread of the knowledge of farming from one group to the next by means of cultural diffusion. The second possibility is that farming was carried to Europe by the gradual expansion of the farmers themselves, who, as in the Bantu and Austronesian cases, gradually encroached upon—and ultimately either absorbed or eliminated—the aboriginal hunter-gatherers who had long inhabited Europe. These two scenarios are, of course, not mutually exclusive; some hunter-gatherers may have adopted agriculture from the expanding farmers; others may not have.

How might one determine which of these two possibilities was the actuality? During the 1970's the American archaeologist Albert Ammerman and the geneticist Luca Cavalli-Sforza devised an ingenious method of testing the two. They reasoned as follows. If the farmers had *themselves* spread from Anatolia throughout Europe, then so too would their genes. As the progeny of the farmers spread through Europe, the original gene frequencies of their Anatolian forebears, which they would have carried, would have been affected by the gene frequencies of the existing aboriginal populations (in those cases where gene frequencies differed substantially in the two populations). The result of such admixture would have been a gradual shift in the gene frequencies that would be reflected as a *cline* running from the southeast corner of the region (Anatolia) to northwestern Europe. Let us assume for example, that the aboriginal populations of Europe, before the arrival of the farmers, had a very high frequency of the Rh-negative gene, whereas the farmers had a very low frequency. As the farmers spread through these populations with a high frequency of this gene, the frequency of the gene in the farming population would concomitantly rise, increasingly so as it progressed through the original inhabitants, ultimately yielding a clinal gradation from the southeast to the northwest.

If, on the other hand, it was not the farmers *themselves* that had migrated, but merely their ideas, then the original aboriginal genetic structure would have been unaffected, and one would not expect this particular cline, or any other. When Ammerman and Cavalli-Sforza analyzed the known genetic data, which in Europe was already substantial, they found that there was indeed a cline running from Anatolia to northwestern Europe (a color picture of this cline appeared on the cover of *Science* magazine in 1978). Because of their findings, I believe, it is now generally accepted that the Anatolian farmers did in fact expand in much the manner of the Bantu and Austronesian families. It was not the *ideas* that had spread; it was the *people themselves*.

But who precisely were these Anatolian farmers? It seems almost obvious that these people who carried their genes and their knowledge of farming to Europe must have been the Proto-Indo-Europeans themselves, for it is today—with very few exceptions—Indo-European languages that are found in the area occupied by the genetically corroborated expansion of the Anatolian farmers. You will no doubt be surprised to learn that this very plausible idea was not proposed until 1987, when Colin Renfrew argued for just this scenario of the origin of the

Indo-European languages. You will no doubt also be surprised to learn that Renfrew's hypothesis has not been well received, and indeed has been rejected by many linguists, archaeologists, and geneticists. Others, however, do side with Renfrew.

If the Anatolian farmers were not Indo-Europeans, who were they? And where did the Indo-Europeans come from, if not from Anatolia? A totally different version of Indo-European origins had developed earlier in this century, a version that had become widely accepted by both archaeologists and linguists. According to this view, first proposed by V. Gordon Childe in 1926 and currently associated with the work of Marija Gimbutas, the original Indo-European homeland was in what is today Ukraine, the recently independent country located to the north of the Black Sea. From these steppes, horsemen were supposed to have swept westward into Europe just prior to the Bronze Age, around 3,000 B.C. These were a people who buried their leaders in large mounds, called "kurgans" in Russian, and, drawing upon this term, archaeologists speak of the "Kurgan" invasions that brought speakers of Proto-Indo-European from the Pontic steppes to the heart of Europe. From these invasions derive the modern Indo-European languages. Such was the view at the time of Renfrew's radical proposals.

Renfrew's proposal, as you can now see, could hardly have been more at odds with the accepted consensus. It placed the Indo-European homeland in Anatolia, across the Black Sea from the Ukraine. It put the date of Proto-Indo-European at 6,500 B.C., not 4,000 B.C. And it connected the spread of the Indo-European languages with the gradual, almost imperceptible, expansion of a peaceful agricultural population, not with the mounted warriors from the steppes who had, according to the traditional view, conquered Europe.

We have examined the line of reasoning that led to Renfrew's proposal, but what is the basis of the traditional model? On what evidence does it base its homeland, its date of dispersal, and its explanation for the cause of the dispersal? The choice of homeland is based on the fact that there were certainly Kurgan invasions from the steppes; the date is based on the timing of these incursions, as well as on the *estimated* age of the Indo-European family; the reason for the incursion was the perpetual battle between the mounted and armed warriors from the steppes and the rich agricultural produce of Europe that virtually called out for pillaging.

Is there any way of discriminating between these two very different proposals? We saw earlier how the genetic evidence from modern European populations could be used to decide between two possible interpretations of the archaeological record. Might we not in the present instance use linguistic evidence to determine the question of the Indo-European homeland, much as linguistic evidence was used to determine the Bantu and Austronesian homelands?

According to the American biologist Jared Diamond, "Renfrew's theory ignores or dismisses all the linguistic evidence" (Diamond 1992: 267). It is certainly true that Renfrew's book overlooked a great deal of linguistic evidence that bears on the question of the Indo-European homeland. But at virtually the same time that Renfrew's book appeared, Aron Dolgopolsky was publishing a masterly survey of the linguistic evidence for the Indo-European homeland, and he found, as had Renfrew, that all the evidence pointed to Anatolia. Neither Renfrew nor Dolgopolsky was aware of the other's work at the time they were pursuing their research.

Let us, then, take a look at Dolgopolsky's linguistic arguments for an Anatolian homeland. First, he points out that the internal structure of the Indo-European family itself indicates an Anatolian homeland. His argument is as follows. As early as 1933 the American linguist Edgar Sturtevant showed that the Indo-European family consists of two branches, Anatolian and non-Anatolian, and he proposed to call the entire family Indo-Hittite, while the branch containing all the non-Anatolian languages would retain the traditional name Indo-European. But what evidence is there that the Anatolian branch is distinct from all the rest? One crucial piece of evidence is that the Anatolian branch has just two genders, animate and inanimate, whereas in the non-Anatolian branch these two genders have developed into three, masculine, feminine, and neuter. (We know that the two-gender system must have given rise to the three-gender system, rather than the reverse, because there are traces of the two-gender system in a few non-Anatolian languages.) This is but one of a number of innovations common to the non-Anatolian Indo-European languages, and taken together they virtually guarantee that the first split in the family was between the Anatolian branch and the remainder. In Renfrew's view this first split occurred when the Anatolian farmers first spread to Greece, 8,000 years ago.

There is thus clear evidence that Anatolian was the first branching in the family—and Sturtevant's Indo-Hittite hypothesis turned out to be correct. But despite that evidence the traditional Indo-Europeanists have rejected the Indo-Hittite hypothesis as staunchly as they have opposed the idea that Indo-European is related to other language families. Some Indo-Europeanists have even gone so far as to adopt the bizarre position that Anatolian was indeed the first branching, but that the Indo-Hittite hypothesis is nonetheless to be rejected! Lest one suspect that I am inventing a straw man, consider what the Indo-Europeanist Calvert Watkins has written in the *International Encyclopedia of Linguistics* in the article on "Indo-European Languages": "A number of archaic features in morphology and phonology set Anatolian apart from the other branches, and indicate that it was the earliest to hive off." In other words, Sturtevant was correct and the Indo-Hittite hypothesis is to be accepted. Well, not quite. Watkins immediately adds: "But Anatolian remains derivable from P[roto-]I[ndo-]E[uropean]; and periodic efforts to situate Anatolian as a sister langauge to I[ndo-]E[uropean], with both deriving from a putative 'Indo-Hittite,' have not found a following." One is left to wonder what kind of science this is, when the view that is acknowledged to be correct has not been allowed to find a following.

Once the Anatolian branch has been factored out, on the grounds just given, where do we find the greatest diversity in the rest of the family—the vast array that Sturtevant called Indo-European? Dolgopolsky argues that it is the area of the Balkans—the extremity of Europe closest to Anatolia—that shows the greatest diversity among the remaining languages. Among the dozen or so recognized branches of Indo-European, almost half were originally found in the Balkans, though most of these (for example Phrygian, Thracian, Illyric) have long since been extinct, having been replaced in historic times by incursions of languages from the Slavic and Romance branches of Indo-European, and by Hungarian. Only Greek and Albanian continue branches from this earliest expansion. In Renfrew's theory the area of secondary dispersal of the Indo-European family, once it spread outside Anatolia, is located in the Balkans, again agreeing perfectly with Dolgopolsky's proposals.

Probably the strongest argument for an Anatolian homeland is to be found in the evidence of loanwords. The presence of borrowings between languages can often be used to tell where and when the two languages were in contact. Had the Proto-Indo-European homeland been in the Ukraine, it would have had different neighbors—and hence would have borrowed different words—than it would if the homeland had been in Anatolia. From what families, Dolgopolsky asked, do the known borrowings in Proto-Indo-European derive? Of all the families that might have been in contact with Proto-Indo-European—depending on the various proposed homelands—Dolgopolsky found evidence of borrowing only from Proto-Semitic and Proto-Kartvelian, both of which would have been virtually contiguous with a Proto-Indo-European homeland in eastern Anatolia. Notable also is the complete absence of any borrowings between Proto-Uralic and Proto-Indo-European, in either direction. Had the Proto-Indo-Europeans in fact been living in the steppes north of the Black and Caspian Seas, as the traditional model maintains, their immediate neighbors to the east would have been the Uralic people. That there were no borrowings between these two groups indicates that they could not in fact have lived side by side. (There were later contacts between the Finno-Ugric branch of Uralic and the Indo-Iranian branch of Indo-European that resulted in borrowings between these two smaller groups, but these contacts occurred much later and do not bear on the question of the Indo-European homeland.)

Examples of Proto-Indo-European words that were borrowed from Proto-Semitic include *tauro- 'bull' (from Proto-Semitic *θawr- 'bull, ox'), *ghaido- 'kid, goat' (from Proto-Semitic *gadj- 'kid, goat'), *woino- 'wine' (from Proto-Semitic *wajn- 'wine, grapes, vine'), *Haster- 'star' (from Proto-Semitic *ʕaθtar (-at)- 'evening/morning star, Venus'), and *septm̥- 'seven' (from

Proto-Semitic *šabʕ-at-u-m* 'seven'). Now if the Indo-European homeland had been in the Ukraine, the Proto-Indo-Europeans would never have been in contact with Proto-Semitic-speakers. How, then, could these (and other) borrowings have taken place? At best they might have been borrowed into the Anatolian branch, but they would never have passed on into the Indo-European family as a whole.

It seems to me that the linguistic evidence presented by Dolgopolsky fits Renfrew's archaeologically based model like a glove. They agree on virtually every point. When confronted with the traditional model, the Renfrew-Dolgopolsky-Cavalli-Sforza model seems to me much better supported by the evidence. It provides a reasonable cause of the spread of Indo-European languages (agriculture). It provides a homeland (Anatolia) and general rate of expansion that can be traced in the archaeological record. The genes of the farmers can be traced to this same homeland. And the languages *now* spoken in the area into which the farmers expanded all (with few exceptions) belong to a family of languages (Indo-European) whose homeland can be traced back to Anatolia. As in the Bantu and Austronesian cases, there is a perfect congruence of genes, languages, and the archaeological record of the expansion of an agriculturally driven migration.

Let us once again compare this model with the traditional view of Indo-European origins, according to which mounted warriors swept westward from the Pontic steppes and brought their Proto-Indo-European language to western Europe. What propelled this migration, according to Diamond and others who support the traditional model, was the invention of metallurgy and the domestication of horses, the combination of which allowed these peoples to invade the lands to the west. I do not doubt that such attacks of the Kurgan peoples took place; similar attacks by the Huns, Turks, and Mongols are known from a later time. But in none of these later attacks did the invaders leave behind any trace of their languages. Yet the earlier Kurgan invasions, which never penetrated farther west than Hungary and left behind no trace of their genes, are supposed to be responsible for completely replacing the languages of the Anatolian farmers who were already occupying all of Europe. How such a massive linguistic replacement could have been accomplished is difficult to imagine. Although it is easy to understand how the languages of an expanding *agricultural* society would replace those of hunter-gatherers—since farming can support a population fifty times greater than that of foragers—we can be sure that it was not by dint of numbers that the Kurgan invaders dominated the farmers. Furthermore, the technology of mounted horsemen developed slowly, and it is probable that these first horsemen rode into Europe bareback, with saddles yet to be invented. I do not doubt that these early horsemen wreaked havoc on the farmers they attacked, just as the later attacks of the Turks and Mongols did, but that they were able to completely replace all the languages then spoken in Europe stretches credulity. I do not believe the Indo-European expansion is to be explained by reference to petty events of this kind, if I may borrow Flight's apt phrasing in commenting on the Bantu debates.

And if the Indo-European languages came from the Pontic steppes in the fourth millennium B.C., then what languages did the farmers from Anatolia bring with them to Europe during the agricultural expansion that began three millennia earlier? Diamond suggests that Basque and a few sparsely attested languages like Etruscan are the remnant languages of the early farmers. But if this were the case, then the languages of the farmers would have been little more differentiated at the time of the Indo-European (Kurgan) invasion than are Bantu languages today, inasmuch as a time interval between two and three millennia would be responsible for the linguistic diversity in both cases. Basque is the only extant, and hence the only well-known, language from this early period, but what we know of Etruscan and other extinct languages of Europe leaves little doubt that they were *vastly* more divergent than are the modern Bantu tongues. Were one to take comparable amounts of information from two Bantu languages (that is, complete information for one of them, and from another an amount comparable to what is known of Etruscan), it would be immediately apparent that both were Bantu languages. This is certainly not the case for Basque and Etruscan, nor for any of the other extinct languages of Europe.

It should be noted that the traditional model adds an extra layer to the prehistory of European populations. Since the Anatolian farmers are claimed to be responsible for the languages in Europe (Basque, Etruscan) at the advent of the Indo-European (Kurgan) invasion, then there must have been completely *different* languages in Europe *before* the Anatolian farmers poured into Europe. With the Renfrew model, by contrast, the paleolithic languages like Basque were *already in place* before the coming of the agricultural Indo-Europeans (from Anatolia), and an extra round of language replacement is not needed.

Finally, when and how did these mounted warriors from the Ukraine borrow words from Proto-Semitic and Proto-Kartvelian as they swept through the heartland of Europe? This seems to me to present the traditional model with an irreconcilable problem.

In the final analysis, I believe the false date of 4,000 B.C. for Proto-Indo-European that has been advocated—and is still tenaciously clung to—by Indo-Europeanists lies at the root of all this confusion. In his book Renfrew discussed the circularity of the reasoning behind this date. The archaeologists have borrowed the date so uncritically conjured up by linguists and used it to support the Kurgan invasion hypothesis. In return the linguists have borrowed the Kurgan invasion hypothesis from the archaeologists to buttress their dating of Proto-Indo-European. Everything fits together neatly, as long as one fails to examine the evidence and ignores the implications. When one faces up to the evidence, as I have tried to do here, it becomes apparent that the traditional model "has been looking for all the wrong people, in all the wrong places," to borrow a line from a recent rock song.

The Origin and Spread of Modern Humans

In what remains here I will attampt to piece together a general outline of human evolution, one that is consistent with the different lines of evidence we have examined in this book. Since no clear picture is to be had from any one field of inquiry, I shall be integrating complementary evidence from all fields. My general conclusions are summarized in Figure 12.

Biological evidence and archaeological evidence both point to Africa as the homeland of modern humans. Shortly after 100,000 B.P. a group of modern humans migrated out of Africa, spreading first to the Near East, then beyond to Southeast Asia and Oceania, reaching Australia by at least 40,000 B.P., and perhaps 10,000 years earlier. Eurasia was at that time already occupied by "archaic" humans, as they are sometimes called, including Solo Man and Neanderthal Man. The relationship between archaic humans and modern humans is controversial, but there appears to have been little, if any, genetic mixture between the two populations. What kinds of languages the archaic humans may have had, if any, is unknown.

It is striking that after these two early splits in the human family tree—the first separating sub-Saharan Africans from everyone else, the second leading to the populations of Southeast Asia and the near Pacific (New Guinea and Australia)—what remained was a single large population that then split into various subgroups, the subgroups eventually expanding throughout Eurasia, though at different times and in different directions.

The subgrouping within this vast Eurasian population is problematic, and that given in Figure 12 will surely be revised as the various lines of inquiry yield additional information. As we have seen, the initial branching appears to have been a Dene-Caucasian expansion that moved both east and west from a base in the Near East, populating Europe but also giving rise to the Sino-Tibetan family in Asia. The later Eurasiatic migration, also probably originating in the Near East, in time replaced most of the Dene-Caucasian languages, leaving Basque as the sole European language surviving from that earlier time. The Caucasian family remained sheltered in the Caucasus mountains, and Burushaski managed to survive in a mountain valley of northern Pakistan. In Asia, the progenitors of the Sino-Tibetan family may also have had a mountainous homeland, in the Himalayas, but they soon spread throughout much of East Asia. The present positions of the Yeniseian and Na-Dene families would appear to reflect later movements, not the original Dene-Caucasian expansion.

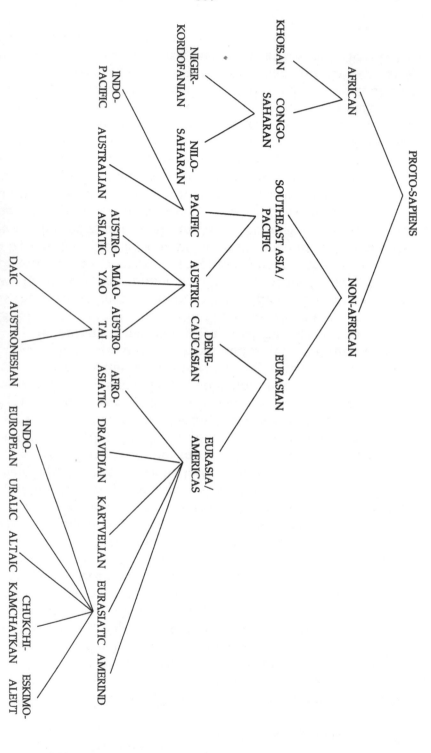

FIGURE 12   The genealogical structure of the human population.

With Dene-Caucasian identified as the third major branching in the human family, we are left with three large, ancient families—Afro-Asiatic, Eurasiatic, and Amerind—and two well-defined low-level families—Kartvelian and Dravidian—whose relationship to the three larger families is unresolved. As we have seen, Russian Nostraticists such as Illich-Svitych and Dolgopolsky include Afro-Asiatic, Dravidian, and Kartvelian with the Eurasiatic families in a single Nostratic family. Greenberg, however, considers these three families to be related to Eurasiatic at greater remove, an opinion that is now shared by Starostin for Afro-Asiatic and Dravidian.

From this Eurasian population one group apparently backtracked to Africa, giving rise to the Afro-Asiatic family, while another group left Eurasia via the Bering Strait around 12,000 years ago and became the first humans to enter the Americas, the forebears of the modern Amerind peoples. The Eurasiatic population that remained in Eurasia disintegrated into a number of distinct families (Indo-European, Uralic, Altaic, Chukchi-Kamchatkan, and Eskimo-Aleut) that eventually came to occupy most of Eurasia, replacing Dene-Caucasian languages in much of this territory and even extending, via Eskimo-Aleut, into North America.

I do not pretend that the genealogical structure shown in Figure 12 will be immune from change as the investigation of human prehistory proceeds. Still, I anticipate that large portions of it will prove to be valid even with the accumulation of additional evidence. In particular, groupings such as Amerind, Eurasiatic, Nilo-Saharan, and Dene-Caucasian will *all* prove to be valid linguistic families, despite the scorn currently heaped on them by so many of the experts. You have yourself seen, in solving the various tables in this book, how such families can be discovered, using only the techniques that led to Indo-European so long ago. Ironically, the linguistic evidence I have presented in this book is disparaged chiefly by a small group of historical linguists. Outside that narrow clique, particularly among geneticists, biologists, anthropologists, and archaeologists, one finds these ideas held in high regard. Perhaps fittingly, I will close with Renfrew's (1992b: 473) current appraisal of the evidence:

> If the lumpers (notably the Russian school including Dolgopolsky and Starostin, and the American school of Greenberg and Ruhlen) are correct, then the broad outlines are already becoming clear. It may even be possible that the unity of human origins may be reflected in the evidence offered for linguistic monogenesis. . . . But if the splitters are right, and if it is indeed the case that languages evolve so fast that no reconstructions of any kind could be possible beyond about 5,000 years ago . . . , then these broad macrofamilies (e.g. Amerind, Austric, Nostratic or Eurasiatic, Sino-Caucasian) would be entirely illusory, and so too in consequence would any supposed correlation between them and the genetic evidence for human phylogeny. . . .

> Time will tell. But already there are sufficient arguments from the fields of archaeology, linguistics, and genetics to suggest that the new synthesis fulfilling the premonitory vision of Darwin and Huxley . . . may be more than a mirage.

Epilogue

Reconstruction, Sound Correspondences, and Homelands

One of the themes of this book has been the contention that different stages in the practice of historical linguistics have been hopelessly confused during the twentieth century, with the end result being innumerable, often bitter controversies based largely on misunderstanding and ignorance. In particular, I have argued that the indispensable first step in the comparative method is *classification*, or taxonomy, which defines all language families at all levels, from the most obvious (for example Bantu, Romance, Germanic) to the least obvious (for example Dene-Caucasian, Indo-Pacific, Amerind). What is usually referred to *in textbooks* as the "Comparative Method" is really the *second* stage in historical linguistics, for it takes the existence of a language family (the first stage) *as a given* and then proceeds to ask specific questions *about that family*. When did the proto-language, the lineage founder, exist? Where was the homeland of the proto-language? What did the words in the proto-language sound like? What historical processes were responsible for transforming the words in the proto-language into the forms we see in the modern languages, the daughters and grand-daughters of the proto-language?

All of these are important questions and deserve detailed study, but they can be satisfactorily approached only when the initial stage in historical linguistics—the identification of a language family—is complete. The attempt to mix or reverse these two levels on the part of twentieth-century Indo-Europeanists and their followers, pretending that family-specific problems like reconstruction and sound correspondences must be used *in identifying families*, has led to the current theoretical impasse in which everything but the obvious is considered beyond the limits of the comparative method.

In this book we have seen many reasons why these constraints and confusions can no longer be countenanced, but it is also important that one not minimize the problems that linguists face in the second stage of historical linguistics—the exploration of issues *within* specific language families. In this Epilogue we will take a brief look at some of these problems.

Reconstruction

The reconstruction of proto-languages has been a prominent theme in historical linguistics since the mid-nineteenth century, when the German linguist August Schleicher attempted to compose a fable in Proto-Indo-European (for a version of this fable in Proto-Indo-European, albeit not Schleicher's version, see Diamond 1992: 274). The reconstruction of a proto-language entails the reconstruction of several different components of the language, for instance the set of consonants and vowels it used, the specific words in its lexicon, its grammatical endings, and the ordering of its various syntactic elements, for example whether the adjective precedes or follows the noun.

Let us consider a few of the problems that linguists face in attempting to reconstruct a word in a proto-language. We will begin with a simple example and gradually make it more complex. Assume we have identified, or someone has identified, on the basis of substantial lexical and grammatical similarities, a language family, call it X, that consists of ten languages, ABCDEFGHI and J. We wish to reconstruct the word for 'finger' in Proto-X on the basis of its reflexes (modern forms) in the ten languages. Let us assume first that a brief inspection demonstrates that the word for 'finger' is *tik* in all ten extant languages. Under these circumstances we would not hesitate to reconstruct **tik* for Proto-X, and we would further posit that this proto-form has been passed down unchanged into all the modern daughter languages. Needless to say, cases like this are rare, since even within closely related languages like those of Romance or Bantu not every language has retained every word from the proto-language, and not every word that *has* been preserved remains unchanged in its sounds and meanings. Rather, what we typically find, as you have seen in solving the various tables in this book, is a collection of forms, in *some* of the languages in a family, that are *similar* to one another, but not necessarily identical, in both sound and meaning. This typical situation raises two distinct questions. First, if a word is not attested in every one of the languages of the family, how can we be sure it actually existed in Proto-X and was not developed later in some branch of Proto-X? Second, what specific form and meaning should we reconstruct for the word in question, regardless of what level in the family—that is, what time depth—it may represent, if the modern forms differ from one another?

Let us begin with the first question: how can we be sure that a word existed in Proto-X if it is lacking in certain languages? This is in fact a delicate question, and the most obvious solution—give each language one vote and let the majority rule—turns out to have disastrous consequences. To see why, let us consider an example from biology. Of all the recent species of mammals, 4,000 bear their young live, and only six lay eggs. Did Proto-Mammal lay eggs or bear their young alive? The odds would appear to be strongly in favor of live childbirth; who could ask for better odds than 4,000 to six. And yet the correct answer, doubted by no biologist, is that Proto-Mammal was an egg-layer. Biologists know this by looking at the nearest "outgroup" to mammals, that is, the group of animals most closely related to mammals. When we survey the closest relatives of mammals, the reptiles, we find that almost all of them lay eggs. So too do most of the less closely related vertebrates, like amphibians, fishes, and birds. The general presence of a particular state (egg-laying) in the nearest outgroup (reptiles) and its presence—even marginally—in the group under consideration (mammals) virtually guarantees that Proto-Mammal was an egg-layer, even though most modern descendants are not.

Similar considerations may be brought to bear in linguistic reconstruction. If, for example, languages A and B in our hypothetical family X have *tik* for 'finger,' while languages C–J show totally dissimilar forms, it may still be possible to show that *tik* 'finger' existed in Proto-X, despite its having survived in only two languages. Let us assume that we know that family X is most closely related to family Y, and that in family Y the usual word for 'finger' is *tik* (or something similar). Since the form *tik* is general in the nearest outgroup (family Y), and at least present in the group being considered (family X), we may safely conclude that *tik* 'finger' existed in Proto-X despite its absence from most contemporary languages in family X.

It was Guthrie's failure to understand these simple principles that was largely responsible for the failure of his Proto-Bantu reconstructions: he reconstructed, for Proto-Bantu, forms that we now know in all probability did not exist in Proto-Bantu, and he failed to reconstruct forms that we know did exist in Proto-Bantu. Guthrie divided the whole Bantu area into six zones, Northwest, Northeast, Central West, Central East, Southwest, Southeast, which he treated as taxonomically equal. Thus, if he found a root attested in all the zones except Northwest, he would still reconstruct it for Proto-Bantu, whereas if a root was found only in the Northwest zone, he would never reconstruct it for Proto-Bantu. The problem, as we have seen earlier, is that the Northwest branch represents one of the two primary branches of the Bantu family, taxonomically equal to all the other zones put together. Furthermore, the "outgroup" for Bantu is the West African languages that Greenberg called Niger-Congo. Now using the considerations given above, it is easy to see that a root that is found in Niger-Congo and in the Northwest Bantu zone may be safely reconstructed for Proto-Bantu even if it is totally absent elsewhere. Yet Guthrie ignored such roots in his Proto-Bantu reconstructions. On the other hand, a root that is absent both in Northwest Bantu and in the rest of Niger-Congo cannot safely be reconstructed for Proto-Bantu even if it is attested in all five of the other Bantu zones. Yet Guthrie invariably reconstructed all such roots for Proto-Bantu.

The outgroup method of determining whether a particular root is primitive or derived depends, of course, on knowing what the nearest outgroup is. This means that the method is not accessible to Indo-Europeanists, who deny that Indo-European *has* any known outgroup. For them, any root found in two different branches is considered to derive from Proto-Indo-European, but we have just seen that this sort of practical solution has little chance of coinciding with historical reality.

Let us turn now to the question of how one determines the original form and meaning of a root whose modern reflexes are similar but not identical. Let us assume that the word for 'finger' in family X is $t^s ik$ in five languages and *tik* in the other five. Which form should we reconstruct for Proto-X? The answer is *tik*, and the reason is that the sound change $ti > t^s i$ (> means "changes into") is abundantly, and frequently, attested in the world's languages, whereas the reverse change, $t^s i > ti$, is exceedingly rare. Linguists know which sound changes are commonplace, as well as which are rare or impossible. For example, they know that a *t-* is susceptible to various stages of phonetic erosion if followed by the vowel *i*: $ti > t^s i > si > hi > i$, that is, *t* is first weakened to t^s, which then may be further weakened to *s*, which may then be reduced to *h*, and in the last stage the consonant disappears entirely. Any change in the opposite direction would be unexpected, and in some cases probably impossible. There are many such chains of phonetic changes that are familiar to all linguists and used in reconstructing earlier stages of languages. Many of the hints I gave you to help in solving the tables in this book were intended to give you some knowledge of these general processes, so that you would be able to better recognize what forms are likely to be cognate. Some of the other general phonetic paths that we have encountered in the tables include $ki > či > ši > si > hi > i$; $p > f > h$; $k > x > h$; $k > ?$ (? is heard in the Cockney pronunciation of 'bottle' as [ba?l]; $d > ð > z$; $t > θ > s$; $i > y$; $u > w$; Vn (V represents any vowel) $> \tilde{V}$ ($\tilde{V}$ is a vowel pronounced with simultaneous nasalization, that is, air is allowed to pass through the nose) $> V$; $Vm > \tilde{V} > V$; $Vŋ > \tilde{V} > V$; $V? > \tilde{V} > V$; $Vh > \tilde{V} > V$; $VpV > VbV$; $VtV > VdV$; $VkV > VgV$.

When one combines a knowledge of these general evolutionary trends with Greenberg's methodology of multilateral comparison, the result is a powerful tool for recognizing cognates. To see why, let us return to the example of Proto-Amerind *t'ina*/*t'ana*/*t'una* 'son, child, daughter.' If one were to compare just two languages—as the Americanists have done *ad nauseam*—then one would probably not attribute any special significance to the fact that one language had the word *t'ina* 'brother' and the other had the word *sin* 'son.' Of course any historical linguist could imagine a hypothetical scenario whereby ordinary phonetic changes might conspire to transform *t'ina* into *t^s'ina* into *t^sina* into *sina* into *sin* at the same time that the semantics was shifting from 'brother' to 'son.' All of these changes, phonetic and semantic, are quite plausible, but the fact remains that *s-* need not derive from an earlier *t'-*; there are numerous other possible sources, including the possibility that it has always been *s-*. What leads one to conclude that Molale (Oregon) *t'in* 'elder brother' is related to Changuena (Panama) *sin* 'brother' and to Pehuenche (Chile) *t^sena* 'brother' is not just the similarity among these three forms taken from languages that are thousands of miles apart, but rather the presence of *all the intermediate forms* between *t'ina* and *sin* in other Amerind languages throughout North and South America. The abundance of such forms on two continents, in contrast to their virtual absence elsewhere in the world, cries out for a genetic explanation.

As an illustration, one may trace the historical attrition of the initial consonant in Proto-Amerind *t'ina* 'brother' through all the intermediate stages that one would expect to find if the three forms cited above do indeed derive from a single earlier form (we ignore a difference between *i* and *e* in the following examples): *t'in* (Molale, Cayuse, Chitimacha, Yana), *t'i* (Southern Pomo, Northeast Pomo, Southwest Pomo, Mazahua), *tin* (Nez Perce, Atakapa, San Buenaventura Chumash, Cuicatec,

Maku, Tiquie, Papury, Ubde-Nehern, Tatuyo, Cuica, Marawa, Atoroi, Yagua, Yameo), *tī* (Puinave, Yehupde), *ti* (Pawnee, Wintu, Maidu, Plains Miwok, Motilon, Dobokubi, Muyska, Tucano, Kamaru, Ramarama, Palicur, Surinam Carib, Apucarana), *tˢ'in* (Yuki, Chorti, Pokomchi, Chontal, Southeast Pomo), *tˢin* (Yurok, Mohawk, Lacandon, Yuma, Southern Paiute, Pipil, Patagon, Pehuenche, Amaguaje, Siona, Yupua, Guato), *tˢī* (Assiniboine, Coreguaje), *tˢi* (Blackfoot, Wiyot, Koasati, Natchez, Northern Paiute, Paez, Taulipang, Tacana), *sin* (Flathead, Santa Cruz Costanoan, Changuena), *šin* (Columbian, San Francisco Costanoan, Mutsun, Kawaiisu, Amuesha), *si* (Qawashqar), *ši* (Tunica). In addition to the various phonetic changes to which these forms attest, there were also slight semantic changes from the original meaning 'son, brother,' to such closely related meanings as 'boy, child, young man, male,' and—with the addition of affixes—to meanings like 'nephew, grandchild, son-in-law, brother-in-law, uncle.' In short, one finds just the range of phonetic and semantic variation that one would expect to find after more than ten millennia of evolution of an original form like *t'ina* 'brother.'

The technique of outgroup comparison can also be used in determining the specific form of a reconstruction. If, for example, half of the languages in family X have *kap* 'cover,' while the other half have *k'ap* 'cover,' which form should be reconstructed as original? Since *k* may sometimes develop into *k'*, but *k'* may also become *k*, there is no clear directionality to the change that can be relied upon. Suppose, however, that family Y, the nearest outgroup to family X, shows the same root in the form *k'ap* 'cover.' Under these circumstances we would reconstruct Proto-X **k'ap* 'cover,' on the basis of the evidence in family Y, and we would postulate that this form has been simplified to *kap* in some languages of family X.

Sound Correspondences

In its modern conception, linguistic reconstruction goes beyond the considerations just discussed in constraining the reconstructed proto-forms by a set of regular sound correspondences that connect forms in the modern languages with the reconstructed proto-form. We have from time to time observed examples of regular sound correspondences in the various tables. For instance, in Table 5 we noticed that the sound *d* in language E (Brahui) corresponds to the sound *n* in language H (Tamil) in the words for 'blood' and 'water.' Further investigation of the Dravidian family, to which these two languages belong, would show that Proto-Dravidian **n-*, at the beginning of a word, has regularly become *d-* in Brahui when followed by *i* or *e*. If one pursued this topic further, one would also find that there was a parallel change of Proto-Dravidian **m-* to Brahui *b-* in the same phonetic environment. In its most general form this sound correspondence states that a word-initial nasal consonant (**m-* or **n-*) in Proto-Dravidian changes to its corresponding voiced stop (**b-* or **d-*, respectively) in Brahui when followed by a front vowel (**i* or **e*).

The important point here is that sound correspondences apply to entire languages, not just to a few specific words. This is so because sound change is regular: when one sound changes into another it does so without exception, at least in theory. Since the question of sound correspondences is so often mixed up with questions of taxonomy—incorrectly, as I have sought to show in this book—it will be useful to place the question of sound correspondences in its proper historical context.

The first Indo-Europeanists in the early years of the nineteenth century, scholars such as Rasmus Rask and Jacob Grimm, were already aware of sound correspondences that connected the various Indo-European languages, and in fact the most famous of all sound correspondences, known as Grimm's Law, was first postulated by Rask. This law specifies how certain Proto-Indo-European consonants had changed into the consonants attested in modern Germanic languages such as English, Dutch, and Swedish. So that you might gain at least a sense of this law (the standard texts dwell at length on the details—and rightly so), let us consider what the law had to say about Proto-Indo-European **t*. According to Grimm's Law this consonant becomes θ in Proto-Germanic, the language from which all modern Germanic languages derive. Thus we find that although Sanskrit *bhrátar-* 'brother' and Latin *fráter* 'brother' have retained the *t* that presumably once existed in this word, Gothic (the first attested, but now extinct, Germanic language) shows *brōθar* 'brother.' Other words in these languages show the same correspondence.

Grimm's Law explained a good deal, but it was not without exceptions. For example, on the basis of Sanskrit *pitár-* 'father' and Latin *pater* 'father,' Grimm's Law predicts that one will find *faθar* 'father' in Gothic, but in fact the actual Gothic word was *fadar*. The existence of such exceptions did not particularly bother Grimm, who wrote that "the sound shift is a general tendency; it is not followed in every case." This was the general conception of sound correspondences up to the 1870's. During that decade a string of discoveries led scholars to the conclusion that sound change, and the correspondences that reflected it, was indeed regular. The German Indo-Europeanist August Leskien proclaimed that "sound laws admit of no exceptions," while his Danish colleague Karl Verner stated the new perspective on sound change as follows: "There must be a rule for exceptions to a rule; the only question is to discover it." And it was in fact Verner who discovered the rule for the exceptions to Grimm's Law.

Verner resolved this puzzling double development within the Germanic branch of Indo-European by looking carefully at the evidence in *other* branches. What he noticed was that the placement of the accent in Proto-Indo-European, as revealed in Greek and Sanskrit, was directly responsible for the two outcomes. If the Proto-Indo-European accent preceded the *t*, then the outcome accorded with Grimm's Law (for example *brōθar*). If, however, the accent did not precede the *t*, then the outcome is *d*, as in Gothic *fadar*. This is, however, just one part of Verner's Law. What must have happened early in the development of the Germanic branch is that *t* changed into both *θ* and *d*, depending on the place of the accent. Subsequent to these changes, however, the Germanic accent shifted to the beginning of the word, thus eliminating the conditioning environment. It is therefore possible to understand what happened in Germanic only by taking into account the evidence of other branches where the difference in accent placement was preserved (compare the placement of the accent in the Sanskrit words for 'brother' and 'father' cited above). Later changes in the history of English have caused the two distinct Germanic reflexes of Proto-Indo-European *t, θ and d, to merge as ð, the phonetic symbol for the -th- sound in both 'brother' and 'father.' In Old English, however, they were still distinct: brōðor versus fæder.

Is sound change, then, absolutely regular, as Verner and Leskien claimed? The answer, perhaps paradoxically, is no, but almost all modern linguists operate on the assumption that it is. The assumption of regularity forces linguists to seek further explanations for recalcitrant data, as Verner did so brilliantly, rather than simply accept the apparent exceptions. But even in the 1870's it was well known that certain kinds of sound changes, often called *sporadic* sound changes, were not regular, but affected only specific words, and these were explicitly exempted from the regularity hypothesis. The various types of sporadic sound change include *metathesis*, where the order of two consonants is reversed (for example, Modern English 'wasp' derives from an earlier 'waps,' and Modern English 'bird' derives from Old English 'brid'); *dissimilation*, in which two similar consonants change so as to become less similar (for example, Classical Latin *peregrīnus* 'pilgrim' had become *pelegrīnus* already in Late Latin, and it is the latter form that is reflected in French *pèlerin*); *assimilation*, in which two different consonants become more similar, often identical (for example, Classical Latin *quīnque* 'five,' instead of the expected form, *pīnque*, is sometimes attributed to assimilation of the first consonant to the second); and *contamination*, in which other, usually semantically related, words influence a word idiosyncratically (for example, numbers used in counting are frequently found to contaminate one another; thus the initial consonant of Latin *quīnque* 'five' is sometimes attributed to the initial consonant of the preceding numeral, *quattor* 'four,' in which the initial *qu-* is normal).

A great deal of work by the American linguist William S.-Y. Wang and others in recent years has shown that sound changes do not necessarily affect simultaneously all of the words to which they might apply, but in fact often spread through the lexicon of a language gradually over time. In some cases, the sound change is arrested before all of the relevant items are affected; at other times, competing sound changes result in a residue of exceptions to otherwise general sound changes. In a word, the mechanisms and causes of sound change are extremely complex, and the outcome of such changes is often a good deal messier than the regularity hypothesis would lead one to expect. Nevertheless, despite the messiness, virtually all modern linguists—including Greenberg, despite frequent claims to the contrary—operate on the assumption of regularity. Irregularity is to be explained one way or another.

Finally, one might ask what all this has to do with the subject of this book, the genetic classification of languages. Actually, very little. As we have emphasized throughout, sound laws are discovered once one has identified a language family by means of the method of comparison of basic vocabulary. It is the transparent similarities that lead to language families, not esoteric sound correspondences of the Armenian *erku* 'two' variety that may be discovered later. Were it not for the fact that contemporary historical linguists endlessly cite sound correspondences as the only "real proof" of genetic affinity, it would not have been necessary to go into these questions in this book. Certainly none of the nineteenth-century pioneers of Indo-European studies ever imagined that the Indo-European sound correspondences had proved Indo-European. This view is entirely a product of twentieth-century Indo-Europeanists.

Analogy

Even if we grant that sound change is regular, we cannot expect regularity in phonetic shifts to lead to overall regularity in a language. On the contrary, regularity of sound shifts often leads to irregularity in other components of grammar. There is, however, another historical process, called *analogy*, that works in effect to eliminate the irregularity caused by regular sound change. Analogy comes into play when the regularity of a grammatical paradigm (that is, a set of related forms such as Latin *cant-o* 'I sing,' *cant-as* 'you sing,' *cant-at* 'he sings') comes into conflict with the regularity of sound change. To see how analogy works, let us imagine an Amerind language in which the original Proto-Amerind kinship system, *t'ina/t'ana/t'una* 'son, child, daughter,' has undergone two sound changes. First, glottalization of the initial consonant was lost (*t'* > *t*) and then the initial *t-* was weakened to *t^s-* before the vowel *i*. Both of these changes are garden-variety phonetic changes; glottalized consonants are often simplified to normal consonants, and *t* is frequently shifted to *t^s* before a high front vowel (*i*). As a result of these two changes, the original system has become *t^{s}ina/tana/ tuna* 'son, child, daughter,' and the masculine form is characterized not only by the masculine vowel *i*, but also by a different initial consonant.

Human languages prefer to represent the same meaning with the same form, as was the case with Proto-Amerind **t'Vna* (in which the variation in the first vowel *-V-* signals the gender). In the hypothetical evolved language, however, we find that we have two forms of this root, *t^{s}Vna* for the masculine form, and *tVna* for both the feminine and the neutral, and the preference of one form for one meaning is violated. Analogy works to iron out these rough edges by once again unifying form and meaning in a single form. Given the fact that speakers of this language perceive all three forms as morphologically related (because they form a paradigm), and given further that languages tend to prefer a single form for each meaning, one way of correcting this situation would be for the language to change the *t^s-* of *t^{s}ina* 'son' to *t-*, a process known as *analogical leveling*. One may think of analogy as a battle between two different forms of a root, each of which wants to take over the entire paradigm and establish its own form, to the exclusion of the other. Which form ultimately prevails (if either, since such irregularities are not always eliminated; compare English 'was' and 'were') turns out to be influenced by a large number of factors. Furthermore, analogy may work in different directions in different languages, with the result that in one language one form of the root may prevail, while in a closely related language it is the other form of the root that emerges victorious. An example of this may be seen by comparing English 'choose' with German *küren* 'choose' (a form now archaic). In earlier stages of both English and German there were two forms of this root, one with z, the other with r. In English 'choose,' the first form, with z, completely eliminated the forms with r; in German *küren*, however, analogy worked in the opposite direction and the z-forms were eliminated.

Let us return now to our original Amerind example, in which *t^sina* 'son' was analogically leveled to *tina* on the basis of feminine *tuna* 'daughter' and neutral *tana* 'child.' We might say that the masculine form was outvoted two to one by the feminine and neutral forms. Imagine, however, that in another Amerind language word-initial *t-* was weakened to *t^s-* before both *i* and *u* (this is a natural possibility, since *u* also can cause weakening of a preceding consonant). In this language we would find *t^sina/tana/t^suna* 'son, child, daughter,' and analogical leveling might lead to the replacement of *tana* 'child' by *t^sana*. But the direction of analogical leveling is not dictated solely by democratic vote, as we have assumed in the examples just cited. The *frequency* of particular forms in daily discourse may also play a role. If one form is used much more frequently than the others, it may prevail even if it is not the most common form in a paradigm. Many other factors are involved in predicting the direction of analogical change, all of them amply discussed in the standard textbooks on historical linguistics (Hock 1986, Anttila 1989).

Locating the Algonquian Homeland

A final topic that is of great interest to historical linguists is the use of linguistic evidence to locate the homeland of a particular language family. We touched on this problem in Chapter 8, with regard to the Bantu, Austronesian, and Indo-European families. Here, let us consider the Algonquian family of North America and try to determine where it originated and how it spread to the distribution it exhibited at the time of Columbus's arrival.

Because the Algonquian languages were spoken along the

Eastern coast of North America from Labrador in Eastern Canada as far south as North Carolina, the Algonquians were among the first indigenous peoples of the Americas to be encountered by Europeans. The genetic affinity of these East Coast languages was so obvious—they are very similar—and was recognized so early by European explorers that whoever was the first person to perceive the Algonquian family is not even known, or at least no particular person is credited in any of the standard references on the Algonquian family. What was *not* immediately apparent to these first English settlers was the fact that the Algonquian family extended westward as far as what is now the Montana-Canada border, where the most westerly Algonquian language, Blackfoot, is spoken. This enormous distribution, shown in Map 9, was discovered much later.

Although the Algonquianists have not yet settled on any particular homeland for the family, Frank Siebert has proposed the area of the eastern upper Great Lakes as the origin of the Algonquian dispersal. Seemingly, the Algonquians would have radiated out in all directions from such a fairly central position, but I believe this proposal is implausible, for the following reasons.

Let us first consider the internal structure of the Algonquian family. Though there is no generally accepted subgrouping of the Algonquian languages—a common situation where the languages constituting a family are very closely related—there does seem to be consensus among Algonquianists that the most divergent language in the family is Blackfoot, the most westerly of the languages, whereas the languages that run along the East Coast, all very similar to one another, form a valid genetic subgroup of the family, known as Eastern Algonquian. But the Algonquian languages spoken *between* Blackfoot and Eastern Algonquian, variously intermediate in divergence, form an undetermined number of subgroups. The location of these three groups is shown in Map 10.

In light of Sapir's Age-Area hypothesis, whereby the area of greatest divergence indicates the original homeland, we may conclude from these facts that Proto-Algonquian was probably spoken originally in the area where Blackfoot is now found, not in the eastern Great Lakes. The initial division in the family left the Proto-Algonquians in place to become the Blackfoot, while the other group spread eastward, initially differentiating into the Algonquian languages found in the Great Plains. These languages then spread farther eastward, with the occupation of the East Coast representing the final movement in the dispersal. This is the view of Algonquian origins that seems to me to make the most sense on the basis of evidence internal to the Algonquian family. It is also strongly supported by external evidence.

We have already seen (in Chapter 4) that the Algonquian

|||| ALGONQUIAN

MAP 9 The Algonquian family.

family's closest relatives were discovered—by Sapir, in 1913—to be the Wiyot and Yurok languages, which are located on the northern California coast (see Map 11). Though this suggestion was roundly excoriated at the time, it is today universally accepted. Somewhat surprisingly—since they are spoken side-by-side—Wiyot and Yurok appear almost as different from one another as each is from Algonquian, and opinions differ on whether the two California languages form a subgroup, called

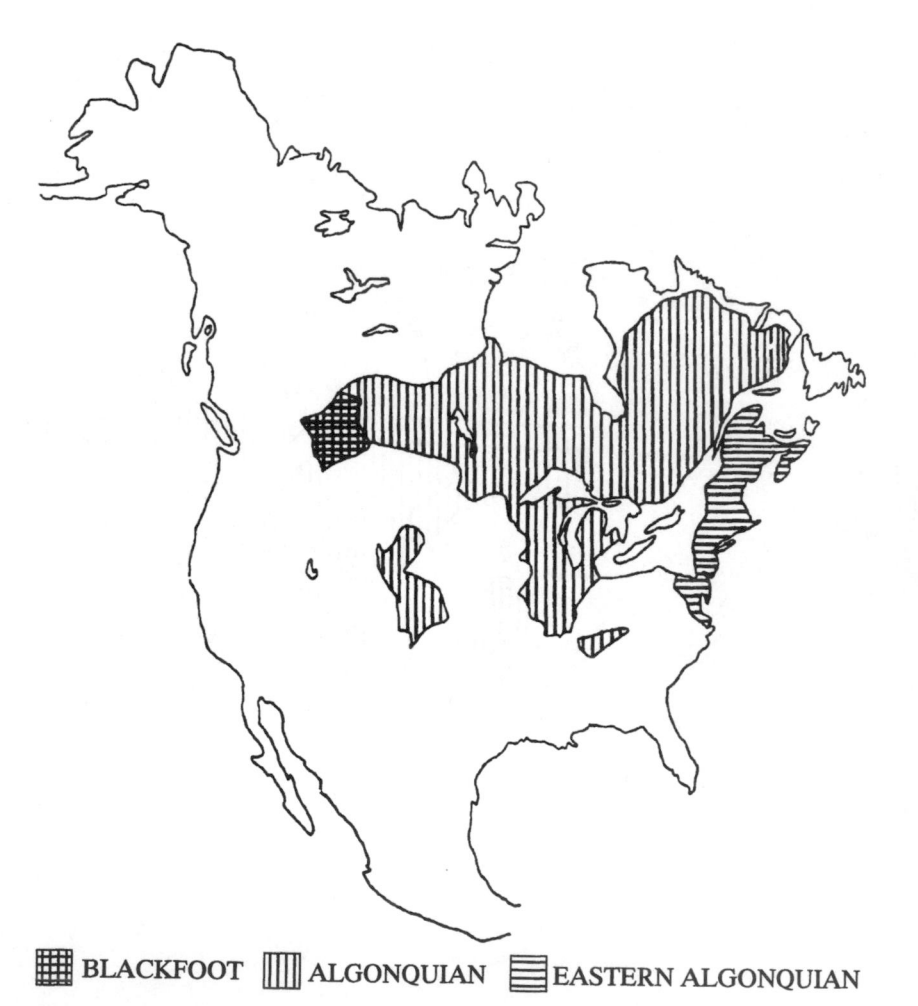

▦ BLACKFOOT ▥ ALGONQUIAN ☰ EASTERN ALGONQUIAN

MAP 10 The internal structure of the Algonquian family.

Ritwan, or whether each is a distinct branch of the larger family, Algic, which embraces both Ritwan and Algonquian. In any event, since Wiyot and Yurok must have branched off from Proto-Algonquian (either individually or together) before Proto-Algonquian itself began to disintegrate, it is more plausible that

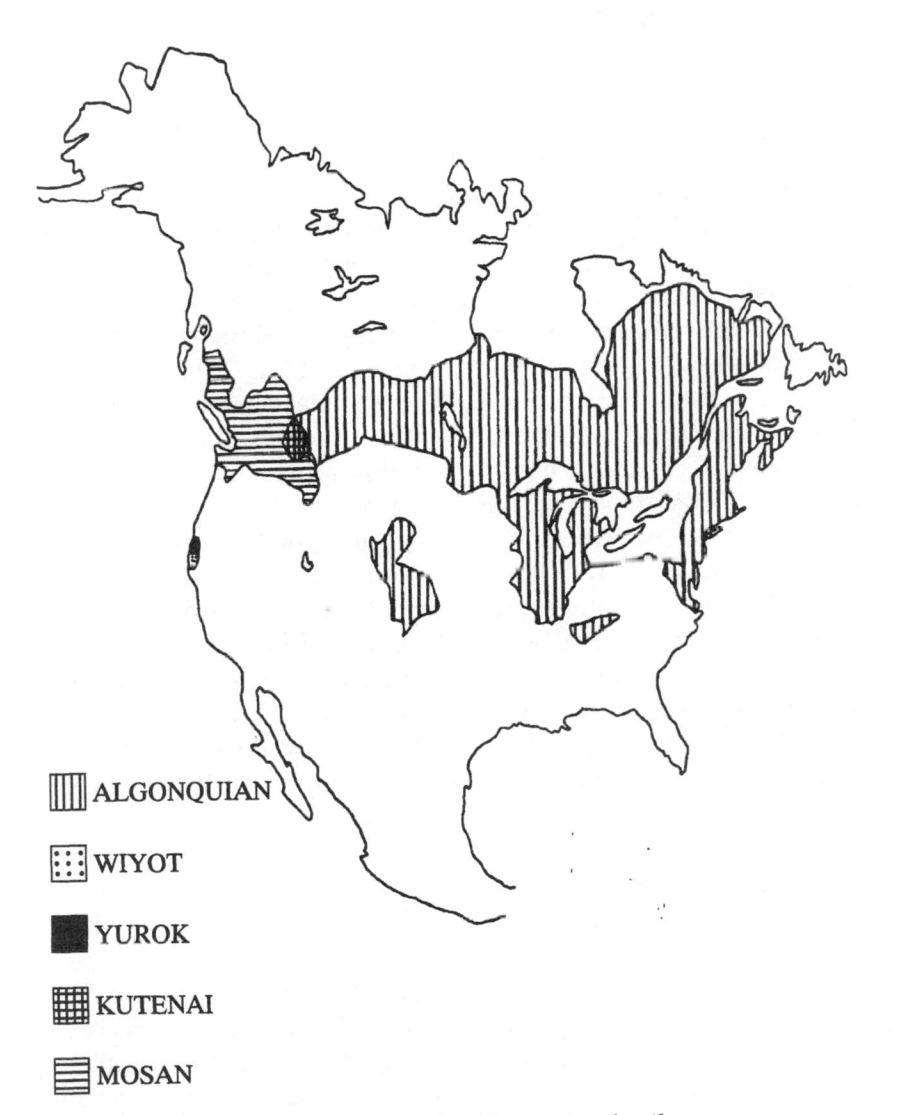

|||| ALGONQUIAN

∷ WIYOT

■ YUROK

▦ KUTENAI

≡ MOSAN

MAP 11   The external relations of the Algonquian family.

they split off from a Proto-Algonquian spoken in the area where Blackfoot is found today than that they somehow traveled to northern California from the eastern Great Lakes, a distance of over 2,000 miles. And if Wiyot and Yurok are really independent branches of Algic (which I doubt), it would be equally incredible that the two broke away independently from a Proto-Algonquian homeland in the area of the Great Lakes and *independently* made their way to the northern coast of California, there to wind up being spoken *in contiguous territories*.

If, then, the homeland of Proto-Algonquian, as well as that of the earlier Proto-Algic, can reasonably be traced to the area where Blackfoot is found today, our next question should be what Algic's closest relatives are. According to Sapir and Greenberg, Algic has two immediate outgroups. One is the Kutenai language, which borders Blackfoot on the western side; the other is the Mosan family, consisting of three subfamilies, Salish, Wakashan, and Chemakuan (see Map 11). The Salish family extends westward from the Kutenai area to the Pacific Coast; both Wakashan and Chemakuan are found along the Pacific Coast. Greenberg has named this more ancient grouping Almosan (= Algic + Kutenai + Mosan), and *its* homeland, as well, can reasonably be traced to the same area of southern Alberta that we have posited as the Proto-Algonquian and Proto-Algic homelands. In sum, then, both the internal evidence of the Algonquian family and the external evidence of Algonquian's closest relatives strongly support a western homeland for the Algonquian family. One might also note that this area of southern Alberta coincides with what would have been the southern edge of the ice-free corridor through which the Proto-Amerinds are thought to have first entered the Americas.

In this Epilogue we have only touched upon a few of the interesting problems that confront historical linguists. We have seen some of the considerations that must be taken into account in attempting to reconstruct the original vocabulary of a language that existed far in the past and left no written records. We have learned that, in general, sound changes are regular— that is, they affect the entire vocabulary of a language rather than just specific words in that language—but we have also found that there are exceptions to regular sound changes, for a variety of reasons. Furthermore, regular sound correspondences may lead to greater irregularity elsewhere in the grammar of a language, and we have seen how analogy can work to iron out such irregularities. We have also discussed briefly how linguistic evidence can be used to locate the ancient homeland of a family. All of these are fascinating topics that are fully worthy of the two centuries of scholarship that has been devoted to them.

Though it should be obvious that these topics can be fruitfully explored only after one has identified a group of languages that appears to constitute a valid family (invariably by inspection of basic vocabulary), there has developed in the twentieth century the peculiar view that reconstruction plays some crucial validating role in the discovery of language families. I have argued in this book that classification of languages—and hence identification of language families—must precede the traditional pursuits of historical linguists that we have surveyed in this Epilogue. And I have also tried to show that once one understands the true basis of the genealogical classification of languages (unencumbered by the currently fashionable mythology), the conclusion that all extant languages share a common origin becomes inescapable.

An Annotated
Bibliography

All of the works cited in the text are given in full here. Several dozen additional works, not cited in text, are also given. All entries are annotated.

Abercrombie, David. 1967. *Elements of General Phonetics.* Edinburgh, Scotland [A standard introduction to phonetics]

Anttila, Raimo. 1989. *Historical and Comparative Linguistics.* Amsterdam. [A standard introduction to historical linguistics]

Barbujani, Guido, Neal L. Oden, and Robert R. Sokal. 1989. "Detecting Regions of Abrupt Change in Maps of Biological Variables," *Systematic Zoology* 38: 376–89. [Investigates the relation between genes and language in a single South American Indian tribe]

Barbujani, Guido, and Robert R. Sokal. 1990. "Zones of Sharp Genetic Change in Europe Are Also Linguistic Boundaries," *Proceedings of the National Academy of Sciences* 87: 1816–19. [Offers evidence that linguistic boundaries in Europe coincide in most cases with gene-frequency boundaries]

Bateman, Richard, Ives Goddard, Richard O'Grady, V. A. Funk, Rich Mooi, W. John Kress, and Peter Cannell. 1990. "Speaking of Forked Tongues: The Feasibility of Reconciling Human Phylogeny and the History of Language," *Current An-thropology* 31: 1–24. [An uninformed attack on Cavalli-Sforza et al., 1988, by a team of scholars from the Smith-sonian Institution]

Bellwood, Peter. 1991. "The Austronesian Dispeisal and the Origin of Languages," *Scientific American* (July): 88–93. [Proposes the expansion of the Austronesian family from Southeast Asia throughout the Pacific, thus providing a study of the Emerging Synthesis in one part of the world]

Bengtson, John D. 1991. "Notes on Sino-Caucasian," in Shevoroshkin, ed., 1991. [Evidence for the Dene-Caucasian family]

Bengtson, John D., and Merritt Ruhlen. 1994. "Global Etymologies," in Ruhlen 1994a. [The most substantial demonstration to date of the monogenesis of extant languages]

Berg, Paul, and Maxine Singer. 1992. *Dealing with Genes: The Language of Heredity*. Mill Valley, Calif. [An introduction to genetics for the nonspecialist]

Bomhard, Allan R. 1991. "Lexical Parallels Between Proto-Indo-European and Other Languages," in L. Isebaert, ed., *Studia Etymologica Indoeuropaea*, Leuven, pp. 47–106. [Provides evidence connecting Indo-European with other language families of Eurasia and Africa]

Bynon, Theodora. 1977. *Historical Linguistics*. Cambridge, Eng. [A standard introduction to historical linguistics]

Cannon, Garland. 1990. *The Life and Mind of Oriental Jones*. Cambridge, Eng. [The definitive biography of Sir William Jones, eighteenth-century British linguist]

Cavalli-Sforza, L. L., 1991. "Genes, Peoples, and Languages," *Scientific American* (November): 104–10. [A popular discussion of the correlation between genes and languages and their import for human prehistory]

Cavalli-Sforza, L. L., Alberto Piazza, Paolo Menozzi. 1994. *History and Geography of Human Genes*. Princeton, N.J. [The standard reference on the distribution of human genes and their implication for human prehistory]

Cavalli-Sforza, L. L., Alberto Piazza, Paolo Menozzi, and Joanna Mountain. 1988. "Reconstruction of Human Evolution: Bringing Together Genetic, Archeological and Linguistic

Data," *Proceedings of the National Academy of Sciences* 85: 6002–06. [Original article on the genetic structure of the human population and its correlation with linguistic families]

———. 1990. "Comment," *Current Anthropology* 31: 16–18.

Darwin, Charles. 1859. *On the Origin of Species*. London. [Relevance for historical linguistics has, until recently, gone largely unnoticed]

———. 1871. *The Descent of Man*. London. [Notes similarities between biological and linguistic evolution]

Delbrück, Bertold. 1880. *Einleitung in das Sprachstudium*. Leipzig. [Presents the views of a prominent nineteenth-century Indo-Europeanist]

Diamond, Jared. 1992. *The Third Chimpanzee: The Evolution and Future of the Human Animal*. New York. [A lucid, informed, and entertaining perspective on human origins]

Dolgopolsky, Aron. 1988. "The Indo-European Homeland and Lexical Contacts of Proto-Indo-European with Other Languages," *Mediterranean Language Review* 3: 7–31. [Presents the linguistic evidence favoring a homeland in Anatolia (modern Turkey) for the Indo-European family]

Excoffier, Laurent, Béatrice Pellegrini, Alicia Sanchez-Mazas, Christian Simon, and André Langaney. 1987. "Genetics and History of Sub-Saharan Africa," *Yearbook of Physical Anthropology* 30: 151–94. [Demonstrates a correlation between genes and languages in Africa]

Fleming, Harold. 1986– . *Mother Tongue*. Boston. [Newsletter of the *Association for the Study of Language in Prehistory*, a group formed to counterbalance the conservatism of Indo-Europeanists and Americanists]

———. 1987. "Toward a Definitive Classification of the World's Languages," *Diachronica* 4: 159–223. [A thorough look at the state of classification of the world's languages]

Flight, Colin. 1980. "Malcolm Guthrie and the Reconstruction of Bantu Prehistory," *History in Africa* 7: 81–118. [A historian looks at Guthrie's proposals concerning Bantu prehistory—and why they were wrong]

———. 1988. "The Bantu Expansion and the SOAS Network," *History in Africa* 15: 261–301. [A look at the Bantu controversy from inside the SOAS]

Gamkrelidze, T. V., and V. V. Ivanov. 1990. "The Early History of Indo-European Languages," *Scientific American* (March): 110–16. [Traces the homeland of the Indo-European languages to Anatolia (modern Turkey)]

Greenberg, Joseph H. 1987. *Language in the Americas.* Stanford, Calif. [The revolutionary classification of Native American languages into just three families]

———. 1990a. "The American Indian Language Controversy," *Review of Archaeology* 11: 5–14. [Answers criticism of his classification of New World languages]

———. 1990b. "Indo-European Practice and American Indianist Theory in Language Classification," to appear in Allan Taylor, ed., *Language and Prehistory in the Americas.* Stanford, Calif. [A rebuttal to critics of the Amerind family]

———. To appear. *Indo-European and Its Closest Relatives: The Eurasiatic Language Family.* Stanford, Calif. [Evidence connecting Indo-European to other language families of northern Eurasia]

Greenberg, Joseph H., and Merritt Ruhlen. 1992. "Linguistic Origins of Native Americans," *Scientific American* (November): 94–99. [A popular account of the linguistic evidence for the peopling of the Americas]

Greenberg, Joseph H., Christy G. Turner II, and Stephen L. Zegura. 1986. "The Settlement of the Americas: A Comparison of Linguistic, Dental, and Genetic Evidence," *Current Anthropology* 27: 477–97. [Original proposal of a congruence in the classification of languages, teeth, and genes in the Americas]

Gregersen, Edgar A. 1972. "Kongo-Saharan," *Journal of African Languages* 11: 69–89. [Proposed joining Niger-Kordofanian and Nilo-Saharan in a single family]

Guthrie, Malcolm. 1962. "Some Developments in the Prehistory of the Bantu Languages," *Journal of African History* 3: 273–82. [Guthrie's view of Bantu origins]

Hock, Hans Henrich. 1986. *Principles of Historical Linguistics.* Berlin. [A standard introduction to historical linguistics]

Hopper, Paul J. 1989. Review of *Language Contact, Creolization, and Genetic Linguistics*, by Sarah Grey Thomason and Terrence Kaufman, *American Anthropologist* 91: 817–18. [An irrational, and uninformed, defense of the status quo]

Howells, William. 1993. *Getting Here: The Story of Human Evo-*

lution. Washington, D.C. [A clear, concise exposition of the origins of modern humans by a leading physical anthropologist]

Illich-Svitych, Vladislav M. 1967. "Materialy k sravnitel'nomu slovarju nostraticheskix jazykov," *Etimologija* (Moscow) 1965: 321–96. [Evidence connecting Indo-European to other language families of Eurasia and North Africa; English translation in Shevoroshkin, ed., 1989a]

———. 1971–84. *Opyt sravnenija nostraticheskix jazykov,* 3 vols. Moscow. [Evidence connecting Indo-European to other language families of Eurasia and North Africa; an English translation and semantic index to these Nostratic etymologies may be found in Shevoroshkin, ed., 1990]

Kaiser, Mark, and Vitaly Shevoroshkin. 1988. "Nostratic," *Annual Review of Anthropology* 17: 309–29. [A summary of Russian research on Indo-European's relatives]

Kaufman, Terrence. 1990. "Language History in South America: What We Know and How to Know More," in Doris L. Payne, ed., *Amazonian Linguistics,* Austin, pp. 13–73. [A defense of the status quo]

Ladefoged, Peter. 1982. *A Course in Phonetics.* New York. [A standard introduction to phonetics]

Lamb, Sydney, and E. Douglas Mitchell, eds. 1991. *Sprung from Some Common Source: Investigations into the Prehistory of Languages.* Stanford, Calif. [Papers from the Rice University Symposium on the Genetic Classification of Languages, March 1986]

Lewin, Roger. 1987. *Bones of Contention.* New York. [An excellent introduction to the archaeological evidence for the origin of modern humans]

Mallory, J. P. 1989. *In Search of the Indo-Europeans.* London. [Traces the Indo-European homeland to the Ukraine]

Mayr, Ernst. 1988. *Toward a New Philosophy of Biology.* Cambridge, Mass. [Essays on evolution by a prominent biologist]

Meillet, Antoine. 1951 [1924]. "Introduction à la classification des langues," in Antoine Meillet, *Linguistique historique et linguistique générale,* Vol. 2, Paris, 53–69. [An Indo-Europeanist perspective on linguistic taxonomy]

Menozzi, Paolo, Alberto Piazza, and L. L. Cavalli-Sforza. 1978. "Synthetic Maps of Human Gene Frequencies in Europeans," *Science* 201: 786–92. [Genetic evidence that the spread of farming was carried to Europe from the Near East by the farmers themselves]

Phillipson, David W. 1977. "The Spread of the Bantu Language," *Scientific American* (April): 106–14. [A look at the Bantu expansion from an archaeological perspective]

Renfrew, Colin. 1987. *Archaeology and Language: The Puzzle of Indo-European Origins*. London. [Proposes that the Indo-European family spread out of Anatolia with the spread of farmers some 8,000 years ago]

———. 1989. "The Origins of Indo-European Languages," *Scientific American* (October): 106–14. [A popular account of Renfrew 1987]

———. 1991. "Before Babel: Speculations on the Origins of Linguistic Diversity," *Cambridge Archaeological Journal* 1: 3–23. [Informed speculation on the correlation between archaeology and historical linguistics]

———. 1992a. "World Languages and Human Dispersals: A Minimalist View," in J. A. Hall and I. C. Garvey, eds., *Transition to Modernity: Essays on Power, Wealth, and Belief*, Cambridge, Eng., pp. 11–68. [Proposal for an Emerging Synthesis among the fields of archaeology, linguistics, and genetics]

———. 1992b. "Archaeology, Genetics, and Linguistic Diversity," *Man* 27: 445–78. [Further discussion of the Emerging Synthesis]

———. 1994. "World Linguistic Diversity," *Scientific American* (January): 116–23. [On the origin and spread of modern humans]

Ruhlen, Merritt. 1988. "The Origin of Language: Retrospective and Prospective," in Ruhlen 1994a. [Russian version in *Voprosy Jazykoznanija* (1991); analysis of the myth that linguistic classification beyond the temporal limits of Indo-European is inherently impossible]

———. 1990a. "Phylogenetic Relations of Native American Languages," in *Prehistoric Mongoloid Dispersals* 7: 75–96. Tokyo. [Linguistic evidence that three separate migrations from

Asia to the Americas led to the pre-Columbian distribution of peoples in the Americas]

————. 1990b. "Amerind MALIQ'A 'Swallow, Throat' and Its Origin in the Old World," in Ruhlen 1994a. [Traces a single word from North Africa, across Eurasia, into both North and South America]

————. 1991a. *A Guide to the World's Languages*, Vol. 1: Classification. Stanford, Calif. [A complete classification of the world's languages, with a historical perspective]

————. 1991b. "The Amerind Phylum and the Prehistory of the New World," in Lamb and Mitchell, eds., 1991, pp. 328–50. [A preliminary attempt to bring linguistic evidence to bear on the Amerind dispersal]

————. 1992. "An Overview of Genetic Classification," in John A. Hawkins and Murray Gell-Mann, eds., *The Evolution of Human Languages*, Redwood City, Calif., pp. 159–89. [A summary of what is known about the classification of human languages]

————. 1994a. *On the Origin of Languages: Studies in Linguistic Taxonomy*. Stanford, Calif. [Essays discussing linguistic taxonomy around the world and across time]

————. 1994b. ' Linguistic Evidence for Human Prehistory," to appear in the *Annual Review of Anthropology*, Vol. 22. [A survey of the linguistic evidence for human prehistory]

————. 1994c. "Multiregional Evolution or 'Out of Africa'?: The Linguistic Evidence," to appear in Emőke J. E. Szathmary and Takeru Akazawa, eds., *Prehistoric Mongoloid Dispersals*, London. [A linguistic perspective on a current debate]

Shevoroshkin, Vitaly, ed. 1989a. *Reconstructing Languages and Cultures*. Bochum, Germany. [Articles from an International Conference on Language and Prehistory, Ann Arbor, Michigan, November 1988; includes an English translation of Illich-Svitych 1967]

————, ed. 1989b. *Explorations in Language Macrofamilies*. Bochum. [More articles from an International Conference on Language and Prehistory, Ann Arbor, Michigan, November 1988; especially noteworthy is Starostin's comparison of Nostratic and Dene-Caucasian]

————, ed. 1990. *Proto-Languages and Proto-Cultures*. Bochum.

[More articles from an International Conference on Language and Prehistory, Ann Arbor, Michigan, November 1988; includes an English translation and semantic index to Illich-Svitych's Nostratic reconstructions]

————, ed. 1991. *Dene-Sino-Caucasian Languages*. Bochum. [Fundamental papers on the Dene-Caucasian family]

Shevoroshkin, Vitaly, and Alexis Manaster- Ramer. 1991. "Some Recent Work on the Remote Relations of Languages," in Lamb and Mitchell, eds., 1991. [Summary of recent Russian work on the overall classification of the world's languages]

Sokal, Robert R. 1991. "The Continental Population Structure of Europe," *Annual Review of Anthropology* 20: 119–40. [Surveys the genetic structure of Europe, its similarity with linguistic families, and the historical origins of these parallel patterns]

Sokal, Robert R., Neal L. Oden, Pierre Legendre, Marie-Josée Fortin, Junhyong Kim, Barbara A. Thomson, Alain Vaudor, Rosalind M. Harding, and Guido Barbujani. 1990. "Genetics and Language in European Populations," *The American Naturalist* 135: 157–75. [Compares genetic and linguistic differences in Europe]

Starostin, Sergei. 1984. "Gipoteza o geneticheskix svjazjax sino-tibetskix jazykov s enisejskimi i severnokavkazskimi jazykami," *Lingvisticheskaja rekonstruktsija i drevnejshaja istorija vostoka* 4, Moscow, 19–38. [English translation in Shevoroshkin 1991; original proposal of the Sino-Caucasian family]

————. 1989. "Nostratic and Sino-Caucasian," in Shevoroshkin, ed., 1989b. [Proposal that language families in Africa, Europe, and Asia are related]

————. 1991. *Altajskaja problema i proisxozhdenije zhaponskogo jazyka*. Moscow. [Provides evidence for the Altaic family, which, for Starostin, includes Korean and Japanese]

Stringer, Christopher B. 1990. "The Emergence of Modern Humans," *Scientific American* (December): 98–104. [Discusses the archaeological evidence supporting an African homeland for modern humans]

Sweet, Henry. 1901. *The History of Language*. London. [Lessons on language now largely forgotten]

Thorne, Alan G., and Milford H. Wolpoff. 1992. "The Multiregional Evolution of Humans," *Scientific American* (April): 76–83. [An alternative view to the African origin of modern humans]

Trombetti, Alfredo. 1905. *L'unità d'origine del linguaggio*. Bologna. [An early attempt to show that all extant languages are related]

————. 1926. *Le origini della lingua basca*. Bologna. [An early proposal that Basque is related to Caucasian languages]

Turner, Christy G., II. 1989. "Teeth and Prehistory in Asia," *Scientific American* (February): 88–96. [Finds that the classification of New World populations on the basis of teeth parallels that of Greenberg based on language]

Watkins, Calvert. 1990. "Etymologies, Equations, and Comparanda: Types and Values, and Criteria for Judgment," in Philip Baldi, ed., *Linguistic Change and Reconstruction Methodology*, Berlin, pp. 289–303. [a defense of the "standard comparative method"]

————. 1992. "Indo-European Languages," in William Bright, ed., *International Encyclopedia of Linguistics*, Vol. 2, New York, pp. 206–12. [A short sketch of the Indo-European family]

Whitney, William Dwight. 1867. *Language and the Study of Language*. New York. [See in particular his Tenth Lecture, in which he decrees the impossibility of ever connecting Indo-European with any other language family]

Wilson, Allan C., and Rebecca L. Cann. 1992. "The Recent African Genesis of Humans," *Scientific American* (April): 68–73. [A popular account of the genetic evidence from mitochondrial DNA for an African homeland for modern humans]

Index

Page numbers in *italics* represent figures; a "t" following a page number indicates a table; an "m" indicates a map.